P9-CIV-547

SLONIM WOODS 9

SLONIM WOODS

9

A Memoir

DANIEL BARBAN LEVIN

CROWN
NEW YORK

Published in the United States by Crown,
an imprint of Random House, a division of
Penguin Random House LLC, New York.

CROWN and the Crown colophon are registered trademarks of
Penguin Random House LLC.

"Pursuit" originally appeared, in slightly different form, in *Provincetown Arts* (2011).

Grateful acknowledgment is made to the following for permission to reprint
previously published materials:

W. W. Norton & Company, Inc.: Excerpt from "Prospective Immigrants Please Note"
from *Collected Poems: 1950–2012* by Adrienne Rich. Copyright © 1963, 1967 by
Adrienne Rich. Copyright © 2016 by the Adrienne Rich Literary Trust. Reprinted
by permission of W. W. Norton & Company, Inc.

Factory Hollow Press: Excerpt from "Mutually Assured Childhood Molestation"
from *Beauty Was the Case That They Gave Me* by Mark Leidner. Reprinted by
permission of Factory Hollow Press.

LIBRARY OF CONGRESS CATALOGING-IN-PUBLICATION DATA
Names: Levin, Daniel Barban, author.
Title: Slonim Woods 9 / Daniel Barban Levin.
Description: First edition. | New York: Crown, [2020]
Identifiers: LCCN 2020047466 (print) | LCCN 2020047467 (ebook) |
ISBN 9780593138854 (hardcover; alk. paper) | ISBN 9780593138861 (ebook)
Subjects: LCSH: Ray, Larry (Lawrence), 1960– | Levin, Daniel Barban. |
Criminals–New York (State)–Case studies. | Manipulative behavior–New York
(State)–Case studies. | Extortion–New York (State)–Case studies. | Cults–
New York (State)–Case studies.
Classification: LCC HV6248.R3914 L48 2020 (print) | LCC HV6248.R3914 (ebook) |
DDC 364.15092–dc23
LC record available at https://lccn.loc.gov/2020047466
LC ebook record available at https://lccn.loc.gov/2020047467

Printed in the United States of America on acid-free paper

crownpublishing.com

2 4 6 8 9 7 5 3 1

First Edition

Book design by Elizabeth A. D. Eno

To the friends I cannot reach

SLONIM
WOODS
9

Daniel Levin
Wed, Jun 19, 2013, 5:39 PM

Dear Angela,

I apologize for the delay in my response. My new life (amazing choice of words) is progressing happily! I'm working for the Department of Education for New York City now, so I am extremely busy, but completely happy.

I have rather unfortunate news regarding your book and it is involved in something extremely disturbing which I have told very few people. I think it might be the last thing you'd expect to hear. I feel obligated to give you ample warning that I am going to share with you something terrifying and awful that I've experienced in my recent past and which I am telling you, if you choose to read it, in absolute confidence. I am only saying this because as someone who is very busy and probably has her own sense of the scope of our relationship, you should have every right to resign yourself to the notion that I just lost your book, take that as you may, and move on. However, I've been roiling over this for a few months because I could just have told you that, and not have to deal with talking about what I'm about to tell you, but I'd rather not lie and diminish my standing in your eyes in the defense of something which has already caused me enough pain and been detrimental to enough of my relationships. So I'm leaving the choice up to you whether or not to go on. I realize your curiosity is probably piqued but I'm really telling you this is something in which you're probably going to feel obligated to get involved, and I would be completely amazed if you had any idea how to deal with it or even comment on it. However I want you to know that I am sharing this with you not just because I want a valid excuse for not being able to return your book to you right now but because I trust and respect you, and perhaps this is unfair to you, but I do not feel as if I could tell anyone else at this moment, certainly not in the hopes of getting some sort of helpful response.

So, after that protracted preamble, here is the basic idea: I know exactly where your book is, but I absolutely cannot go retrieve it because it is at the apartment where I lived off campus during the summer after sophomore year, the summer after junior year, and the first semester of senior year. When I lived there I was a member of what I can now call a cult.

— 1 —

THE ALARMS KEPT SCREAMING, and we ignored them. While we lined the path waiting for the all clear, Santos and I collected rocks, which we were piling to build a makeshift wall against the cliff outside our dorm. False alarms were frequent and familiar occurrences at Sarah Lawrence, and I'd grown accustomed to pretending a whole building hadn't just begun to squawk when I walked past one on the way to class. Our dorms were called Slonim Woods; they squatted at the bottom of a cliff on top of which was a copse of trees—the "woods" for which the dorms were named. In the brisk New York autumn air, herded into the canyon formed by the buildings and the cliff, Santos and I constructed our wall.

All the residents of Slonim were wearing what looked like costumes of our normal selves, having been rushed out of a shower or roused from an afternoon nap. Santos and I were managing a prodigious stack of rocks, what had turned out to be a surprisingly sturdy monument to our boredom. We had no way of knowing how long it would take the firefighters, who were probably as frustrated as we were, to identify which oversensitive alarm had been set off by some toaster crumb just large enough to have become kindling.

"It's unbelievable," Santos said, handing me a rock. I considered the cliff for best placement. "What's happened to them is insane. Talia looks like she's this scrawny girl or something, but she's the toughest person I've ever known. Growing up in the Bronx was nothing compared to some of the stories she's told me from the shelter." Santos and I had been friends ever since we'd been randomly assigned to live together in our first year. He'd been the best roommate you could ask for. He had tough, Dominican parents, which was why, I guessed, he cleaned our whole room practically every day. He didn't smoke, he didn't drink, he didn't even really listen to music. I did every single one of those things, and tried my best to introduce him to them.

The rock I had just placed on the top of the wall wobbled, a little too big. "In my elementary school, we were building something like this at recess once, and two kids were carrying a heavy rock and it slipped," I told Santos. "One of them had to have the tip of his finger removed. Everyone always made fun of him after that. I can't remember why exactly. They said he smelled bad, I remember that. I think they said his finger was rotting or something, and that's why he smelled." The alarm continued to wail, muffled through our house's brick walls. "Do you know Talia's dad at all? I mean, have you met him?"

"No, not besides what she's told me. I know he was in the marines and everything, and he's done some intelligence work. When they've talked on the phone, Talia's put him on speaker with us. Me and Isabella."

I looked up. In the woods on top of the cliff was a ropes course no one used. Mostly people would just sit up there and drink or smoke weed as they watched people stroll by on the path below. In the summer before the school year, our roommate Gabe flew out from California a week early by accident. He tried to secretly camp in this little strip of woods until classes started. He barely avoided getting kicked out of school for that.

"Larry's really excited to see her again," Santos continued. "Everything that happened to them is so unjust. He's really, really smart and has battled through so much."

"Right."

"I think that's why Talia is the way she is. She blows my mind sometimes."

"He gets here next week, right?" I asked. "He's staying with us?" The wind blew stiff down the path, dislodging a couple of the more precarious stones. They clattered among the bright yellow leaves at our feet. The air was brisk enough to wear jackets, the sun hot enough to sweat underneath them.

"Yeah, I think he's going to stay for a little bit while he figures it out. They just haven't seen each other in so long."

"That makes sense," I said. I thought it did. I wondered how high we could build the wall before it would fall. I wanted to build something that would be here long after we'd moved into new dorms, or even after we'd left the school. The alarm stopped. The strange silence it left behind was broken only by the click of Santos placing one last stone on top, and then the clamor of everyone rushing back into their buildings to continue the day. In the year after I graduated from Sarah Lawrence, when I was still going back to visit, I chanced a walk down that path, and I saw the wall we built there, slumped into the cliff behind it. It had been picked apart, perhaps by other students, but it was undeniable evidence. We had been there. It had all really happened.

—⊣⊢—

When I first arrived at Sarah Lawrence, I'd been placed with four other freshmen in Hill House: Santos, Gabe, Max, and Kyle. The suite quickly came to resemble a ruinous, burgeoning landfill. The layer of detritus on the living room floor was so thick you couldn't see the blue carpet, and the smell in the kitchen never recovered after Gabe spent forty dollars on a deep fryer, used it once, then left the oil and batter to go rancid. Only the room Santos and I shared persisted as a haven of cleanliness.

From the beginning, I felt out of place, constantly anxious, like I didn't know how to embrace this new way of living. I wasn't cut out for college, I knew that. I would often sit, legs hanging over the side of my twin bed, the standard-issue plasticky mattress originally designed for bed-wetters crunching beneath me, and think about how I had gotten here. A series of lucky breaks.

One day, back in New Jersey, where I spent the first eighteen years of my life, my mom was driving me home from high school. It was the spring of my senior year. Halfway home, the four-lane asphalt of Route 78 yielded to thick greenery, roads that dipped and curved blindly over hills and little stone bridges, fields dotted with horses, the woods where I spent most of my adolescence trying my best to get lost. Just like she did every day, Mom stopped to check the mail when we reached our driveway. "Something for you!" she exclaimed. She seemed genuinely excited as she handed the envelope to me in the passenger seat.

It was from Sarah Lawrence, the eighth and final letter to come from the colleges I'd applied to. The first seven had all been rejections. With each notice of my failure I'd grown a little more numb. I couldn't think about the future anymore; it didn't exist. I took the envelope. It was thin. As I stomped up the stairs I hated myself for every day I had spent ignoring class, talking to my friends; for the months and then years of accumulating anxiety; for that one time I hid from a teacher under a cafeteria table and he'd found me, and the other times I'd managed to avoid my teachers, just slipping around corners or up stairs, because I hadn't finished an assignment or written an important essay; and almost worse: all the time I'd spent thinking about girls who didn't like me. What had it all led to? This thin envelope that weighed as much as every textbook I'd never read.

My stomach felt like it was losing a fight with my other organs. I went straight into the bathroom and opened the letter sitting on the toilet. I read it three times. A handwritten note in the margin expressed the dean's excitement to meet me on moving-in day. It was like a knife had been pulled out of my gut. I couldn't tell if this was a good or a bad thing.

Sarah Lawrence was the college my mom went to, which was why, I was pretty sure, I'd gotten in. Her class was the first to go officially coed. The campus, I knew, was adorable: steep hills adorned with oversized dormer cottages and black squirrels scrambling up gnarled willow trees, a place families from the tri-state area used to send their daughters for a slightly more progressive education than they would receive at Radcliffe or Wellesley.

By the time my mom started there in 1968, things had changed. One of the new male students rode his motorcycle onto the middle of campus and circled the stone cottage in the middle of the quad. In 2009, the legend on campus was that Joseph Campbell had held meetings in that cottage to talk with students about the hero's journey, developing his theories of comparative mythology. By then, the cottage had been repurposed into a teahouse, that motorcycle-riding student was a history professor at the school, and the student body was a collection of weirdos, punks, performance artists, and the like, mostly the offspring of liberal coastal elite parents who wouldn't bat an eye at the fact that their child was studying at a school with no majors where they might split their time between philosophy and painting.

I was just one of many kids who had grown up with house-poor parents; disaffected, I blundered my way through a fancy high school I couldn't handle and which my parents couldn't afford, and landed at SLC. When I entered my "first year studies," a home room led by a teacher who would be my "don"—Sarah Lawrence lingo for an adviser—it became clear that I was one of the least weird people at the school. I was a little boring by comparison. The unofficial school slogan was, after all, "We're different, so are you."

My first year studies was a poetry workshop. I had chosen it because it sounded easy, and because I had written some poetry for English classes in high school. It was one of the few things I did that seemed to make teachers notice me. When I'd graduated high school and flipped through the commencement program listing preppy kids lauded with awards endowed by their families, announcements about Ivy League acceptances, and superlatives for the beauty of their eyes, the only recognition I received was for writing poems.

On the first day of college, I got lost on my way to the workshop. Luckily, I had left early. I'd printed out my poems at home in New Jersey, and jammed them among clothes and toiletries in the bag I'd brought to college and unpacked the day before. I gripped the papers sweatily as I wandered the back roads of Bronxville. I knew from the brochures that the student population at this school was three-quarters people who identified as female. Someone had also told me that "at

Sarah Lawrence, poetry is like football." I didn't have a chance in high school, but here, maybe, I would matter. As I walked down the road lined with towering houses sporting impossibly tall, tapering shingled roofs and impeccable lawns shaded by gnarled oaks and maples, I was reminded how small I was. I turned a corner, saw a building with a Sarah Lawrence sign outside, made a lucky guess, and went in.

The class took place around a huge circular table in a wood-paneled room. The fireplace in the corner was cold and dark. I sat and waited among the other students, with whom I would be spending the whole year. A girl next to me with dyed red hair and the palest skin I'd ever seen turned to me and said, "Hey," drawing out the end of the word through a voice that sounded like it was polishing gravel. "I'm Moriel," she said, just as languidly. On my other side, another girl leaned across me, practically bouncing in her chair, and exclaimed, "I'm Hailey!" Before I could introduce myself, the door creaked open and in rushed our teacher, wearing a soft blue blazer and thin gold spectacles. His beard looked more suited to the face of a Confederate soldier than that of a poetry teacher.

It turned out Moriel and Hailey both lived in Hill House, so after class we walked back along Kimball Avenue together. It was a straight shot home, which didn't help how stupid I felt for having brought my clutch of poems—the class was just supposed to be for introductions. But the teacher, seeing the stack of copies in front of me, had insisted we read one of the poems and talk about it.

"I liked the part about the golden telephone," Moriel said, lighting up a cigarette she'd rolled with dried lavender the moment we stepped out of the building, saying, "I'm trying to get off nicotine." As we walked, Hailey explained that she was at Sarah Lawrence mostly for modern dance. Later in the year, on a midnight run to pick up munchies, I would find her on a lawn where she had arranged fallen cherry blossom petals into a huge circle. "It's a dance ring to honor the moon goddess," she said. I shrugged, dropped my things, and danced interpretively with her lit by nothing but the full moon.

As freshman year progressed, I became close friends with Santos. He'd met Talia and Isabella in class, and they started hanging out all the time, clustered on his bed in our dorm room. At some point, he and Talia started dating. All I really noticed was that Santos and I hung out less, because there swiftly wasn't a "Santos" anymore; it was always the three of them, and Talia and Isabella stressed me out. They constantly wanted to talk about serious things, about our responsibility to justice, to truth, and it made me want to lie down, so I let them all, including Santos, drift into the periphery.

Gabe got me a job driving the on-campus student shuttle from midnight to three A.M., which mostly involved me finding the highest speeds I could reach on the straightest back roads or idling in some dorm driveway, listening to Sufjan Stevens as I watched the wind buffet the pine trees. Once, while circling the campus, I accidentally hit a possum as it darted across the road. As I waited at a light, I kept glancing at my rearview mirror, where I could see its body bending and snapping like a beached fish. For hours, I had to drive the same route over and over, passing the circle of dark red blood that grew around the corpse as snow slowly began to fall, which turned the ball of dark fur into a pink lump. I prayed that no one would get into the van, forcing me to explain what had happened.

Other nights, I recorded the midnight radio show I ran with Gabe and Max, *The Endless Pajama Cycle.* Max had the most eclectic music taste of anyone I knew, and we let him run the music most of the time. Otherwise, the three of us joked on air about school, riffed on imaginary scenarios, discussed our ideas about life, and took the occasional phone call from one of our six listeners. We would draft the strangest Facebook messages we could think of and send them out to everyone at school to drum up interest.

> In the upside down ocean of another utopia grows a neutral tree which is mostly calcified. In it is a steadily disappearing tabby cat whose misgivings are mostly undeserved. He tells you he is unsure if you can handle the destabilized bureaucracy of revolutionary red pandas on the road ahead. On your travels, you encounter an underground fighting force of axe-wielding badgers, a wise red hound who runs the moving for-

> est with a compassionate fury, and a black bear who can only be awakened by the utterance of his true name. The badgers give you a traveling axe, which comes with a convenient carrying case. The hound shows you the ways of the forest, and gives you a bowl of finely ground mushrooms, only to be used in the direst of situations. Finally, the bear gives you a smallish transistor radio, the music of which is the only sound capable of penetrating his endless sleep, besides the sound of his true name. If you'd like to listen, click on this link. To take advantage of the magical transistor radio's ability for two-way communication to call in, use these numbers.

The rest of the time I watched *The Office* with Max and his friend Raven, who by the end of the year would begin dating. There wasn't much time for studying, so I left most of it until the last minute—we all did. There was a name for it: "conference week," when everyone actually wrote the papers they were supposed to have been working on all semester.

⊣⊢

On one of many occasions just like it, I got back to my bedroom in the middle of the night and heard through the door Santos, Talia, and Isabella having one of their long philosophical conversations, which always seemed to be directed by Talia. I could never quite figure out what they were talking about or why it mattered so much to them: politics, how to be a good person, what they had learned in one of their philosophy classes. I turned around and headed to my friend Claudia's apartment at the end of the hall. She let me in and we chatted on the couch in her living room for hours, not even noticing that the night had ended until the room started lightening up on its own.

As the sky grayed, we banged around in the kitchen, suddenly ravenous. The cat Claudia had smuggled into the apartment, an aggressive unspayed gray stripey thing named Darja, rolled around somehow angrily on the linoleum. Pets were barred from campus and assiduously hunted down by campus security. Darja, so far, had survived undiscovered. Claudia plunked down at the small laminate kitchen table while I rooted around the fridge for eggs. Every Sunday morning back in New Jersey my dad and I would make breakfast together, so this should have been a cinch. I hadn't cooked at all this year, if you didn't count failed attempts at deep frying with Gabe. I threw an egg in the pan, then grabbed curry powder, cumin, and cayenne off the counter and dusted haphazardly. We ate greedily off the two cleanest plates we could find. It was delicious. With a little yolk in the messy facial hair I'd let grow in over the past few weeks, I looked up to see Claudia's roommate Vita pass across the living room and out the front door, probably on the way to her first class of the morning. "I've got to go," I said to Claudia as I grabbed my backpack off the floor and rushed after Vita. "I'll see ya later."

In the greasy light of the hallway, I heard the stairwell door slam closed just as I exited Claudia's. Damn. Our apartment was just down the hall, and it was well past time for me to take a shower and get my things together before class. This building was on the edge of campus, right on the line between Bronxville (the fancy, "just a hop, skip, and a jump from the city" suburban retreat for Manhattan elite) and Yonkers (the disenfranchised suburb of the Bronx). All of the brochures for Sarah Lawrence squarely located it in clean, flowery Bronxville, but its location would be more accurately described to me by one teacher as "Bronkers."

When I got back to my apartment, I couldn't stop thinking about Vita, her pale hair, how she'd looked when I saw her the other day ordering a cup of coffee at "The Pub," our on-campus café, or how graceful she was when she played ultimate Frisbee, a sport I'd taken up partially at Gabe's urging, but mostly because she was on the team. The other day I'd watched her run for a pass that was a bit too long, dive for the Frisbee, catch it in midair, and fall into a perfect roll. Someone told me she'd studied acrobatics and circus in Europe before coming to Sarah Lawrence, which felt simultaneously incomprehensible and inevitable.

I pushed dirty dishes out of the way in our kitchen sink to make enough room to fill a glass with water. Vita would never like me, and why should she? Whenever I saw her, I couldn't think of a single thing to say. I believed there was some quintessential person, a confident, impressive version of myself chained up inside, trapped by my fear, who said with ease the things that I imagined myself saying when I was lying awake at night. Feeling useless, I crossed the room to my dresser, tiptoeing so as not to wake up Santos, who was softly snoring in his twin on the other side of the room. By now the sun was glimmering above the hill for which the building, I assumed, had been named. I picked up a briarwood pipe I had purchased at an antiques shop on St. Mark's, the touristy avenue where you could find a sanitized, nostalgic version of the East Village's former seediness, packed it with a mix of tobacco and weed, and smoked by the window.

I had my literature class at eleven A.M. Perched on the windowsill was a potted flower I'd bought at the Bronx botanical garden, now dead, and a surprisingly healthy weed plant I'd propagated from some scrap seeds. Shit. *I have my literature class at eleven A.M.* I hadn't thought about that when I'd started almost automatically to smoke. I felt plastered to my bed. I looked at the ceiling. There was a rusty stain just above my head, from what? I was more than halfway through the school year, and it barely made sense to me how I had gotten here. I couldn't quite track the days, and felt like I was floating through a strange version of life, a life that did not feel like my own. I certainly didn't feel like I had earned it. I barely registered my classes as they came and went. In fact, my whole life felt like a class I hadn't done the homework for, like there had been a day, or multiple days, of orientation I must have missed. Often I would nod off partway through a class, exhausted from lack of sleep, but I'd mastered the art of propping my head on my fist in such a way that it appeared I was paying attention, or so I believed. In Sarah Lawrence's classes of ten to fifteen students, all seated around one big table, I probably wasn't getting away with anything.

The literature class I had this particular morning was different. Angela, the teacher, made books feel tangible, like soil to dig into, like they were composed of these vast, interlocking mechanisms that were impossible to diagram all at once. She made them sexy, somehow. In one class, she pointed out that the soaked-through napkin under a beer glass in Hemingway's "Hills Like White Elephants," not to mention the beaded curtain through which flies would pass, was a symbol for a ruined prophylactic. She used that word, "prophylactic," which I couldn't remember ever having heard, and others like it: "liminality," "mimesis," "diaphanous." For the first time since before high school, I felt like I was actually learning. I was so excited, I'd begun actually reading all of the homework, which I hadn't done for a class in years. In one of the individual conferences between students and professors that Sarah Lawrence requires, I'd shared with this teacher the one thing I thought made me stand out, the one thing I was good at: a poem I'd written. I'd chosen one about my mom. We'd ended up sitting in her office for hours talking about literature and family.

I managed to swing my legs over the side of the bed and stand. I opened the top drawer of my standard-issue dresser. As I stared at the rows of socks and boxers, I could see the overwhelming array of possibilities before me: this next hour before class, this day, the rest of this year, the rest of my life. It felt like I didn't know who I was. What was I defined by? What I thought other people wanted and a weed habit? I didn't know what I was, but "stoner" didn't feel right. Everything in my life suddenly was wrong: I had made the wrong choices, and now I couldn't even relate to the things I owned, the clothes I was wearing, the thoughts in my head.

I was standing on a precipice, in what my teacher would call a "limen," ahead of me the branching paths of my future getting narrower and narrower, behind me an open field of seemingly random, inexplicable events that had led here. What would happen if I kept going in the wrong direction: chose the wrong pair of socks, the wrong underwear? What made anything happen, and over what did I have any control? I tried to narrow it down, and got nowhere, the anxiety mounting until getting dressed, much less leaving the dorm, felt impossible. I didn't make it to class that day. I sent an email explaining that I was coming down with something.

As freshman year was winding to a close and my nineteenth birthday approached in June, my romantic relationships, or lack thereof, felt more and more important. Summer was around the corner, and I spent the hot late-spring days sitting on the floor of my room with the window open, ripping printer paper into tiny squares, then folding those into intricate triangles. I'd read online about a Japanese tradition of making five hundred tiny pieces of paper into a giant swan and giving it to your beloved. I had been doing origami since middle school, making small boxes, then more intricate flowers, frogs, turtles. I would fold paper in school assemblies or under my desk in class. It felt better to do something with my hands than to just . . . be there.

When I finally finished the swan a few weeks before the end of second semester, I walked it down the hall to Claudia and Vita's room. Vita, I knew, would be going back home to California for the summer once the semester ended. The moment I knocked on their door, I realized how insane I looked. How would I explain this? What would I even say? I tried to hold the swan casually despite its delicacy. When Claudia answered the door, I quickly gave her a hug with one arm, holding the swan slightly behind my hip. As surreptitiously as I could, I sat down in their living room and placed the swan on the floor next to my chair. Vita's bedroom door opened, and she sat next to Claudia on the couch, resting her head on Claudia's leg. From that vantage, it was almost impossible for her not to see the swan. As we chatted about summer plans and the impending conference week, during which we had to produce a twenty-five-page paper for each of our three classes, I felt the cheap polyester couch inhaling me. Darja the cat wandered out from the open doorway and presented herself in the middle of the room. She was going through heat, which I'd never seen before. My cats growing up were boys, neutered. Claudia laughed. Finally, I saw Vita's eyes narrow, and she asked, "Hey, what's that thing?"

I coughed. "Oh, this! Yeah. I've just been making it and I thought I'd show you. It's an origami swan."

They both nodded. "That's really cool, Dan," Vita said. I didn't know what else to say, or what I'd wanted. I'd thought somehow she would know it was for her. But she didn't, and the conversation moved on. I couldn't believe that for weeks I'd thought it made perfect sense to bring this monstrosity here, a physical representation of my inability to just say the words "Do you want to go out sometime?" Unsure what to do, I made up an excuse for going back to my apartment, hoping no one would notice the swan on the floor until it was too late and Vita had no choice but to take it home with her.

A few minutes later, Claudia knocked on my door. Under her arm she had the swan, which she held out to me. "You forgot this," she said. Later that week, I gave it to my literature professor as a farewell gift.

—||—

It seemed obvious that, if we could pull it off, the loose group of friends who had formed around the third floor of Hill House should try to find a way to live together in our sophomore year. When we talked about it in our apartment, Talia took the lead. According to her, Slonim Woods would be the best place to live on campus. We'd each get our own private room and would have a big modern living room and kitchen to share. We'd be pretty much at the center of campus. All we needed were eight people for the application, so we gathered them: Gabe, Max, Santos, and me from our original apartment; Talia and Isabella, Santos's friends; Claudia from down the hall; and, finally, we rounded out the eight with Juli Anna, a friend of mine from poetry class.

When sophomore year began, I stood on the second-floor landing of Slonim Woods 9, looked down on our living room, and thought, *This is perfect.* The floor was a strange gray-beige tile, broken in places. The walls were all exposed brick. Next year, my junior year, I would study abroad—by some fluke I had gotten into a school out in the English countryside, a concept so inconceivable to me that I wouldn't think about it until it happened—but for now, I had everything I could possibly want. Our windows looked out on a cliff and trees, the curated nature of Sarah Lawrence. I still didn't know Talia and Isabella all that well, but I was living with my friends. People I loved. People who were full of energy. People who were complicated but kind. People who liked to do the same things I liked to do, like play Super Smash Bros. on my GameCube and throw parties and dance on the coffee table.

We did all of these things as the year began. Then Talia gathered us all in the living room to tell us that her dad was getting out of jail.

⊣⊢

By coincidence, Talia and I had attended the same high school back in New Jersey. She was a few years older than me, so we'd never crossed paths. What I didn't know, but would learn later on, was that she hadn't finished high school. When her parents divorced, Talia's mom, who according to Talia was evil and abusive, had stolen Talia's younger sister, Ava, and devoted all of her energy to destroying Talia's dad, Larry.

Larry, we'd learned, was an incredible human being. He'd been a marine, and then spent years working for the Defense Intelligence Agency. He'd been a liaison for Mikhail Gorbachev when he visited the United States. He'd helped negotiate the end of the Kosovo War, and had a letter to prove it, thanking him for his invaluable contribution. He'd become close friends with Bernie Kerik, the police commissioner of New York, and was even the best man at Kerik's wedding. However, Talia informed us, when Larry discovered that the commissioner was involved in some corrupt dealings, he went to the FBI. Just as Larry was taking the risk of going up against one of the most powerful law enforcement officers in the country, Talia's mom divorced him. She then worked with Kerik to frame Larry for custody violations, landing him in jail and giving her an impenetrable case to take their two daughters.

Talia, still in high school, had rejected her mom's custody and emancipated herself in a show of loyalty to her dad. Minutes from the mall in Bridgewater, New Jersey, where I'd been seeing Sacha Baron Cohen movies, eating orange chicken in the food court, and trying out iPods in the Apple store, Talia was living in a homeless shelter.

Talia had told me and everyone else all of this again and again. If you sat with her in the living room, if you tried to grab a plate from the kitchen cabinet while she was cooking, if she cornered you in the hallway outside the bathroom, whenever we might interact with her, it was like a lecture series on Larry and Talia's misfortune you had signed up for. I blamed myself for my own discomfort around her—if I were a better, less selfish person like Isabella and Santos, I would've sat down to listen more often. But it was undeniable: Talia was a hero. Larry was a hero. And now he was getting out.

—II—

Talia's dad arrived in the morning, and he wasn't alone. The front door of Slonim Woods 9 opened to a landing, then up a few steps and you were in the wide-open living room. We knew he was coming. It was Talia's big day, years of waiting building to this: the return of her father. As usual, most of us were strewn around the living room, while some were at class or seeing friends. I happened to be coming down from upstairs when the door opened. He looked small, at first. Maybe it was because he was still standing in the entryway. Maybe it was the backpack strapped to his back, which in some ways made him look like a schoolkid. He was round, I noticed, his head gleaming like a tan cue ball. As he stamped up the steps, with friends filing in behind him, his daughter rushed across the room and jumped into him, pressing herself into his chest.

One of the men stepped forward and introduced himself as Lee Chen. Lee had a long, black ponytail reaching down the back of his dark suit. Behind him was an older man who seemed gruff, but whose eyes watered as he introduced himself as a detective and an old friend of Larry's. Bringing up the rear was Iban, in his twenties, tan and sharp-edged, who Larry referred to as a "fellow marine." These men made a point of shaking each of our hands in a sort of procession, as Talia disappeared further into her father's thick arms, almost invisible in his embrace.

Isabella hovered to the side. She was leaning against the wall, tall and thin, looking down, her dark brown hair falling in front of her pale face, her angular jaw, her icy eyes. She could have been anywhere—sitting in her parents' trailer in San Antonio, tuning out a philosophy class down the hill, perched on a stool in a bar somewhere on the Lower East Side waiting for someone to buy her a drink. Larry unwrapped an arm and reached out, gently squeezing Isabella's shoulder.

"Thank you," he said, "for being a friend to Tal when she needed you." He turned to the rest of us, moving Talia to his side–she looked like an extension of him, something growing out of his hip. "Thank you to all of you for looking out for my daughter this past year." Everyone was silent, unprepared for this moment. Most of us had barely paid attention to Talia, beyond knowing that this reunion was all she'd been talking about for over a year. How were you supposed to react to something like this, a family separated unjustly and now reunited after years? We had all chosen willingly to leave our parents, to come to this imaginary world, to study subjects we had never heard of, and to live, for the first time, exclusively with people our age. We couldn't imagine being separated from our families against our wills. We couldn't understand how such a thing was even possible. Larry had an arm around Talia and Isabella now. They were still standing barely inside the room, bordered by the men who had delivered him to our door. "Now, let me make you all some real food," he said, grinning.

2

THE SUMMER BEFORE SOPHOMORE year, Claudia and I had made a plan—I was going to fly out to Los Angeles, where her parents had a house, and then we would drive all the way up the coast to Seattle to stay with our friend Raven, Max's girlfriend. We would take Claudia's dad's car, and I would drive the whole way there and back. Claudia had told us all on a number of occasions about the bombastic ways in which she had failed the driver's test over and over and over again, until they wouldn't let her take it anymore. She had jumped a curb and crashed into a mailbox or she had accidentally grabbed the instructor in a way that was interpreted as inappropriate or she had fallen asleep at the wheel, having taken the test after an all-nighter. Her stories were always hilarious and outlandish. I thought of Claudia as someone who attracted the unusual, whose life was chock-full of wild experiences, which contrasted with her unassuming appearance, her hair not quite red or brown, her eyes a mix of every color at once and so, somehow, no color in particular.

When I landed at LAX, Claudia and her friend Roger pulled up to meet me. I immediately liked Roger; he leaned silently against the car, a stone in the whitewater of airport traffic, horns blaring, the afternoon light of Los Angeles turning everything molten as Claudia ran across the pavement and hugged me. I lifted her up and swung her around. I was enjoying this trip already. I felt hyper-saturated. It was my first time in California.

As Roger navigated the startlingly fast, close-quarters highway traffic and we neared Pasadena, the landscape began to transform from recognizable to alien. The road bounded over vertiginous hills; walls of scrub grass and bungalows billowed into the distance, eventually dwindling into the San Gabriel Mountains. "Roger is like my chauffeur," Claudia said. Roger grunted. "Well, like all of our chauffeurs. Roger has always driven all of us around when we go for tacos and stuff like that." In a half-serious singsong she said, "Thank you, Roger!"

"I guess you would drive if you hadn't put your driving test instructor's car through a mailbox," I said, laughing.

From the back seat I could see Roger's pale, brown beard twitch. "What?" he called back to me.

I felt nearly sick from the roller coaster of crisscrossed highways. "You know, because Claudia failed the driver's test three times. And they wouldn't let her take it anymore." I paused, confused. "Right?"

Roger sighed loudly and glanced at Claudia in the passenger seat, where she was shrinking. "Claudia . . ." he said.

Later, as Claudia and I drove up the coast, it was easy to ignore what I had learned from Roger: that Claudia had never even taken the driving test; she was too afraid of driving to even try. She'd made it all up. The larger implications of this strange lie were then confirmed for me by Claudia's other friends from back home: She had a problem with telling stories as if they were real, which had been well known among her old high school friends, but which her college friends hadn't picked up on yet. As I learned all this, I became acutely aware of how briefly I had actually been friends with Claudia, and how little I knew about her, compared to the people who had been a part of her life for so long. I realized, too, how little she knew about me.

After a day on the road, we stopped talking about the lying thing—it seemed to make her squirmy and uncomfortable—and eventually I decided to pretend it didn't exist. I didn't know what else I could do. I distracted myself with unplanned stops. We climbed a hill overlooking the Pacific coast on the side of the road. We traipsed around tide pools on the edge of the frigid ocean. In Oceano, we bought pounds of succulent California fruit to eat as we drove, and then threw away the leaking paper bag of untouched rot as we reached San Francisco.

When we arrived in Seattle, I steered Claudia's dad's car onto a ferry that would take us across Puget Sound to Bainbridge Island, where we would meet Raven, and spend a few days together. On one of those days, Claudia, Raven, and I wandered the beach, which was unlike any I'd seen: a shore of round, flat stones, the water black and cold and apparently concealing orcas. Claudia kept running into the woods, then coming back to tell us about the ferns she'd found. Raven and I rolled our eyes as we sat looking at the water. Raven pointed at a dot on the horizon, which started to grow larger and larger until it took the shape of a boat. "Is that boat coming straight for us?" she asked.

"No way," I said.

The boat kept expanding, and we started to scramble back on the beach, until it roared to a puttering halt at the edge of the water. It turned out to be Raven's dad, and some of his colleagues, who had been drinking flutes of champagne on the Sound when they spotted us hanging out on the shore. The contrast between how fancy and adult they were, and how scrubby and young we felt, was startling. After they left, we broke down laughing at how absurd it felt, to be on this island among the ferns and the humongous driftwood, to talk to besuited businesspeople in a boat from the shore, to pretend, absurdly, that anything we did felt normal.

That evening, the last before Claudia and I began our return to Southern California, Claudia and Raven took out all of Raven's makeup. Raven was, perhaps, the sparkliest person I knew—she spent what seemed like hours on nail art and her lips always popped with bold color. She was loud, brash, and hilarious, and her style matched. We were all lying around on a shag rug in Raven's room, which hadn't changed since she'd lived in it as a teen. I was staring at the ceiling, thinking about our day, when I heard Raven and Claudia giggling conspiratorially. "Hey, Dan," Raven said. "What do you think you would look like as a girl?"

I didn't glance up. "I don't know, why?"

Raven and Claudia came into my frame of vision, blocking the light. It took me a second to realize they were holding Raven's lipstick, powder, and mascara. "Let's find out!" Raven said. Claudia was near-bursting with laughter. As far as I knew, Claudia didn't normally wear makeup, and I couldn't help but think that she was playing along with Raven's girliness to fit in or, in this case, to participate in overpowering me.

"Oh, I don't really know, guys," I said. Something clenched in my stomach. "Let's not, maybe?"

When Raven and I had been alone on the beach, Claudia wandering somewhere in the woods, I had wanted to reach out and touch her hand, to pull her into me. Lying in her bedroom, which was decorated the same as it had been when she was a teenager, I couldn't stop feeling it, this kind of magnetic pull. I wanted her to see me as someone she could touch. Someone she could want to touch. "Let's just try it," she said. "Just a little bit." I looked at her. If I wasn't game for the makeup, I would be a letdown. Boring. That would be worse. Maybe I could somehow play it off.

I took a breath and let out half of a laugh. "Sure," I said. "Just a little bit."

Claudia and Raven giggled on either side of me, patting a brush into a coin of powder, twisting a column of red out of a lipstick tube. They kneeled gently on my arms, pretending to pin me to the shag. The clench in my stomach didn't go away. I couldn't stop thinking about how to play this off, how quickly I could wipe my face. At the same time, I relished the contact. I liked it when Raven leaned over me, her face above mine, urging me to stay completely still as she lined one eye and then the other. Claudia admitted she didn't really know how to use makeup. Raven showed her where to apply blush, then laughed at how much she put on.

When they were done, they cracked up as they brought me to the mirror. I looked, predictably, clown-like. It was a relief. My fear was that they would actually make me look like a girl. Instead, I looked like a joke. That night, we all slept on a pile of blankets on the carpet. We talked later and later into the night, until Claudia eventually nodded off. Raven and I lay next to each other in the half-dark, and I rolled a little toward her. My arm pressed against her arm. She smelled like candy, or like something that smelled like candy. I knew she had a deep and abiding appreciation for Britney Spears. I wondered if what I was smelling was Britney Spears's perfume. She whispered something, so as not to wake up Claudia, which I couldn't hear at first.

"What?" I whispered back.

"I think about you sometimes," she said, a little louder. "Is that bad?" Her fingers interlaced with mine.

"No," I said. "I don't think it's bad."

—||—

When Claudia and I drove south the next morning, the balance of everything had tilted. I wanted to ignore my feelings, to stop thinking about how much fun I had when Raven was around. Everyone else seemed to exist on the other side of a filter, saying things because they wanted you to react a certain way or feel a certain way. Raven seemed to say exactly what she thought and felt: She was vivid; her feelings were sudden and unexpected and undeniably real. As Claudia and I cut inland from the Oregon coast on a whim toward Crater Lake, the deepest lake in the country, the mix of guilt and desire made my mind go static.

—||—

A few months after Claudia and I made our way back to L.A., the summer over, and as we returned to school again for sophomore year, Raven and Max broke up. Not long after that, Raven and I began to date, and somewhere in the mix of everything changing, of trying to navigate whether our group of friends would fall apart or coalesce again, Larry arrived at Slonim. By the spring of second semester Raven and I had been together almost six months, and though she lived down the hill in one of the suburban Westchester homes Sarah Lawrence used as dorms, she was almost always in my room upstairs at Slonim.

Small things changed for reasons I couldn't figure out. One day, Gabe wrote a play for the radio show he'd been hosting with me and Max for over a year. He asked us to read it on air, sight unseen. At the end of the play, Gabe's radio DJ personality died tragically, and in real life, the instant his persona died, Gabe walked out of the studio and never came back. From then on, Max and I hosted the show without him.

Sometimes, when I walked into Slonim Woods 9, or when Raven would scream my name from upstairs, calling me away from hanging out, I noticed Isabella and Talia, even Santos, whispering to one another, looking at me, giggling. Raven and I would talk about her life, her family, who she was back at home and beyond the orbit of Slonim, but in those moments I couldn't understand anything beyond what I thought she wanted from me, what I thought a boyfriend was supposed to be.

Max, Raven, and I still hung out together, as we had freshman year. In fact, we became more inseparable than we'd ever been before. Everyone else had gotten a little weird, a little cold. Claudia would spend more and more of her time with Santos, which meant that sometimes I would see the two of them at the table eating dinner with Talia, Isabella, and Larry, staring admiringly at Larry as he talked.

Larry was in and out of the house, arranging dinner for half of my friends more often than not. Sometimes Iban was there as well, installing shelves, maybe sleeping over on the floor, but I didn't really notice, and if I did, I didn't really care.

I wanted so badly to understand Raven, to get close to her, and yet it always felt there was something I couldn't push past. Sometimes I could see something like pain in the way she might chew the inside of her cheek, or how the edges of her eyes wrinkled in something of a wince, at seemingly random times, when we were talking about family, or the past, or just being a person in the world, something I wouldn't clock as important. There would be evenings she would explode with rage and despair, and it felt to me as if it came out of nowhere. If I didn't give our relationship all my attention, I thought, things would spin out of control.

One night, we were getting ready in her bedroom before heading to a concert at the Blue Room, Sarah Lawrence's music venue, which was across the road from Raven's house and for which Max booked touring bands. One second Raven was standing in front of the closet picking out an outfit to wear, and then a moment later when I looked over she was crying in a pile of her clothes on the floor. I tried to calm her down, and she pounded her fists against my chest half-heartedly. Not knowing what was going on, feeling almost half-there, I dragged a chair into the center of the room, just to get her off the floor. We sat there together, her head on my shoulder, sometimes murmuring to each other but mostly sitting in silence. After a long time had passed, we had sex in the dark, illuminated only by the strange, bluish light from the streetlamp outside that cut across her bare room, strewn with clothes.

Not long after, we would sit in the grass near Slonim, and I'd float the idea of breaking up, tell her that I felt overwhelmed, that I didn't understand what was going on, and Raven would threaten to kill herself, then insist she could change, be better. I didn't even know what being better would entail. I was the one who couldn't be good enough. I couldn't imagine that the pain and confusion Raven had been expressing might have nothing to do with me. I wanted her to be alive. That mattered more than anything, and I thought it was up to me, somehow.

—ıı—

One night, Gabe, Santos, and I were sitting around the living room playing Super Smash Bros. The windows–the kind you unlatch at the bottom and then angle out vertically, which you find almost exclusively in high school classrooms–were swung open to the path, so that people walking by could see us furiously clacking away at buttons and joysticks. Gabe would occasionally shout, or Santos would throw his controller onto the coffee table in frustration. We had reached a level of excellence I hadn't imagined possible when I'd played this game as a kid. I heard scrabbling against the lock of the front door, which then swung open. Claudia lurched in, heaving. "You guys," she said, walking up to the couches as if barely able to maintain her balance, and then plunking down across from us, "you won't believe what I just saw."

I paused the game and the screen froze mid-fight. "Come on!" Gabe bellowed, standing up and walking over to the kitchen. His voice was always a little operatic. Santos and I ignored him. "What's going on?" I asked Claudia.

"I was walking down the path coming home, you know." We nodded. "And I just had this feeling there was something watching me."

"I hate that feeling," Santos said, his brow furrowed.

Claudia didn't seem to hear him. "So I looked up above the cliffs, and I saw this *thing*." She paused, waiting for us to lean in further.

Gabe rustled around in the fridge. Nothing in there was his. Every shelf was packed with white Styrofoam clamshell containers full of Italian takeout dishes Larry had ordered. Most of the time, I didn't think about Larry or know he was there until I'd come home to find our dining room table overflowing with pastas and salads ordered from Rosie's in Bronxville. Isabella, Talia, and Santos would all be listening rapt as he talked at an impossible clip about topics ranging from tomato sauce to the military. Talia had been Larry lite, it turned out. I knew that lately they had all been wrapped up in something dramatic to do with Isabella. "We've got to take care of our Iz. Her family certainly won't do it," I'd heard Larry say to Talia one night over dinner, his hand on Isabella's shoulder, while I'd sat in the living room plucking away at my ukulele.

I didn't think much of any of this. All year Talia and Isabella had been complaining about dishes we'd leave on the sink or the counter, the mess we'd make in the living room, but now that Larry was here he would clean up after us, so it was a relief not to worry about that anymore. Only a few months before, Gabe, Max, and I had tossed around the idea of dumping a big bag of sand out in the living room and throwing a beach party, but Talia shot that down pretty quickly. I got used to seeing Iban around, and learned that he was Talia's ex-boyfriend before Santos. Like Isabella, he had become an adopted member of their family. Iban's put-on southern lilt, which I came to associate with his time as a marine, joined the clamor of Slonim 9. Anytime Larry was there,

Iban was too, like a bodyguard or a military escort. Tonight, though, it had seemed to be just us, and for at least the time being the house had felt, briefly, normal.

"What was it, this thing?" I said.

Claudia was looking pale and clammy on the couch. "It was like this glowing . . . ball. I just felt this chill wash over me. This deep, heavy, cold feeling in the pit of my stomach. It wasn't like fear, it was dread. It was *cold,* you guys. I had to unstick myself from the ground, like it was pinning me there somehow, and turn and run down the path until I got home." Claudia's voice was shaking, holding on to every syllable before she let it go, drawing out the drama. Gabe snorted in the kitchen. I couldn't tell if he was expressing disbelief or just trying to breathe through one of the colds with which he seemed perpetually afflicted. Claudia didn't seem to notice. "I went to my room to see if it was still out there. And it is, you guys. It's out there on the cliff. This glowing thing. Like it knew where my room was. I could feel it again as I looked at it, that sinking, cold feeling. It was like it was looking into me."

I shook my head, unsure what to do. I had no idea if she believed what she was saying. I thought it might be like finding someone sleepwalking in the kitchen–waking them up would be more dangerous than just letting the dream play out. But letting the dream play out made me feel, at least a little bit, like I didn't know what was real.

"We just need to go upstairs to see if this thing is still outside," I said to Claudia and Santos, and we rushed up the stairs and into Claudia's room. We stood around the window, peering into the dark, where there was, of course, no glowing orb.

"Where is it?" Claudia seemed genuinely panicked.

Santos looked at her, concerned. "Why don't you tell Larry about it?" he said. "Maybe he can help explain."

I felt something click into place. When Santos and Claudia tried to answer the question "What should I do?" Larry had become part of the answer. I'd never noticed that before. Maybe they were right, for all I knew. Maybe Larry could help. I had no idea how to handle Claudia's stories, or fantasies, or delusions, or whatever they were. We needed some kind of guidance. I didn't want to talk to Larry myself. I'd seen the way Talia, Isabella, Iban, Santos, and now Claudia spent almost all their time with Larry when he was around. It seemed like being friends with Talia's dad necessitated a huge time commitment, time I didn't have.

Claudia looked worried, but also a little excited. "Yeah, maybe I should talk to him," she said. "Do you know where he is?"

Santos grimaced. "He's been in Isabella's room all night, actually." He looked at me. "I can't really talk about it, but she's having a really hard time. Larry's helping."

I cocked my head. It was close to midnight. "Wow, all night this has been going on?" I realized I hadn't seen either Larry or Isabella around for the past day.

"He's really dedicated to helping her," Santos said. "Especially after she looked out for Talia while he was in jail and everything. He's been giving up a lot of his time, honestly. It's part of what's been slowing down the process of him getting a place. He's been helping me get clarity on some stuff with my family, too." He smiled at Claudia with half of his mouth, somehow. "I really think you should talk to him about this orb thing, or whatever it is. You should talk to him sometime, too, Dan," he said, looking at me. "He can help you, I bet."

3

COFFEE GRINDERS ARE, TRULY, the sound of insanity, I thought. Chairs scraped across the floor as people shifted in front of their computers, or murmured to their friends. A barista shouted, "Law-rence!" and from across the table, Larry looked at me. "Why don't you get it, Danny?" he asked. I didn't let anyone call me that, normally—Danny. It would be rude to say anything now, though. He'd insisted on buying me a coffee when he'd strolled through the door of Starbucks so I owed him at least that much. Plus, he was my friend's dad, and he'd agreed to sit down with me and dispense a little advice.

Somewhere between deciding to talk to him and setting up this coffee date through Claudia and Santos, I'd lost track of what I needed advice on. The main thing on my mind was finding a place to live in the city on my dwindling funds from driving the Sarah Lawrence shuttle, with the prospect of a part-time job at an ice cream shop downtown coming up. I'd been dragging around the weight of trying to find a place to live in New York for weeks, ever since school ended. I didn't want to spend another summer at home in New Jersey, especially while my friends lived in the city. The whole point of going to a college near New York was to get out of the woods.

I'd reached out to the paltry group of New York City dwellers I knew, trying to find rooms for Santos and me, but nothing was panning out. Somehow Larry had lined up an apartment in the city, so maybe he'd be able to point me in the right direction. Sure, if he could help me figure out how to make things work with Raven that would be great. Something about his tone when he'd somehow both asked and told me "You want a coffee," made the fact that I'd been waiting at this little corner table for almost forty minutes past our agreed-upon meeting time seem like the least important thing imaginable.

"Grab us some half-and-half, will you," he said without looking at me, after I brought the coffee to the table and sat down.

Confused again, blundering because I wasn't used to being commanded like that, I went over to the counter where they had containers of milk and cream. I looked back. The black backpack I'd seen him carry around all year at Slonim was hooked on the back of his chair. He tapped some pills out of an orange bottle into his hand, then threw them back. I brought the half-and-half back to the table, and as he took it, the edges of our hands touched. His fingers were so thick the handle of the carafe practically disappeared. He poured pale mushroom clouds into both of our coffees until they turned the color of his skin—an almost-too-perfect tan—then he took a big gulp of coffee. It struck me, somehow, as a manly way of drinking.

"Sit down, Danny," he said. He put the half-and-half on the table, where it stayed. I wondered if anyone else in the café would need it, but it didn't seem to matter. The whites of his eyes were impossibly white, the irises little sequins of light. "Are you happy about how this school year has gone?" The grinding of the coffee machines and chatter of other Starbucks patrons got a little quieter. Our table was an island. He was looking through my face, it felt like.

"Yeah, I mean, I would say so. I think so." I crossed my legs, then checked, covertly, I hoped, how he was sitting: both feet flat on the floor, legs uncrossed. I uncrossed my legs.

"Would you put your signature on it, this year?"

I cocked my head. "I'm not sure what you mean."

"Danny, everything you do, you put your signature on. You know that, subconsciously, even if you don't know it. Every act, not to mention every *year* of your life, is the evidence of yourself, your being. It's the trail you leave behind in the world." His tone said he was repeating obvious information, things my parents must have taught me a long time ago. "Every single thing I do is deliberate. There is no action I take that I don't embrace as my own, that I wouldn't put my signature on. Little things, too. The laundry you fold or leave unfolded on the floor, the bed you make or leave unmade, the food you eat, the things you say or keep to yourself—all of this is what makes you who you are, and every day you move through a world of your own creation. You're making choices constantly, and when you ignore that, you're doing a disservice to yourself. What about today? Would you put your signature on this day? What about this year? Really, would you?"

"I guess not. I wouldn't put my signature on this past year, no. It hasn't felt like . . . mine, in certain ways."

"Why not? Talk me through it. I understand from Claudia and Santos you've been having some trouble. Good kids, by the way, your friends."

"Oh yeah, they're great, totally. I'm not sure I would go so far as to call it trouble. I don't know what Claudia and Santos told you. They said you might have some advice." I barely knew him. Even if he'd been living in my house for months now, we weren't exactly close.

He smiled. "I could have helped you much earlier, Dan. I take it you want to talk to me about your relationship."

It was oddly relieving for him to say it. It wasn't really what I was here for, but yes, I could feel it already: It would be a relief to at least talk about it. I couldn't talk to anyone—the way things had begun was too complicated, and it felt impossible to imagine how they might end. I hesitated, like I was looking into a freezing lake from the top of a cliff, my friends already down below, urging me to leap. "I guess I can't really figure out what's wrong—"

"What do you think is wrong, Dan?"

"Well, no, nothing's really wrong, exactly. Sometimes, with Raven—"

"Not with Raven," he interrupted. "With you. What do you think is wrong with you?" His voice was warm. He took a sip of coffee. It was shocking, his directness, and I felt more *there,* more in the room than I had been before, less conscious of what my hands were doing or the noise my chair's legs would make if I tried to adjust it. I wondered all the time what was wrong with me, it was true. I could try to explain. I bit the inside of my cheek. *The way Raven does,* I thought. She chewed the inside of her mouth so intensely that on the outside you could see a subtle pattern of dimples and pocks of inverted bite marks.

"I'm scared," I blurted. "All the time."

"Yes," he said, "I know." He was nodding as if it was the most obvious, normal, and acceptable thing in the world. "Tell me why."

How does he know? I thought. *Is it that obvious?* A wave of relief flooded over my brain. I wasn't totally alone. "I don't know, I'm always trying so hard. When I talk to people I feel like I think so hard about what they think, or what they want to hear, that it's like it's not me talking, but a projection I've made of the version of me that I think they want to hear from." His shoulders were tucked back, his whole body leaning forward over the table a little bit. It was around two P.M., the shadows in Manhattan were long, and he was blocking half the light from the window behind him, through which Ninety-second Street was bustling. "Since I was a little kid I've felt almost like I was saying stuff because I wanted a certain reaction or I wanted a friend or a girl to feel a certain way about me, so it was kind of like the actual *me* disappeared more and more, and I don't even know what's left–some kind of manipulative amalgam of the imagined expectations of–"

"Hold on a second."

My chest was pounding. It felt like he had stopped my heart midbeat. He was looking down at his phone, texting. It felt possible, somehow, to tell him these things, which I hadn't ever even put into words before. He just seemed so cavalier about it, like it was nothing he hadn't encountered countless times before, so casual that now he was interrupting me to text. "I'm sorry, Danny, you understand," he said without looking up. "Someone from the DIA."

"Oh, that's okay," I said. I'd heard him talk about the Defense Intelligence Agency before, at Slonim. I'd been insulted, momentarily, that he was texting during this conversation, and now I felt ashamed. The fact that someone so important and professional, a real adult, whose job this was not, was even making time for me, some kid, some friend of his daughter's, was really generous. He'd bought me a coffee.

He snapped his phone shut and looked back up at me. "You were saying you feel like you manipulate people."

"Yeah . . ."

He held his hand in the air between us, moving one finger at a time, as if he was slowly flipping a coin between them. "Do you know what this is?" he asked.

"No, I'm not sure," I said.

"That's manipulation. Digital manipulation. Just movement. I'm manipulating each of my fingers. You use those fingers to manipulate things in the world around you. So what? They're all a part of my hand. They're supposed to move together. Now, are they moving, or am *I* moving *them*? Does it matter? Manipulation is how the universe moves. It's how things change. I'm a master manipulator, it's why I was so valuable to the U.S. government. It's not something to be ashamed of, it's something to be proud of. That's not what's wrong. Tell me what it really is." he said.

"Right . . . yeah, I guess not." I felt frustrated. I didn't know what exactly was going on, but whatever it was, I wanted to do well at it. Maybe I had said those things because they were what I thought he wanted to hear, and he could tell the difference. If he wanted something true, I would find something true to give him. Something deeper. "Well, I guess to go further, sometimes I wonder if that means I'm a sociopath," I said. "Because I don't really feel things, I just feel what I think other people want me to feel, or what I need to feel to get through the day or a conversation, even. I've been wondering that for a really long time. Since I was pretty young."

He sighed. It was as if I had said both exactly what he'd expected and not what he wanted to hear. Was he getting bored with me, with my problems? My thinking felt like a Möbius strip, it always had, flipping over and over with no end. I needed to figure out what the truth was so that I could tell it to him, and I needed to tell it to him in order for him to help me figure out what the truth was. "If you want me to help you," he said, "I need you to tell me what's really going on. Can I try something?"

"Okay," I said, relieved to let him take more control.

"Growing up, as a kid–I need you to really focus, Dan." His hands were flat on the table; they looked strong enough to push his fingers through the wood if he wanted. "Did you have any toys that were important to you, any stuffed animals?"

"Yeah, I did."

"Tell me about the one that mattered to you most."

"I don't know. I don't remember."

"Yes, you do. You remember."

"I don't think so." There had been a pale blue blanket that I'd brought with me everywhere. When it was beyond cleaning, my mom would take her fabric scissors and snip off the soiled, ragged edges so the blanket got smaller and smaller until it disappeared.

"Why do you think you don't remember? What happened?"

"My mom threw them away."

"Why would she do that? There was one that mattered to you most, wasn't there? What kind was it?"

"A dog, I think."

"You think? It was a dog, wasn't it?"

"You're right. It was."

"Of course it was." He smiled and nodded meaningfully.

Of course it was, I thought, convinced, as he seemed to be, that that made perfect, undeniable sense. There was a story about this I had grown accustomed to telling. I didn't know for sure how accurate it really was anymore, but I thought it helped to explain my relationship with my parents. I wondered if I'd told it to Claudia or Santos and they'd passed it along. "It was at dinner one night. I don't know why, but I remember looking up at my parents–they were complaining about something going on at work, some adult problem, maybe politics–and I said something like, 'You know what's the worst? When you can't really sleep because your stuffed animals are taking up too much room in your bed.' Just to have something to say. When I came home from school the next day, my mom had thrown them all away."

"Tell me what happened next."

I thought hard. "I don't know. Nothing happened next."

"Yes, it did," he said, as if he had been there. "Do you remember?"

Maybe it was okay to unearth it together, his hand on top of my hand, which was on the handle of the shovel digging into my brain. "I ran down to the end of the driveway," I said.

"It was a long driveway. Keep going. What happened?"

I was searching. "I looked in the trash can. It was taller than I was." It must have been. "It was empty. I remember looking down the road and seeing the garbage truck turn the corner and disappear. It was trash day. Thursday." I thought it was what had happened. It could have been. His eyes were half closed, like he was partially there in the café and partially in the past with me.

"Why do you think you told them about the stuffed animals? That wasn't true, was it?"

I took a breath. I felt energy rippling through me. Maybe it was the coffee I wasn't used to. Maybe it was talking about things that I rarely, if ever, talked about. Things I didn't even know were there to talk about. It was scary but also exciting. He looked at me, waiting.

"We just sat there. Eating dinner. We just ate, as if nothing had happened. As if my mom wasn't sick, as if these weren't the chairs where she routinely sat barely holding on to consciousness while we tried to convince her to take a glucose tab or drink some orange juice and she yelled at me and my dad to leave her alone. Which would have meant letting her die. And if I looked down I would see the floor, this stone floor, underneath me, where I'd found my mom so many times passed out, soaked in sweat. Halfway through a meal she would say something that didn't make sense, the way someone talks when they've fallen asleep but don't realize it. I'd always notice first. My dad didn't know how not to get frustrated. I guess he'd been dealing with it way longer than I had. Sometimes he would just tell me to leave and I'd sit in my room, hoping she'd be okay, that I wouldn't come downstairs later to ambulance lights turning the kitchen red, which happened sometimes. We didn't talk about it, is the point. It felt silent all the time, because of the things we didn't talk about. So, I don't know, I just wanted to fill the void, the imagined void, I guess." I didn't know if I was getting all the details right. It didn't matter. I had already started, and he was listening. I wanted to tell him. I wanted what I was saying to matter to someone else as much as it mattered to me. I wanted to be worth his time.

"Your mom has diabetes, is that right?"

"She has MS, too."

He nodded knowingly. "Danny, you know as well as I do that something is going on in your family beyond your mom's physical illness. We're just talking here. What do you think it is?"

It was like unreeling a tightly wound skein of yarn. "She's so sick, it's true, but I also feel like she makes herself sick. Something makes her sick. She's constantly hurting herself, falling down the stairs, spilling boiling water on her hands, it's always something, always horrendous. I started to wonder if she was doing it on purpose." I didn't even know that much about the actual illness she had, or what mixture of illnesses, even though I'd been living with her my whole life. This wasn't how it was supposed to be, I thought, though no one had explained to me how it *was* supposed to be.

"Why would she do that?"

"For attention, I guess."

"Would you say that's the same way you brought up your stuffed animals? For attention? Who do you think is really the problem in your family? It's not your mom. She's a sweet lady, isn't she? Wouldn't you say so? What if I told you I could help her? What if I told you that helping your mom is crucial to clearing the clouds in your mind and helping you achieve clarity?"

For so long I had thought everything was my mom's fault. Her fault when we barely made it off the highway on our way home, her head lolling as if it couldn't stay balanced on her neck, then waking up after we'd slammed into a snowbank, me having to zip up my winter coat and wander off into the snow to find a neighbor who could help. It was her fault the ambulance drivers knew our house, that the 911 operators seemed to know my voice on the phone. Her fault that the neighbors knew what it meant when I showed up at their front door. It was a relief to take that blame off of her. I wasn't sure what my mom needed. Help had been out of the question for years; it was just something we lived with, something I'd left back home. I had given up without realizing I had given up. The thought that there might be a way to undo the knots of guilt and anger and blame inside of me was a brand-new idea, and the possibility that the confusion I felt—I couldn't deny I felt it—might have to do with that, was a revelation. I had been nodding slowly without realizing it.

—⊣⊢—

"Can you feel it? Something feels better already, right? I told you earlier I was texting with the DIA. You know I was recruited to work in intelligence because of who I am, because of what I can do with people?"

"Yeah, Santos and Claudia said, and you did earlier, about the manipulation."

"I assure you, I am very, very good at this. If I want to, I can help your mom. I'd like to do that for you. But I know why you really wanted to talk to me. Let's talk about Raven. Danny," he said knowingly, seeming disappointed, "you can do much better. Why do you think you cheated with her on your friend Max?"

I felt a little nauseous all the sudden. "I don't . . ."

He looked at me. I didn't want to call it that. Earlier in the year, back at school, she and Max had still been dating, at what turned out to be the very tail end of their relationship, and there had been that match struck between us over the summer, and then on the back path behind the dorms, as we were walking between classes, a kiss that felt somehow much worse—violating the campus, the school year, the place where their relationship was real. Was it guilt I had been feeling all this time, that had been making me almost sick, or fear that I'd have to deal with the consequences?

"You know why you did it."

It was all falling apart. I had tried to break up with her, I had, and she'd said if I broke up with her I would have made her do that to Max for nothing. The words climbed out of my throat. "I was scared. I've just been scared." He raised his eyebrows and looked a little sad. I felt like if I could have anything in the world at that moment, it would be him grabbing me, wrapping me in a hug, holding me for a long time. I felt so tired. I'd just wanted her. It was selfish. She wore tight, low-cut dresses and bright makeup. She was there and I was an asshole.

"You were scared of being alone."

"Yeah."

"You don't have to be alone. You could be with anyone, Dan."

"I'm not sure I can be. Even when things do happen with someone, I don't know, even if I am intimate–"

"Sex. If you're fucking," he interrupted.

". . . if I, yeah. Even then I feel like they're only with me because I somehow tricked them into it." I'd almost said "manipulated," but caught myself. "I get nervous, too, like physically, and that can be a problem. All of that gets in the way."

"Nervous about what?" I squirmed in his gaze, which felt like it hadn't left me for hours. "What are you worried about, your size? What are we dealing with here, Danny?"

I coughed, wondering for an instant if anyone could hear us, then that thought drifted away, out to where any other patrons might be, on a shore a thousand miles away, on another world. I put my coffee back down on the table. This kind of thing came up. At sleepovers, at boys' summer camp. You never really told, not exactly. You learned not to compare, not to even really be naked in the same room, so you never really knew what was "normal." This was why it was such a relief to be dating someone for once, because I was sure that everything was acceptable. "I worry I'm kind of small."

He gestured in the air and leaned back. "So does everyone. Tell me what you're working with, Danny, and I'll tell you whether it's small."

Suddenly I felt naked, sitting there across from him in Starbucks. It didn't matter if I wanted to tell him or not, whether I wanted to talk about this or not. He would already know. I had tried measuring, everyone had measured. But I didn't ever really know where you were supposed to measure from or whether it was supposed to be hard or soft. I'd compared it to the distance from the tip of my thumb to the tip of my forefinger to see if what kids in school said was true. It wasn't. In the locker room in middle school as we were changing for gym class I'd seen a brief glimpse of the way my friend's penis hung down between his legs. Mine didn't do that. So I figured it was small. "Like five inches," I said.

"Dan, that's normal," he said. "Not a problem." I heaved a sigh of relief and laughed nervously. I was acting, kind of. I just wanted this part of the conversation to be over. It felt like talking to a version of my dad that didn't exist, about things my actual dad and I had never discussed. Instead of a sex talk growing up, I'd found a book about sex in the middle of our basement floor, left out there for me to find. "What matters is how you use it. What about Isabella? You've never slept with her?" His neck was almost as thick as his head. I could see some of his chest hair, graying, out of the top of his polo.

"No, we never . . ."

It seemed almost like he didn't believe me, or he thought I was wrong, somehow. "Why not? She was around all the time, wasn't she? You think she's good-looking."

"Yeah, I guess, but that's not really . . ."

His nostrils flared as he waited for me to explain.

"I get really nervous."

"So you lose it, right? You can't stay hard?" It felt like he was getting impatient with me, as if all of this was so typical that it could be simply brushed away. These fears had calcified in my brain since I had even started to think about sex. The fact that he knew what I was thinking before I even said it made everything seem run-of-the-mill, predictable. "Also perfectly normal, Danny," he said.

My mind drifted. I found myself thinking about a time I'd been driving the student shuttle last year for the graveyard shift, and a girl got into the shuttle at two A.M., then stayed until the end of my shift, when she reached forward from the back seat and started to touch my neck. I'd looked at her in the rearview mirror—no one had ever been so forward with me—and she'd insisted I come to her room, which I did. At that point I was exhausted, the morning would arrive any minute, and I didn't know her at all, her name even, and I was so new, so barely in the world, and when she reached for me my body didn't respond. After a while, she started yelling at me, this stranger, asking why I didn't find her beautiful enough, and when I wasn't able to change anything, she kicked me out into the dark, and I walked home, ashamed.

"Yeah, that does happen."

"Why do you think that is?"

"I think too much. I'm in my head. Why am I here? What am I doing? Do they actually like me? What am I supposed to do? What happens now?"

"I'm going to let you in on something. That's what you think you're thinking. But it's not what you're actually thinking. I want you to tell me *why* you're asking those questions. When you were younger, and you'd think about sex, before you ever actually had sex, what were you afraid of?"

I thought. I could see myself in my bedroom back in New Jersey, looking out the window at the oak tree, the string of crushes I'd had that had led to nothing, the poems I'd written about unrequited love, the deep longing at the center of it all. "I was afraid I wouldn't be any good."

"That's not it. What were you afraid of?"

I was still in the house in New Jersey. Down the hall from my dad's office. Even younger. My friend—we had been friends since first grade—was over for a playdate. My parents were downstairs. We played detective. A detective had to have a secretary. We were in my dad's office. My friend played my secretary, I played his detective. The same friend whose penis, years later, I would see hanging down between his legs in the locker room and find myself, by comparison, inadequate. Something went wrong in the case we were investigating. He sat in an armchair while I paced across the room. *What are we going to do, Mr. Detective?* he asked in a high, girlish voice. *I have one idea,* I said dramatically as I threw myself onto him. *Forget the case,* I whispered into his ear in a voice deeper, older than I was. *Oh,* he said, his voice fluttering.

I looked up at Larry.

"I was afraid I might be gay."

Larry smirked, then started to laugh. It took me a second to understand he was laughing at me. I'd never felt the kind of overwhelming lust for a man the way I had for a woman, like my whole body was an arrow pointed at her, like she reverberated with multicolored light; she was Las Vegas and Jerusalem, and more than anything, I understood her as a door for me to walk through. Like I would be sick if I couldn't meet the shining secret on the other side of her. That was true. But I wondered if, maybe, that kind of sick, toxic attraction was a wall I put up to hide a more difficult truth from myself.

"You're not," Larry said. "I can tell you you're not gay. You're not a sociopath. You don't have a small penis. You just need to relax. Trust me, I am professionally trained to evaluate people, to walk around the inside of their minds. That's easy for me. I want to use that to help you, okay? Would you like that?" I took a breath. If I believed him, if he was right, then I didn't have to worry about anything. I could just get over it. I could maybe move forward with my life without feeling so twisted up inside all the time.

"Okay," I said. "Yeah. I'd like that."

"Then let's get out of here," Larry said. "They're closing up soon."

I looked around us. The café was practically empty. The light was artificial; when had the sun gone down? I got up with Larry, and as we walked to the door I pulled my phone out of my pocket and checked the time. It was almost nine o'clock; we'd been talking for six hours. I couldn't believe it. No wonder I felt so hollowed out, the energy coursing through me so thin and weird.

"Walk with me back to my apartment," Larry said. "It's just a block or two." I felt like I couldn't say no anymore. I knew I should get back to my brother's apartment in Brooklyn, where I was staying, but there wasn't really any rush. It was only a couple blocks. We emerged from the closing Starbucks into a warm summer night. It felt like the first time I had ever walked in New York. Larry walked slowly by my side. Claudia and Santos weren't wrong; there was something extraordinary about him. Even though he was shorter than me, it felt somehow like I was looking up when I talked to him. We passed underneath some scaffolding, and as we strolled past a wall of blue-painted post-no-bills plywood, Larry stopped to give some money to a man with one leg who was squatting on a low stool. "How's it going, Henry?" Larry asked.

"Same, same," Henry said.

"What are you doing this summer?" Larry asked me.

I had to slow my pace to match his. I tried to make sense of the Alsatian pizza restaurant we were passing on our left. "I've got this job downtown. A nondairy ice cream shop in the East Village."

He grunted. "All this stuff about Raven," he said. "Let's clear that up. You know you can just break up with her, right?"

"I don't think I can do that, though, just break up with her. I've tried." I wished Larry could help her. I wished Larry could fix everything.

"You can. You have to. Whatever she says, that's not your responsibility, okay? You don't answer. She'll call you, she'll text you. *You don't answer the phone.* That's not your responsibility anymore. You need to move forward. Your only responsibility is your own life, how to be a good person, how to be whole. You want my advice? Cut it off."

I'd thought I could find a way to end things with Raven that was reasonable. I didn't know what I had imagined. That we might agree, mutually, to be friends. Somehow it'd turned out to be a decision between dating and suicide. Maybe Larry was right.

"Do you have a place to stay?" Larry asked. I knew Santos and Claudia had been splitting their time between their parents' places and Larry's apartment. It wasn't that far off from our arrangement in Slonim Woods except reversed, as if Larry was paying back our generosity in letting him park his life in the corner of our college experience.

"I'm staying at my brother's for now. I figure I'll go back to my parents' in New Jersey for a bit—I'm supposed to spend next week there with Raven. After that, I don't know."

"Well, if you want, you can always stay at my apartment until you find a place."

I had no idea how to find an apartment in New York, and had been having so much trouble that I was thinking about just staying with my parents and making the three-hour commute into Manhattan to work at the ice cream place. Maybe then I'd be able to save a little money and find a place after a while, maybe even split it with Claudia and Santos, at least for the second half of the summer. I could stay with my brother on the weekends, but he'd just forwarded me an email from my sister-in-law that listed the things I'd left dirty or ruined in their house: mold in the shower from not closing the curtain, a bath mat left sponging the wet floor, crumbs on the kitchen counter, and my stuff piled in the corner of the living room attracting roaches. I felt like I was the roach. I needed to find a place where I wouldn't be in anyone else's way. "Thanks," I said. "That's really generous of you."

"Here's everybody," Larry said. We'd rounded the corner onto Ninety-third Street, where a stretch limousine idled on the corner.

I followed Larry as he opened the limousine door and crawled inside, where Santos, Claudia, Talia, and Isabella waited. It looked like they had all been laughing so hard they'd been crying. I'd only ever been in a limousine for prom and for funerals. I squeezed in between Isabella and Larry, near the front. "How'd it go?" Isabella leaned into my ear. I was immediately aware of her soft angles pressed into my side.

"It went very, very well," Larry answered. "Didn't it, Danny?"

"Yeah, it did." I smiled at everyone. It was true. I felt new. They were all looking at me, thrilled. It was as if I was everything they had been waiting for. I'd been in the audience of this show for so long, and now I had taken my spot onstage. I wouldn't find out until later that they had all been waiting in the car, sitting there for the entire six hours that Larry and I were in the Starbucks.

"Should we get some dinner?" Larry leaned toward the window that separated us from the driver.

"Sorry, I should probably get back to Brooklyn," I said. If I returned to my brother's too late, I'd have to wake him up to let me in.

Larry rolled his eyes. "Danny wants to go back to Brooklyn, everyone." He embarrassed me for the first time that evening. I blushed and didn't say anything. He turned back to the driver. "Take us down to L'Express," he said. He put his hand on my shoulder. It seemed gigantic. He squeezed. "Remember what I said? You just need to relax." He smiled, and everyone else did, too. I looked at him. I didn't understand what had happened, but now I was going with them—I could no longer say no. It wasn't even an option.

4

THE NEXT WEEK, AS I sat on the slab of a bed in my old bedroom at my parents' house in New Jersey, my back resting against the off-white wall still patchworked with posters, Raven began to stir next to me. I thought I should take her for a walk in the woods. When I came home, I often found ways to spend as little time as possible with my parents, especially if I came home with someone else. In front of an audience, the discomfort of my family became unignorable. The cloudy silences that gathered over meals were suddenly interminable, every clink of ice in a glass like the thud of blood behind a bruise. Raven and I had already been here for a few days, so we could afford to avoid breakfast with my parents without seeming too ungrateful, though we had spent much of that time squirreled away in my room.

I knew that I must be naive about my parents. I felt frustrated by the knowledge of my lack of knowledge. They were surely extremely complicated, deeply layered—they had to be. My impressions of them must be merely superficial, I thought. That's what drove me crazy. What were they really thinking, really feeling, under those glassy exteriors? What was trapped in there? Would I ever find out?

As I sat waiting for Raven to wake up, I wrote a poem that described my parents lying in the sun, absorbing light, while the vultures that lived in the rotting trees around our house danced above them, casting shadows. I thought it was the best poem I'd ever written, but I always thought the latest poem I'd written was the best poem I'd ever written and, knowing that, I immediately hated it. I watched the gray morning light, veined with the shadows of tree limbs, inch across the blue carpet. On the windowsill, making its own awkward shadow, was a small ornamental bucket filled with seashells Raven had spent a long afternoon collecting for me on the beach in Mexico. She pushed her cheek into my thigh.

I was not entirely there. After New York, this place, being in the same room as Raven, didn't feel altogether real. It felt harder, anyway, like I had to put effort into existing—whereas with Larry, it was like he did all the existing for you; he held us all up. I finally got what Santos and Claudia had been talking about this whole time, but I still knew how it sounded from the outside. I thought I would never be able to explain.

I leaned over Raven, somewhere between knowing and not knowing what I was going to do. Her face was all soft and closed. I was naive about her, too, though I couldn't figure out how. I couldn't see beyond what I thought she wanted from me, and the retribution I feared if I ever said the wrong thing. I knew there must be an explanation for why she'd had a meltdown and thrown a shoe at me the day before, for example, which had left a hole in the wall I'd had to move one of my posters to cover, but Larry said it wasn't my responsibility to figure that stuff out anymore. After this week, she would fly back home to the Northwest, then in the fall she would go to Florence to study abroad for a semester. I was going to England. So it didn't make any sense for us to stay together; our relationship was already over. That didn't mean I had any idea how to end it. "Let's go outside," I said.

It was later than I thought; my parents had already abandoned the kitchen. Raven stepped past me through the screen door. Her sandals flapped against the stones of the patio. "You should've worn long pants," I said to her. She looked down at her dress, short and splayed out at the waist. It was cute—she was always cute. I didn't know what to say. I thought the woods would explain it for me.

"I'll be fine," she said.

As we crossed the yard, we passed a small log that was covered in white lichen and jutted vertically out of the ground. I paused. "This is where I buried my cat," I said. We stood facing the log, which had frozen and then thawed again over the winter.

"Weird gravestone," she said. It was. I'd come home from college over winter break last year and my parents had warned me they had bad news. "Where did you put it?" I'd asked, and my mom, after making a surprised face, had gone to fetch the trash bag where she had thrown our dead cat. I'd gripped the edges of the bag in my fists and looked into it: an orange moon at the bottom of the black plastic night. I'd walked out to the edge of the woods and stabbed at the frozen ground with the log until I'd made a deep-enough hole, buried the cat in the trash bag, then stuck the log there.

"This way," I said, carefully pinching the vine of a pricker bush and pushing it aside to expose a faint path.

"Where does this go?" she asked, as she started off ahead of me.

"Nowhere really. The deer make these paths in the woods and I just follow them." It felt good to be dramatic and mysterious, the boy from the woods with the inexplicable upbringing. The path traced along the lip of a cliff that overlooked a stream. It was strewn with boulders deposited by a glacier that had passed this way eons ago and left the valley suspended in a state of tumbling. I reached up and tapped a piece of

quartz in the joint of a tree where I'd lodged it years ago, then stood looking down over the valley.

"This is where I used to sit and meditate in high school." She peered through the trees, a tapestry of green extending up to a ceiling carpeted with gray-white cloud. Everything was upside down. The air was dense with summer humidity and the roar of cicadas, summer's cacophonous pulse. Any kind of real conversation was impossible; we would have to either yell or whisper.

"You can see the road," she said, loudly. She was right. The dotted line of asphalt through the trees shattered the illusion we were somewhere wild, animal, where anything could happen. I turned into the deeper part of the woods and she followed.

We emerged in a small clearing, a wide patch of tall, overgrown straw in the middle of the thick forest. The light was suddenly fluorescent. Raven was untangling the hem of her dress from one of the pricker bushes on the edge of the clearing when she noticed I had stopped. "What?"

"This is it," I said.

"This is what?"

"What I wanted to show you. I used to come out here when I was younger. These are deer beds, where they sleep." Around us were craters where deer had used their bodies to flatten the grass. At night, fawns slept cradled by their mothers while bucks stood at the edge, keeping watch. I knew that. I had seen it. I sat, and she hesitated, then quickly lowered across from me. The grass rose above our heads, and everything disappeared.

I realized I was trying to make the day beautiful, but everything felt hollow. She smiled, her lips pressed hard. She closed her eyes and leaned back on her hands as if the weak sunlight was a rope tugging her upward. I stared at her, arched like that, and it took me a minute to register what was moving. There were tiny green insects, the size of a pinprick—dozens of them crawling up her dress where it had settled on the ground. I reached over and brushed them off.

"What is it?" she asked without opening her eyes.

"Nothing," I said.

—ıı—

I waited until she flew back to Seattle to call. I told her I had been thinking about breaking up the whole week we were in New Jersey. She was bewildered, and said I sounded totally different than I had when we'd been together. She said I didn't make any sense and called me a liar. She said that there must be something that I wasn't telling her. "Well, I talked to Larry," I finally admitted.

"Fuck Larry," she said.

"He told me if I wanted to break up, it wasn't fair to you or to me for us to stay together."

"Fuck you," she said.

I didn't say anything.

"Larry's a fucking creep, and it's weird that he hangs around with Claudia and Santos and Isabella. It's fucking weird," she said.

I remembered something Larry had said over dinner that night, after our conversation in the café. I tried to repeat it back, as best I could. "Raven, Larry cares about me and wants what's best for me. If you don't live what he has to say, then logically, you must not care about me."

"Oh, go fuck yourself," she said. "At least I don't have to anymore."

—ıı—

"Primavera." The man sitting across from me on the subway was shouting at no one. "Primavera. PRIMAVERA." New York was about negative space, I had learned. Where you could and couldn't look. The laser beams of your glance could intersect with others', you could stare into the infinite emptinesses between people, and you could even meet another person's eyes, but only rarely. Men yelling on the subway were definitely among those I tried to avoid making eye contact with, or any other kind of contact, for that matter. "THIS IS A REAL WORD," the man picked up volume. "WHAT DOES IT MEAN?"

My eyes met those of the girl sitting next to him. She smiled and did not blink, then looked back down at her book. You can learn not to hear what's happening in the same room as you, the same subway car, just like you can learn not to see what's happening around you even with your eyes open, looking straight at it. Almost exactly one year before, at the end of my freshman year at Sarah Lawrence, I had been moving home for the summer, already in a mood, exhausted from packing, resentful that I had no choice but to spend the next few summer months with my parents in New Jersey. Laden with luggage as I entered the subway station beneath Grand Central, I made the mistake of making eye contact with another group of people I tried to avoid: the police, who were stationed around a gray plastic folding table.

The officers made me stop before the turnstile to perform a search of my bags, which I heaved onto the table. Faced with the choice of suspicious silence or suspicious nervous chatter, I elected for chatter, and when I was mid-prattle about my first year of college I remembered what was in my bag. Time slowed down. The sound of the officer unzipping my backpack became like a ratchet tightening in a series of clicks. The weed plant from my windowsill. I'd placed the plant into my backpack with the intention of taking it home to New Jersey and planting it somewhere in the woods, less because I cared about growing weed, and more because I didn't want to kill a living plant. The police officer unzipped the bag and looked into its shadowy interior. My life and its possible outcomes and endings, one of which was a felony conviction, tipped on a razor's edge.

Then the officer zipped it closed. "We just stopped you because of the instrument case. Sometimes people keep guns in those. You'd be shocked: pistols, machine guns, bazookas even," he said. "What's that for, a violin or something?"

I gulped. "A ukulele." My train roared into the station behind him. The world seemed to arrive and return to its normal course.

Even now, sitting on the train a year later, I hadn't learned the distinction between privilege and what I perceived to be luck. I smiled to myself, thinking the answer to the yelling man's question ("spring").

"THAT GUY SMILED!" He pointed at me. *No secrets in New York,* I thought. *Not even thinking can be private here.* He was wearing a hairnet over his beard. "Primavera," I would learn later from Larry, when he became obsessed with exotic timber, is also a type of Central American tree, the raw wood of which changes color upon exposure to air.

I got off at Union Square. Passing through a New York City subway station in summer, the heat of the earth close by, I trotted up the sweaty steps onto Broadway. The sun reflected for a moment off countless mirrored windows; the street shimmering like a mirage. I crossed to the marginally shadier side, and walked the few blocks over and down to the East Village. Below Fourteenth Street, the city started to wane, the buildings shrank to more comprehensible scales. Stuyvesant Street was a diagonal rift in the grid, forming a triangular park across which St. Mark's Church-in-the-Bowery stared into Stogo, the ice cream shop whose owner, Junie, had looked past my paltry résumé and offered me a job. A woman named Bethany was working today, and waved at me as I practically fell into the air conditioning. I had worked in the shop for a few shifts, and was slowly becoming less petrified. Bethany was cool, pretty, older than I was, and friendly, which was confusing. Beautiful, older city girls were supposed to be scary, I thought. "What's up?" she asked.

"Not much," I said. "Ready to sling some cream."

She laughed. "Gross. You want something? I just invented it—oatmeal raisin soyshake," she said.

"Jesus Christ," I said. "Yeah, make me one."

Stogo was a nondairy ice cream shop, which meant the clientele were vegans, people with aggressive allergies and equally aggressive attitudes about their allergies, or people who had made some kind of mistake. Over the course of my shift, the customers changed from the occasional family or pair of tourists in the afternoon to the roaming bar-hopping crowds of the East Village at night.

"I'm out of here!" Bethany shouted from the back as evening fell, untying her apron. It was a weeknight, so there would be only one person closing—me. It was my second week, and no one had told me how to close, but I didn't want to say anything and look stupid. Maybe I was supposed to know, somehow, or maybe someone had told me and I had not been listening or had forgotten. It must be pretty self-explanatory anyway.

Around ten, a group of men hanging on to one another as if for dear life came in through the tinkling door. They were laughing at something as they swayed toward the counter; one of them had his eyes locked on me. He leaned into the cold glass case. "Can I have a sample of the Mexican chocolate?" he asked. "And your number."

I blushed and mumbled, "Sure, yes, I mean here's your sample," handing him a tiny fluorescent green spoon and trying not to touch his reaching fingers. "I'm not . . . I date girls," I said.

He smiled. "Of course you do. Give me some of that salted caramel instead, babe." I felt thrilled, and I felt weird about feeling thrilled. I wanted to tell someone, but Bethany was gone.

Closing time was creeping up so I decided to start putting things away. A laminated index card marked CLOSING PROCEDURES was tacked to the wall in the back. I'd never looked closely at it, and now that I did I blanched. The instructions looked like they had been written in marker and then dipped in a bath—all the thick lettering was smudged and had run together illegibly. It was too late at night now, nearly midnight, to call Junie. So I made a series of guesses. I brought the chalk sandwich board in from the sidewalk, turned all the chairs up onto the tables, and shut off the lights. Standing in the doorway, I looked around. It looked like an ice cream shop that was closed for the night. Good. Except that industrial whir in the background. The air conditioning. I paused for a second. I knew that Junie was freaked out about money all the time, and she would be furious if I left the AC running all night. Grateful that I'd noticed, I went back and shut it off, then locked the door and headed uptown for the night.

⊣⊢

"I'm going up to Larry Ray's apartment." The doorman of the Waterford building on the corner of Second Avenue and Ninety-third Street nodded without looking up, as if expecting me, or accustomed to kids heading to the fifteenth floor. It was around midnight when I'd finally gotten uptown, but they said they'd leave the door open for me. When I arrived at 15E, I pushed the door open gingerly. I was surprised to see the lights on, and to hear the sound of Santos guffawing. *I guess they're up late,* I thought. *Larry doesn't mind? I guess not, even on a weeknight.* During that first dinner downtown, which went far past midnight, I had come to understand that Larry intended to get the most out of his freedom. I heard the distinct timbre of his voice around the corner in the living room; he was saying something to Santos. I shut the door behind me, and emerged from the little hallway.

"Danny! Come sit here with Santos," Larry said as I came into the room. He had positioned Santos on the black leather couch, which faced out into the room, catty-corner to the big-screen TV. Throughout most of my time living there, the TV would stay on, muted, twenty-four hours a day. The apartment so resembled a page out of some Manhattan high-rise condo catalog that it looked practically two-dimensional. The walls behind the TV formed a corner of plate glass. "I need you to listen to this," Larry said. Claudia, Isabella, Talia, and Iban were positioned around the room, half-watching, half-pretending not to watch. Behind them I could just see the kitchen, which was small, practically a notch cut out of the apartment. The mood was bright; it smelled like cooking had been happening very slowly and for many hours, and now, as far as I could tell, it had stalled for some sort of demonstration.

Larry faced the two of us on the couch, and the room seemed to swell up toward him. He leaned forward. I thought he might do some kind of magic trick. "It's time for Santos to understand music," he said. "Real music. The way that music and the mind are aligned. Music has powers, magic powers, and can change you. You know that music is frequently used in therapy?"

I smirked. It was kind of silly, sitting there, but I was happy to listen. Larry must have seen my face, because his gaze locked on me, and he went on, "But did you also know, Danny, that music is used, frequently, by our U.S. military, for torture?" I shook my head. There wasn't much else I could do. Larry was practically vibrating with passion. I knew from our first year living together that Santos barely listened to music at all, didn't seem to have an interest in it, and so I assumed this must be what had inspired the diatribe I had walked into.

"You have a mind, and you have a self," Larry said. "Before you know how to navigate between them, before you've even learned the languages they speak to one another—music can bridge that gap, translate between the self and the mind." I nodded. A mind and a self. I was familiar with not understanding what was going on inside me, not being able to name it, and finding that a song's lyrics might be able to do that better than I ever could myself. "Lean back," Larry said again, this time forcefully, as we had both leaned forward automatically. I felt awkward and vulnerable fully reclining into the thick, pillowy leather. I was used to crossing my legs, crossing my arms, hunching a bit. This felt totally exposed. "Close your eyes," he said. We hesitated, then did as we were told.

"Don't open them."

I sat there in the darkness. I could hear Isabella whispering something to Claudia, then Larry harshly shushing them. When the music started, I knew I was supposed to feel like something extraordinary was happening. I tried to focus as hard as I could, to forget Santos sitting next to me in the same supine position, everyone watching. If Larry wanted some kind of revelation, I was going to give it to him. The song started with a piano and drumbeats, then a high voice floated in. It was Neil Young. My parents used to play Neil Young in the car and on their record player, but somehow the only song I ever seemed to hear was "Keep on Rockin' in the Free World." It drove me nuts. In that song, his voice sounded to me like he had died and been brought back a few times.

On Larry's couch, I tried really hard to listen, to be open to it. After the first verse, the song hesitated, just for an instant, then crossed a gap of silence and rose up into the chorus: "Don't let it bring you down. . . . It's only castles burning," and maybe I did feel something. Maybe.

The song ended, and we started to open our eyes, started to see the blurry shapes still sitting in the same places, watching us. "Keep them closed!" Larry said. "Santos, what did you feel?"

"I don't know," he said. "It was really nice, I think." I rolled my shut eyes. I had tried something not unlike this with Santos a dozen times before, showing him music, and I knew how he sounded when he lied to be nice.

I couldn't help wanting to be a little better than him at this. "It felt ghostly," I said. "Like something floating that you can never reach, but the music, or Neil Young somehow, made it possible to go up there, to fly above it, to see this city."

"He gets Neil Young," Larry said, winking at Isabella. "Now those lyrics, that was poetry, wasn't it?" I started to answer yes, but he continued. "There are words that in the right combination can transcend. Words can change people, a lot of people, if they're deployed correctly. There are books that access a level of consciousness which eclipses most people's understanding. *Finnegans Wake.* You know *Finnegans Wake*?" I shook my head. "I laugh out loud page after page reading that book. It knows something most people don't. Joyce is one of those people able to gather up the strands of human consciousness and put them together into one thread, a thread you can pull on if you know how to. Neil Young, too. Would you like to know how to do that?" I thought I could hear Santos nodding beside me.

"What about, 'Blind man running through the light of the night with an answer in his hand'? What do you think that's about?"

"I don't know," I said, giving up.

"It's about you, Danny. And you, Santos."

—||—

That night, after Santos had gone home to his parents' house in the Bronx and Claudia to her parents' apartment just a few blocks away, I stretched out on the couch, draped the blanket Isabella had given me over my bottom half, and sloughed off my jeans. Talia, Isabella, and Larry had said good night around three A.M. and vanished behind what I learned was the bedroom door. They all slept together in a king bed, which at first struck me as odd. But it seemed to be a norm everyone had accepted, so I did too. Talia and Isabella were best friends, and Larry and Talia had a really close father-daughter relationship, and with him having not seen her in jail and everything, it made enough sense for me to accept. Especially since it meant I got a couch to sleep on. For now.

As I settled back into the weird, skin-like leather and stared up at the ceiling, which flickered with light from the TV I'd felt it'd be too intrusive to ask how to turn off, I heard the bedroom door open. Isabella emerged, wearing her pajamas: a soft cotton shirt that seemed barely to serve any purpose, and underwear. She crept over to the couch, where I had sat up. "Hey, what–" I started to say, but she shushed me, putting her hands on my legs as she knelt in front of me. I understood what was about to happen, and it felt like everything inside me hardened, like I was suddenly in the wrong place at the wrong time, like I would die if I moved an inch.

I looked over at the bedroom; the door was still ajar. I had many thoughts very quickly, and they all made perfect sense. Larry had sent her out here. He and Isabella had had hours and hours of conversation; she must have told him she had a crush on me. After I'd talked to him the other day, he must have told her I was too afraid to do anything, that I needed some coaxing. He had convinced me to break up with my girlfriend. He had convinced me to stay here in the apartment, where Isabella was also staying. Even though Claudia and Santos stayed over most nights, he had sent them back to their respective parents' places. And now this. She was an extension of him. What she was doing now, he was doing. I tried to relax, but couldn't really. She pulled down my boxers. He had made this happen. She leaned forward, and swallowed me.

—||—

In the morning, I woke up to my phone ringing. It was Junie, from the ice cream shop. *Am I late?* No, my shift wasn't until that afternoon. I picked up. "Junie? Is everything all right?"

"Hi, Dan. No it's not. Did you turn off the air conditioning last night?"

My heart started to speed up. "Yeah, I did. Was I not supposed to? What's wrong?"

"Everything's melted, Dan. All the chocolate, everything's a mess.

We've had to clean it up all morning, I couldn't open on time. I called Bethany to figure out who closed. We came in and it was like a hundred degrees in here."

"Oh my god, Junie, I'm so sorry, I had no idea–"

"That's fine, Dan, we'll just, why don't you come in now, you can help out, and we'll talk about this when you get here."

"Okay, I'm coming! I'm coming!" Relieved to still have a job, and petrified that by the time I got downtown I might not, I pulled on my jeans and rushed out the door, quickly writing Larry a text message as I waited for the elevator. "Had to rush to work. Thank you so much for last night." My finger hovered over the send button. If I had to, I could go back to my brother's place, but he really wanted me to stay there only on the weekends, and I always felt like an imposition. Larry had made it very clear I was welcome in his apartment for as long as I needed, that there was absolutely nothing for me to be worried about. But I couldn't shake the feeling I'd had last night. I sent the text to Larry and typed a new one to Claudia. "Hey is it cool if I stay over with you and your parents tonight?"

5

CLAUDIA'S PARENTS' APARTMENT WAS fashionably academic, the type of place I'd like to live if I could have a place in New York. Pale morning light angled through the tall windows and caught motes of dust as they drifted from one pile of books on a desk to another stacked on the table. I crept back into Claudia's bedroom with a glass of water I'd drawn from the tap, then dropped cross-legged onto the blanket where I'd slept the night before, and waited. I'd been waking up before people at sleepovers my whole life. Being in a room with other people, conscious people, felt like clinging to a cliff. The brief, early morning before anyone else woke up was a private paradise. When I lay back down on the floor in Claudia's room, and scanned my eyes across the bookshelf, the ceiling, the diaphanous curtains quivering against the cracked-open window, I felt calmer than I knew I'd feel all day, having to deal with other people.

What was wrong with me? I'd learned at those sleepovers growing up that if I sneaked downstairs and ate breakfast with my friends' parents as they got ready for work, I could keep up a polite, precocious conversation, and end up making their parents say things like "If only our son was as grown-up as you are!" That felt easy. Having to be a full person, an adolescent with an identity, who had fun, who did things, who had interests and preferences that I expressed around my friends—*that* felt like trying to carry my own self up a hill every day.

I didn't have a shift at the ice cream shop to get to—I still had a job, thankfully, though Junie had taken most of my paycheck for the damages—so I just sat on the floor, waiting, sipping water and looking around. Claudia's room was half filled by the bed; the rest was bookshelves and the bit of floor where I'd camped out. Her crumpled white duvet shifted as her arm flopped over the edge, followed by her face, which asked me if I wanted coffee.

I pointed to my water and shook my head. Suddenly everyone liked coffee. She groaned and stepped over me, then returned a few minutes later with a steaming mug in her hand. I put my chin up on the bed, and she ruffled my hair like a dog's. "What are you up to today?" I asked her. "Do you want to hang out downtown?" The New York City in my mind was a cloud of unconnected dots, the East Village, my brother's apartment in Brooklyn, Larry's apartment on the Upper East Side, and now Claudia's parents' apartment. I wanted to feel moored to something, to understand New York as one contiguous, inhabitable entity.

Claudia was sipping her coffee on the bed and nodded into her mug. "Totally. I was just thinking we could stop by Larry's first and say hi, and then whatever." I shrugged. Talia and Isabella were there, I knew, and maybe Santos would drop by. "Did you have a good time the other night?"

"I did, yeah." I knew I shouldn't say anything, but it'd been on my mind all morning. "If I tell you something, can you keep it a secret?" I leaned over and let myself fall to an elbow so I was staring at the underside of Claudia's bed, rather than being at face height. "Isabella and I hooked up that night."

"What!" The bedsprings strained and hopped around. "Dan! What happened?"

I sighed. I hated the way her voice sounded. Like an actor giving an unconvincing performance with a gun pointed to their head. Who cared why she felt compelled to pretend she was excited? I longed to be with someone who felt authentic, like how they appeared was, in fact, a reflection of who they were. But no one was that way, not really. "I feel like Larry . . . engineered the whole thing, though." The light through the window was truly bright now, filling up the room.

Claudia shifted, the springs buckled further down the bed. "I don't get that. What do you mean by that?" Now it was really weird, her voice skipping across the words like they were burning hot.

"He and I had that whole big conversation and he convinced me to end things with Raven, and he was asking me stuff about Isabella and whether I liked her. I don't know, it's stupid, but I've always kind of felt like she liked me, and I hated that, to be honest with you. That's probably more my issue, that I immediately dislike anyone who likes me." Claudia's forehead crumpled. "Anyway, he probably talked to Isabella and told her I'd broken up with Raven. Maybe I said something that made him think I was interested in Isabella, so he told her that. Maybe he encouraged her to come out and hook up with me, because it would be 'good for her' or whatever. Or good for me. I don't know, it just felt weird. It made me feel weird."

Claudia put her mug down and sat on the edge of the bed. "Dan, I don't think Larry would do something like that. Or if he did, you're misunderstanding it. Maybe you should talk to him."

I shook my head. Why would I talk to him, about him? "No, I don't think so. That's okay."

Her voice was getting higher. "You didn't see him tell her to do anything, did you? She didn't say that or anything. So you probably shouldn't say that. I just don't think it could be true, and by saying something like that out loud, you're putting it out into the world. You're making it real, by saying it. So you need to tell him, Dan, so he can fix it."

I had no idea what she was talking about. "Okay, jeez. Just forget it. It was probably nothing. I was being weird." She looked away, but seemed to accept that.

—ıı—

The sun's heat had settled into the concrete by the time Claudia and I walked to Larry's apartment. The sky looked high and tight, like the skyscrapers didn't come anywhere close to scraping it. A new doorman nodded us through the lobby of the Waterford building, we took the elevator fifteen floors up, and Claudia rapped her knuckles on 15E. Santos swung the door open and smiled; his whole face had a way of becoming whatever expression he was making—his eyes actually twinkled, his cheeks turned a little pink, his joy to see us was soft and dimpled and right there. I wondered if he was that kind of person who was authentically himself, but if so, how tragic. It felt that way, like he had no choice but to be entirely *here,* a puppy so adorable you wanted to squash it, just a little bit. Isabella and Iban were hanging out around the glass table with cups of coffee, Isabella looking like she had just woken up, wearing everything soft, Iban sitting as straight as his military crew cut. Isabella's light eyes and the long line of her lips made her smile look the way a python smiles at a pig. "We're talking about Tal's birthday," she said, keeping her voice low.

Santos started to squeeze past her chair to sit on the opposite side and as he did, Isabella shouted, "Get away from me, you perv!" cackling as she grabbed the lip of the table and pushed her seat back into him. He tensed and slipped past her, flopping awkwardly into the empty chair. "Just kidding, San-tos." She rolled her eyes, over-pronouncing his name, as if spelling it out in the air, pointing at it, calling it strange. "We're going to do dinner. Something really fancy. Talia deserves it after everything, right? Now that we're all together we can really show her she's got a family. We'll all dress up and go out and give her something nice."

"Oh yeah!" Claudia glommed on. "Let's get steak. Tal loves steak." It felt awkward to hear Claudia use the nickname I had only ever heard Isabella or Larry use. It meant you were a member of the family, in a sense. You couldn't just pretend it belonged to you; surely you had to earn it.

Isabella nodded anyway, chin jutting. In the absence of Larry and Talia, she was in charge. "This is ridiculous," she said. "Where is my man?" She strode to the speaker, plugged in her phone, and put on Nirvana. Iban winced, clearly preferring silence over Kurt Cobain.

⊣⊢

Talia shuffled in, wearing thick slippers and pajama pants more than a few sizes too big. She looked like a nine-year-old girl born with the face of a twenty-year-old, worn out, as if the wrong side of the bed had folded over and flattened her for a few hours. Larry, on the contrary, looked and sounded positively cheery as he followed her through the door into the living room. "Good morning, everybody! Iz, where's my coffee?"

"Right here, Lare!" It was in her hand already, as if by magic, or she had readied herself to start pouring him a mug the instant the bedroom door began to inch inward.

"We should go out today," he said, looking not out the windows, through which the sun was gleaming, the whole city gilded, but instead directly at me. He was sitting at the table now, and I realized Claudia had popped out of her seat to make room for him and was leaning against the wall. The whole apartment moved when he moved.

"Claudia, come talk with me for a second." He indicated the bedroom with his cue ball head. "What is this shit, Iz?" He looked up into the air, sniffed the music.

"This is my man, Kurt!" Isabella said, scandalized. Kurt was singing: "I'm so lonely but that's okay, I shaved my head, and I'm not sad."

Larry's face was inscrutable. "I like it," he said. "Leave it on. Grab your coffee, Claud!" She hastily poured herself a cup, and followed him through the door.

⊣⊢

I wasn't sure what to do in the meantime, so I wandered over to the couch and looked at the bookshelf. "Are you looking for something to read?" Talia asked me. "Has my dad told you about *The Conquest of Happiness* yet? It's one of our favorites. Here, it's in my bag. She started rustling around, and handed me a yellow paperback. Sinking into the couch, I paged through the introduction and preface until I reached the first page, where it opened:

> Animals are happy so long as they have health and enough to eat. Human beings, one feels, ought to be, but they are not, at least in a great majority of cases. If you are unhappy yourself, you will probably be prepared to admit that you are not exceptional in this.

I looked up at the room, my friends dotted around it, and I wondered whether they were happy. I wondered if I had ever wondered if anyone besides myself was happy. Isabella came over and sat next to me, and I tensed as she grabbed my arm. "You boys are looking fit!" she exclaimed, looking at Santos. I laughed, feeling awkward. Back at Slonim, Larry had given Santos a workout routine from the marines, ten sets of forty push-ups every morning, and I'd agreed to do it with him. I couldn't help but enjoy that it had been a little easier for me than for Santos to wake up and do the push-ups on the dirty tile, to wait for him more and more mornings as the semester pushed on and he slept through his alarm. Now that it was summer I'd been eating mostly dairy-free ice cream milkshakes and gluten-free pizza around the corner from work, and had been frequently skipping meals altogether to save money. Even without paying rent, I could barely afford New York. When I looked down at my body I felt like I was some kind of Tinkertoy, all blobs and sticks.

Talia pulled up her sleeve at the table and flexed her wiry little arm. "We're tough too, though!"

"Should we do it, Santos?" I was half joking. Isabella cheered over Santos's groan.

"You're doing what?" Iban didn't move, but I could feel him looking down over us. His face was small and boyish, his mouth often twisted a bit, like he had a wry comment he could make, but wouldn't.

"Forty push-ups," I said, getting down on the carpet next to Santos. Santos checked his form against mine. "Ten sets." I guessed Iban liked knowing he was better than these soft, private school kids. He was, I thought.

—⊣⊢—

The carpet came in and out of focus. Santos panted next to me. I balanced on one arm for a second, wiping a bead of sweat out of the corner of my eye. “My dad used to do push-ups with me sitting on his back,” Talia said. “I’d come into the room when he was having meetings. It didn’t matter who it was or what was going on, honeyboy let me come in whenever I wanted. I would ask him to do push-ups while I sat on him, and he would do it.” Isabella nodded, as if she had been there.

“That’s right.” Larry’s voice filled the room. From down on the floor, I hadn’t seen him come back in. Trailing behind him, Claudia looked stony, like she was staring at something floating right behind Larry’s knees. He slumped down at the table with a big sigh that sounded burdened and satisfied. “Claudia has something she wants to say to us, don’t you, Claudia?” She nodded, looking down through the table at something else altogether. “She just told me something very interesting,” Larry went on. “Go ahead.”

“I just told Larry something about Isabella and Daniel. I lied about it. About them.”

A pressure in my ears started to creep down to my jaw, which locked in place. Isabella was less stunned. She looked like she could smash Claudia through the table. “What the fuck are you talking about?” she said.

“I’m sorry.” Claudia looked like she was being wrung out.

“Excuse me,” Talia said. “What *are* we talking about?”

Larry smiled. “It’s okay. Claudia, you need to calm down and just tell everyone what you told me.”

“I told Larry . . .” She looked up and was halted by Isabella, who had gone from hot to cold, and was now looking down, an impenetrable curtain of hair. Larry nodded at Claudia, encouraging, prodding. “I’m sorry, Iz! I told Larry that you and Dan hooked up and—”

“How did you even know that?” Isabella’s voice seethed.

“I . . .” Claudia paused as if searching for the right answer. I couldn’t believe what was happening. The pressure in my jaw had moved into my actual mouth; it felt like I was biting down on a rock. “Dan told me this morning.”

Larry put his hand on Claudia’s shoulder. “It’s okay, Claudia,

Danny. This is good. It's good for all of you. Go ahead." He sounded so self-assured, so calm, it made me feel like throwing up. Isabella was still furious, her eyes broiling the wall.

"He told me this morning, and then I told Larry, and–"

"What did you tell me?"

"I told you–"

"Tell them, not me again, Claud."

Her eyes were pleading as they seemed to dart toward and away from each of us, like it would be dangerous for our gazes to meet, like something might be accidentally communicated. Santos shook his head sadly while Iban sat stock-still, the slightest curl at the edge of his lips.

"I told Larry," she said, nodding along with her thoughts, "about Dan and Isabella hooking up, but I told him that Dan said that Larry engineered the whole thing."

"What the fuck?" Isabella was standing up. "What the fuck, Claudia? What the fuck!"

"Izzy, sit back down," Larry said without turning his face, which was locked on Claudia. She sat.

No one was looking at me, asking me if it was true or not. Talia seemed genuinely confused and curious, her head cocked as she took in what Claudia was claiming. "I'm sorry, what? Why would you say that? Dad, why would she say that to you?"

Larry's eyes passed from his daughter to Isabella then back to Claudia. "I agree, that is very strange, isn't it?" I could've sworn he had the ability to make his eyes twinkle like freshly sharpened metal on command. "Why would you say that to me, Claudia?"

I shouldn't have told Claudia, that was stupid. But I shouldn't just be worried about myself. I shouldn't have said it at all, to anyone. He offered me this place to stay, which is making my whole summer possible, and now I'm going to lose that. Or no, that isn't the problem. The problem is that it wasn't fair to him, wasn't kind. I could see Claudia struggling, and it was because of me. She was still staring through the table into something that wasn't there, flickering into focus when she looked up, then back out when she saw our faces. "I'm sorry," she said. She sounded like she was about to cry. "I didn't mean–"

"Why'd you do it, Claudia?" Talia's voice was raised, and the annoyance at its edge snapped Claudia to some kind of attention.

"I don't know why I did it! I'm sorry, Tal. I lied. I was jealous. Not like that! Not jealous of them or anything. I think that's great, I do. It's just that, it was this secret and I wanted Larry to know I knew, and I wanted to make it—"

"You wanted attention?" Talia asked.

Claudia nodded, head bowed again.

Larry looked back at his daughter. "You see?" he said. They shared a knowing glance, as if they'd had some prior conversation about this, about Claudia, about all of us. I was trying to clamber back onto solid ground. Somehow no one seemed to be mad at me. As if he knew, Larry turned to me. "Danny, it's okay. You're overwhelmed. You should be. You didn't know this was going to be brought out into the open, did you? But that was Claudia's choice today, and I decided to try to handle this in a way that would help all of you. You're attracted to Isabella, right?"

I looked around, confused, and then nodded, because there wasn't anything else I could do. They believed Claudia had lied. Maybe even she believed she had lied. But she hadn't. I knew she hadn't.

"That's why the two of you got involved. Danny, do you mind if I talk a little bit about what you're going through, to help this make sense to Tal?"

Again, there was nothing else to say, the maze had become a hallway, so I nodded.

"Thank you, Danny. See, everything that happens here happens because you want it to, when it is right for you. Why do you think you're all here? Not because I brought you together, or called you up and asked you to be here, or called up your parents and signed you up. You're here because you wanted to be here, and because you needed to be, because you knew you needed to be. Danny has been alone for years. He's felt profoundly empty, empty and alone, like nobody wants him, and anybody who does want him—there must be something wrong with them for wanting him. He's very smart—especially smart, just like all of you. And like all very smart people, you're each especially capable of walking yourself into corners, building these byzantine cave systems of thought inside yourselves, spinning yourselves up. You can feel it coming off him, can't you? His fear of being together, being with us, of having family, of people who don't want anything from him. When these things combine, all of you, like different volatile chemicals, there are going to be risks, combinations that bring out reactions you wouldn't expect. But I expect them. I know what's coming. You need it. Danny needed to express himself to Claudia, Claudia needs to confront her desire to be seen, to be the center at any cost. Isabella, when we first talked, you, me, and Tal had a conversation about helping these people, about taking them in, and I said that none of this would go forward unless you said it was okay. That was a promise, and I meant it."

"Well, I think this is totally fucked up," Isabella said. Then, after a pause, "But I do want Claudia to get better."

"What about you, Tal?"

Talia raised her eyebrows. "That was a really weird thing for Claudia to do. It doesn't really make any sense."

"I told you the way their minds work is not going to make sense to you. I'm able to understand that kind of disturbed thinking, but you won't have access to it. You've been raised with me, with total clarity since the beginning. Taking apart a broken mind, navigating that brokenness, and giving them clarity is going to mean living inside it. My skill set has been breaking minds, creating loops it's impossible to get out of. That's what I did in the DIA, that's what I've been tapped for. But I also have the ability to unravel the knots people have made in themselves. I told you I was going to show you how it works, so you could understand, or even do it yourself."

Talia seemed to think on that for a moment, and then shrugged. "Okay. That was super weird, Claudia! You're going to need to apologize to Isabella and my dad. You can't do stuff like that, okay?"

"I won't! I mean, I did, but I won't! I'm sorry."

"It's okay, Claud," Larry said. "You see, we all have to help each other. We have to be willing to give things up to make progress. I had plans this afternoon, but now I've dedicated my day to this, to you."

Claudia grimaced. "I'm more than happy to take my time to help all of you, because ultimately, it helps Tal. She needs to understand how your minds work, what it is like to be a person living without clarity, so that she begins to see how her own mind started to malfunction while I was gone, and where she was headed without me." He paused, suddenly seeming choked up. "Talia, you tell them."

Everyone leaned in as if they had learned a while ago how to listen to this story. Talia seemed to lean in, too, somewhere inside herself. "This last year at Sarah Lawrence, even after my dad came back, I had been fighting for so long, it was my whole life, I devoted everything to the truth. There had been so much loss, so much terror. . . . We had been completely cast out of society, and I just couldn't abandon it—the truth. Dan, did you know that when the FBI raided the place me and my dad were staying, they broke my dad's arm?"

I shook my head, and everyone else nodded.

"I would have gotten my life back if I lied and went along with what the lawyers and investigators and everyone wanted and said none of it happened, that my mom hadn't abused me and my sister, that Bernie Kerik hadn't conspired with her to put my dad in jail, but I knew it did. It happened. What I had to do got bigger and bigger inside me. My choice wasn't between the truth and a lie; it was between the truth and my life. If it weren't for my dad, I would have died clinging to that belief. He finally confronted me in Bronxville; he could *see* it. I'd had this impulse inside of me, to take my own life, to kill myself, and it had been brewing. Without even thinking, not consciously, I had been planning it, how to do it, putting things in order, slowly giving more and more of myself over to the impulse. I was going to take my life, which had already been taken from me. But my dad saved me."

Larry's eyes were wet. "Talia didn't realize her mind was putting everything in place to make it possible for her." He looked at Santos, Claudia, and me. "What do you think I've been helping Isabella with?"

Isabella laughed acidly. "Oh hell yeah, I've been thinking about killing myself forever. Because of my family. I came to school to do it there, away from them. Talia saved me freshman year, and Larry's been helping me work through it."

Iban jumped in. "I've had suicidal impulses, too, for a long time. Larry's been talking to me, helping me through it, even from jail."

"You see? Who arranged your whole housing setup at Slonim? Tal did. I marveled at the power of her mind when I first saw it. She brought you all together, people with the same issue, but she didn't know why. She surrounded herself with people who wanted to die, too, so she could. It made the choice possible, to kill herself. Right, Santos?"

Santos had been looking down into his empty coffee mug, and his eyes snapped up. "Yeah, I also dealt with depression, all through high school and stuff."

"Come on, Santos. You need to be honest if you're going to get better. Talia, Isabella, and Iban all just shared something very personal. Do you want my help or not?"

"Yeah, sorry. I do! You're right. In high school I also tried. I attempted suicide."

I looked at him—Santos, whom I had lived with throughout freshman year, who was quiet but so quick to smile, who seemed to be laughing half the time. Now his chin was practically impacting his chest, he was nodding so hard.

"And you, too, isn't that right, Danny?" Larry smiled softly at me.

"Not really. I mean, I'm sorry, I just haven't tried . . . or anything like that."

Larry frowned. "Danny, I already know. You can just admit it."

They were all looking at me. I had almost lost all of this a few minutes ago, the place to live, the access to this man who, no matter what I might believe, had some kind of unique power. I might not be exactly the same as all these people—I certainly didn't think of myself as suicidal—but look at how he was helping all of them, helping them face something so difficult. Maybe he had decided to help me whether or not I spread rumors about him, and he'd found a way for me to stay here, and for everyone to still want me to be here. Only a few minutes ago, I'd been willing to go along with him and pretend that I wasn't so messed up that I would say a girl wanted to hook up with me only because someone had manipulated her into it, which would be clearly insane, and that I would pin that on him, putting everyone in such a weird position. Clearly it was important to him that I say this. So why shouldn't I? Sometimes when I was standing on the subway platform, it was true, I would imagine stepping into the empty air as it filled with the light of an oncoming train. I thought about it, made it bigger inside me, let that light, that desire, get bigger, until it felt like it could be everything. Maybe I *was* suicidal! This coal of sadness had been burning through me my whole life, and I just wanted to get it out, for it to be over. I swallowed, and looked up at all of my friends gathered around the table.

"Sometimes, I do think to myself, *'I don't want to exist anymore.'* Sometimes I imagine my funeral, and I think about how it would feel better to be dead, what people would say, all gathered around me, how they would miss me, like somehow being dead would make it not so bad to be alive, as if I could be both at once. I don't know, it doesn't make sense. Yes, I've thought about it. I've wanted to kill myself."

Larry leaned over the table. "What do you really want to say?" he asked me.

It took me a second to understand what he wanted. I revised my statement. "I *want* to kill myself." Everyone relaxed at once. I was there, finally, with them. Everything fit together.

"Do you see?" Larry asked, looking around the table at us. "Now you're all interconnected, you became interconnected the moment Talia brought you all together at Slonim. I have to protect my daughter, and to do that means protecting all of you. If any one of you goes through with your plans, if I let your impulse to hurt yourself get its way, then we'll have a domino effect. At the end of that chain is Tal, my honeygirl. So you can believe me, as a father, as a man. I will keep you all safe."

—ıı—

Larry had sent Iban and Isabella over to the Fairway on Eighty-sixth to pick up ingredients for lunch so, unsure what else to do, I sat back down on the couch with Talia's book. Where I'd left off, Bertrand Russell was dividing humanity up into categories: "Self-absorption is of various kinds. We may take the sinner, the narcissist, and the megalomaniac as three very common types." The sinner, he wrote, "is perpetually incurring his own disapproval. . . . When he falls in love, he looks for maternal tenderness, but cannot accept it, because, owing to the mother-image, he feels no respect for any woman with whom he has sexual relations." The narcissist, conversely, admires everything he does and, incapable of loving anyone else, obsessively desires that everyone love him. "The megalomaniac," Russell writes, "differs from the narcissist by the fact that he wishes to be powerful rather than charming, and seeks to be feared rather than loved. To this type belong many lunatics and most of the great men in history."

I had trouble telling the difference. Wasn't each of us–including me–a mix of all these things? I wanted to escape self-absorption, the way Larry had. Or maybe the meaning of his specialness was that he'd never been self-absorbed, had been born selfless. All I wanted was to be like him. To never be unhappy or unsure about anything, ever again.

That night, when Isabella came out of the bedroom and sat on the couch, when she pushed me back into the leather and her legs vised my waist, I–knowing that she must believe I had never questioned this, not even for an instant, that it had only been some lie Claudia had told–grabbed her and pulled her into me. I'd said that I wanted this; I'd claimed that as the truth. I wanted the reality Larry had presented. It was different from mine, but easier to believe in. It was simple. It was a reality in which I could be happy.

6

I know it's gonna be a lovely day
lovely day
lovely day
lovely day

lovely day
lovely day
lovely day
lovely day
lovely day

A lovely day
lovely day
lovely day
lovely day

lovely day
lovely day
lovely day
lovely day
lovely day

MY EYES BUZZED INSIDE their sockets as the world turned back on. I tried to remember falling asleep. At some point in the night, Isabella must have crept back into the bedroom. Or maybe we hadn't been together last night; it was hard to say.

Slowly the evening came back to me: Larry had gotten Santos to open up more about his depression. After a while Santos had admitted that sometimes he went into the closet in his bedroom and sat on the floor and closed the door, just to sit in the dark. I didn't think he ever went into the closet in our dorm, but I had no way of knowing. It was like that in his brain, he said, an empty place, an interminable gap of air between him and everything else: "The Land of Nothing," Larry had called it, and Santos had agreed, but by then it'd been hours of us all sitting in a ring in the living room, talking, talking, hours of talking, the sky dusty with morning.

Nothing was really resolved with Santos yet, Larry said, with any of us, and it was never good to let something so sensitive stay open. The idea that it should be exposed to air was all wrong, he said; instead, you really have to cover it with Neosporin and a bandage. He talked about cellular regeneration, how with the right help and conditions your body can make new, better flesh on top of a wound, without any scar, and didn't we want that for our wounds of the mental variety? Then he'd talked about "mental management"—that thinking was a conversation and you had to learn to manage that conversation to achieve some semblance of clarity—but Santos was different, Larry explained. He was sitting silently in the dark closet in his brain, and he needed help walking out so he could meet himself.

Even though it wasn't ideal, Larry had said, he would let us go to bed, and that was when I'd finally been able to stretch out on the couch. So there hadn't been much of a night for Isabella to creep out from the bedroom where she slept with Larry and Talia, which is what we had been doing over the past few weeks—pretending we had something private, though nothing, really, was private anymore.

Larry was sitting at the table, Talia was cooking something in the kitchen, and the pitch of the music made me want to sob. The singer kept holding out the word "day" so long it could have been a year. I peeled myself from the couch and sat up.

"Morning, sunshine," Larry said, smiling at me. This is why I always liked to wake up before anyone else. I didn't like how vulnerable I felt.

"What're we listening to?" I asked over the music.

"Bill Withers, Danny, come on. 'Lovely Day.' Doesn't it just make you feel excellent? It lines up your mind for the day. Listen to it, it just makes you happy."

"Right." I rubbed my eyes. He was drinking coffee. He took a pill bottle out of his backpack and tapped out two orange pills.

"There are things about this song you can't understand, Danny, that will make you feel better, that will make *you* better. You choose your unhappiness, your being stuck, you *choose* it. You make your world what it is—closed, small, weak, empty, bleak, barren, and that's the energy you send out. They don't see it, but I see it, I can feel it there, and everyone else will start to feel it if they're around you long enough. We need to put you on rails toward clarity. You have to start choosing happiness, so you can start to see what the world is offering you. You can be capable of caring about other people. Izzy and I put this playlist together, and it's going to help, even if you don't understand how. You're going to trust me; you're going to listen to it every morning. In order. In order, always. She's got perfect taste in music, you know that? Incredible, I've never seen anything quite like it. Still dead in there," he said, indicating the bedroom, and winked at me. "Lovely Day" faded out and the next song came on, the tumbling, frenetic organ intro of "Baba O'Riley."

—||—

Later that morning, Larry cloistered himself, as he often did, in the hallway bathroom with his laptop. It was the only place he could achieve the necessary level of privacy to do his work for the Defense Intelligence Agency, he said, and once he was in there, he couldn't be interrupted at any cost, and he wouldn't be out for hours. This was another sacrifice that he made—having us in his house meant he had to work in the cramped bathroom all day. No matter that it was the only bathroom we were allowed to use—the one in the bedroom was completely full of boxes of his and Tal's stuff. I'd really wanted to take a shower, but that was irrelevant. I wasn't the one making sacrifices; I was the one getting a free apartment. Talia and Isabella were chatting in the bedroom with the door closed. For the moment it was as if I was alone, just with every door locked and someone behind each of them, and the inaccessible, unaffordable, lonely endlessness of New York City outside.

I had no idea how anyone found a place in the city who wasn't rich or living with someone rich. In a sense, I was homeless, but I couldn't think about that. I walked into the kitchen, the cold, white tile sucking at my bare feet. I leaned against the kitchen window. The world 150 feet below lurched away from me. I felt a little dizzy, but still let myself lean there, the only thing keeping me from falling this pane of glass, which I rapped my fingers against now, my chewed-down fingernails making an unsatisfying thumping sound.

New York City was all windows reflecting back at each other, and people like me hidden behind them. I wondered how many had looked out of their apartments and seen this window and had no idea my whole world existed behind it. All my belongings were stuffed into a backpack I'd had since high school, and the things that were flat enough–notebook, laptop, book–I'd slid under the couch. I wanted to make myself as small and as temporary as possible. I wanted it to be easy to move on, though I'd given up looking for an apartment, and neither Santos nor Claudia seemed at all interested in finding a place, either. More and more I was knit into the fabric of this apartment.

I returned to the living room, sat down on the couch, reached between my legs, and pulled out my notebook. I flipped to a poem I'd written for workshop at Sarah Lawrence. It was called "Pursuit."

I was irresponsible
almost obsessively so
I watched the grass grow green on the back porch
then turn gray with the stone
It took me almost a month
to brush off the dust
and breathe in a cloud
of something new gone old
It feels like I've spent a long time
coughing up a lover
from the very bottom of my throat

I tried adding punctuation, then removed it again. My brain bypassed some barrier when I wrote poems; I'd bring them into a professor and every time, in the process of analyzing my poem, they would tell me something about myself I didn't know, or that I knew, but had never said out loud. I thought of writing as a process of definition—each poem was like a new word that described something which had yet to be described. It was like discovering a plant, and figuring out what it was called, so that when you said the name, someone else would know what plant you were talking about. Put enough poems together, and you had a kind of encyclopedia of the self.

Once I had the words for a feeling or an experience, I'd found, it was like I could see where it ended and everything else began, as if that feeling or experience, now made out of words, emerged from the background, and in that way became recognizable, or real, even. So, in a sense, words were unimaginably powerful. That's what I liked to believe, anyway. This poem, however, made no sense to me, and since Larry had talked often about his deep knowledge and love of literature—I couldn't imagine when he'd had time to become a Joyce scholar while also doing intelligence work overseas—I'd shown it to him, thinking maybe, at least, he might want to talk more, about the poem, about me. I ached for that warm spotlight he'd shone on me in Starbucks, without all these other complications, everyone else desperate for his attention, the sexual relationship with Isabella, not knowing how to explain everything to my parents, to my friends outside this room. I just wanted another conversation like that one. Something in me clamored for that feeling: time vanishing, that warmth washing over me, being able to share my secret fears, being told—convinced, rather—that everything would be all right. After he'd finished reading the poem, he'd asked me only if I noticed when I started my sentences with "I feel" as opposed to "I think." Subtle differences in language, he'd said, reveal the place in your brain from whence your utterance is actually derived. Is it a real, valid thought, or is it emotional? I looked back at the poem and crossed out "It feels like."

—||—

Santos and Iban showed up later that afternoon, and Talia came out of the bedroom to join us. I sat back on the couch with my book, squinted, and closed it again—the light through the windows had dimmed to the point that we were practically sitting in darkness, but no one had turned on a light. I wanted to, but maybe there was some reason no one had. Maybe Talia liked the natural, indoor sunset, or perhaps she had a headache and would resent anyone who turned lights on. I didn't want to accidentally do something wrong—if every action was deliberate, even subconsciously, then what would it mean if I turned on the light when no one else, apparently, wanted to? Better to do nothing.

"My back hurts so much," Talia groaned, leaning forward on the couch.

I gestured for her to turn around so that her back would be facing me. "I'm really good at massage," I said. She scooted over, and my hands swallowed her shoulders. It was like touching a fragile bird; her bones were small and knobby, while her skin was warm, almost hot underneath the fabric of her shirt. I moved down her back, holding her sides and feeling the muscles give under my thumb and resist where they were tense. I worked gently in circles over the knotted muscle that clung to her spine, thinking this would be easier if she were not wearing a shirt, not saying that, then working back up her side. Feeling her bra strap, I carefully pressed beneath it, like rubbing a dog under its collar. Then the bathroom door finally opened and Larry came around the corner, still holding his open laptop in one hand, his backpack hooked over the other.

"Why's it so dark in here?" he asked, dropping his bag and reaching for the light switch. I didn't want to immediately whip my hands into my lap, so instead I froze, my hands resting on his daughter's back, and patted her gently. Talia hummed, "Thanks, Daniel," and I withdrew slowly. With the light on, I saw Iban and Santos watching me.

"You giving Tal a massage?" Larry said. He said it like it was the most natural thing in the world. That's how it had felt to me when I'd suggested it at least. Why couldn't I just relax? "I've got to show you how to do that properly sometime. Do we have groceries?"

"I think we need to pick some stuff up," Talia said.

I quickly rummaged through the compressed layers of my backpack, managed to pull out some clean underwear, and said, just as quickly, "I'm going to take a shower," before anyone could ask me to go to Fairway and I missed my chance. I rushed to the little hallway, boxers balled in my hand, and pushed the door shut behind me. It was jarringly bright and cramped. I breathed—I couldn't believe he worked in here all day. And yet, I also wondered if he felt like I did—as small as the bathroom was, it was such a relief to be alone.

Leaning into the mirror, I looked at myself, and it was hard to see who was there. Back at Slonim, my hair had been long. Raven had cut it when we were in New Jersey to a kind of Seattle skater cut, long in the front, short everywhere else, and once I was in New York it'd found its way back to how it'd been in high school—sort of the same everywhere. My skin looked dark, oddly tan considering how much time I spent inside now, but it always got a little almondy over the summer.

I turned on the water in the shower and let it heat up, then watched myself in the mirror slowly fade into fog before stepping in. The water was so hot it made my toes feel frozen, my chest like it was rippling. I let myself fall forward, my forehead gently meeting the pink marble shower wall. I leaned like that for a while, the water lashing my back, a little Dr. Bronner's I'd grabbed from a bottle on the floor in my hand, until I worked up the nerve to touch myself.

When I got out of the shower, my body steaming, I was finally relaxed, and I realized, because it returned the moment I reached for the bathroom doorknob, that the only thing I'd felt for weeks had been a clenching across my whole body. But I was just anticipating the cold and having to be moist and half naked while I pulled on the rest of my clothes in the corner of the living room, I thought. Larry was sitting on the couch looking at his laptop, and when I came into the room, he looked up and shouted, "What, were you jerking off in there?" I started like an animal the moment after it's tasted food that turns out to be bait, too late to escape. *No,* I thought, *impossible for him to know.* "Five minutes to shower, that's all you should need," Larry said. "If you take six in the marines, you're completely fucked, isn't that right, Iban?"

Iban was sitting at the table, his back to the night sky outside. "Yes, sir. In and out, five minutes, shaved and dry. You look more like a black Q-tip with that mess on your head and face, by the way."

I laughed, trying to seem like one of the guys, not knowing what else to do, not wanting to lie and not wanting to admit the truth. I pulled on my clothes, which caught and resisted on my still-wet skin. Isabella peeked her head out of the bedroom. "Dan, could you come in here, please? I need help with something." She smiled, her head kind of dangling there, as if it'd been removed, then closed the door behind her.

⊣⊢

The mattress felt damp underneath my skin. How long had Isabella and I been together in the bed? An hour? Less? It was a miracle no one had come in. I was naked, and Isabella, wearing just her underwear, crawled over me. "Stay there," she said, and disappeared into the small connected bathroom. The gigantic bed was the only empty space in the room. At its foot, stacks of boxes left a narrow pathway to the closet, in which clothes were crated, piled, and hung two, three, four to a hanger. Most of the closet was occupied by a group of IKEA boxes labeled CLOSET ORGANIZING SYSTEM. The windows were only partially visible past the stacks, which obscured the black masses of skyscrapers and the light-polluted dark.

Isabella came back into the room holding a safety razor and a can of shaving cream. She nestled between my legs and tucked a hand towel underneath me.

"What are you doing?"

"I'm going to clean you up a bit." She shook up the shaving cream then sprayed it into her cupped palm. She dropped a razor blade into a gleaming, chrome handle, then tightened a screw at the bottom. I'd seen a safety razor for the first time soon after moving here when Larry came out of the bedroom, his face dotted with whips of white foam and patches of sandpapery skin, and insisted on showing me the way a man properly shaves. I'd always associated those razor blades with suicide, those little metal rectangles that looked deceptively harmless, and yet either edge was so sharp it'd practically fall through flesh, the kind you see in movies on the corner of a porcelain sink or the edge of a bathtub, the water blooming with blood.

She spread some of the white lather on me, brought the line of the blade into its center, then pulled. Blankness trailed in the wake of the blade. I felt as if she were grooming an animal, something separate from me, that we were both watching through a window as a dog was shaved to protect it from some disease. The tiny, sharp black hairs mixed with the foam and mounded at the back of the razor, which she wiped and patted on the towel between my legs. I wondered if she had done this before. When she was done, she wiped me off with a clean edge of the cloth. She touched me, examining her handiwork, then, apparently satisfied, flounced to the bathroom, discarding the towel somewhere. There was a knock at the door and it began to open. I found my boxers and pulled them on just as Larry came in.

He was holding his laptop, in the midst of hanging up the phone, and his backpack was dangling from his forearm as he pushed through the door. He saw me huddled in the bed in my underwear and didn't react, as if it was entirely expected, and said, "Iz, help me with this," handing her the backpack so he could flip his phone shut. Isabella must have put on her bra and underwear in the bathroom; she came out and took his bag. I started to apologize, but he cut me off saying, "Don't worry about it, Danny." He sat on the edge of the bed, which Isabella crawled back onto as he looked at his computer. I felt bizarre, unsure where in the room my clothes were, whether I should feel strange about us both being half naked with Larry, but they seemed utterly relaxed. I was trying not to touch the pillows with my bare back. It felt impossible to get out now.

"That's my boy, Danny!" Larry said. He clapped me on the naked shoulder. "Are you using protection?" he asked.

Isabella laughed and playfully pushed Larry's shoulder. "I'm on the pill, silly. You know that."

"That took a lot of work, didn't it? Izzy was on entirely the wrong birth control when we met, Danny, and her doctor had no idea what she was talking about. But I taught Izzy all about the chemistry of the different compounds of each pill and how they affect your hormones, and how that affects your cognitive function. She had no idea that the pills she was taking were impacting her hormones, her period, and making her depression worse. Can you believe that?"

He wasn't looking at me. I shifted a bit on the bed, felt the hot, damp spot on the memory foam beneath me. "I had no idea."

"Danny, I hope you know it's fine that you were masturbating in the shower earlier. That's perfectly healthy, natural stuff. Izzy loves masturbating, don't you, Iz? She loves porn, too; she's obsessed with it." He laughed. "I bet you think no women like porn, Danny. Most women are freakier than you or I. Izzy used to hate her body, though, and sex—found it all repugnant. You wouldn't believe how many women hate, *hate,* their vaginas, Danny. It's a travesty, a really sad thing. Izzy when we met was one of the worst I've ever seen. I mean it was awful, she didn't even wash properly at all, which is really typical, a really common issue. When she would bathe, which wasn't often enough, she would just skip her vagina, imagine that—the smell! I have an incredibly sensitive sense of smell, Danny, the DIA called it superhuman, my nose. Dogs have about three hundred million olfactory receptors; how many do you think we have? Six million. Think about that. That's forty times more sensitive than you, one of your five primary senses. Of course, how many senses do you think there are? Five, right? You have no idea how many more senses there are, and how attuned they all can be. You know a dog can smell how you feel? Can smell fear? Can smell diseases before a test can confirm it? That's true, Danny, look it up. I can smell about twenty times better than most people, half of a dog. Boy, the dogs would come running when Iz walked outside, isn't that right?" Isabella laughed and pushed him again, lightly. She still hadn't put on clothes. "She's come a really long way, and that's opened up something else entirely. It's healthy, but we need to work on it. She masturbates so much, she's constantly thinking about it." He sniffed. "If you're going to jerk off in the shower, you've got to make sure you actually get clean, too, while you're in there. What do you use for lubrication?"

I'd only been in the shower for twenty minutes at most—a normal length for a shower, I thought. Maybe, though, this was a lesson that was more complex than I could comprehend. I needed to relax, let this happen, trust him. "I don't really use anything," I said.

"You're going to want to use something," Larry said. "The pH of New York City water is on the hard side. It'll give you tiny lacerations on your pecker, and you don't want that."

I shifted. "Well, to be honest, I used a tiny bit of the Dr. Bronner's that was in there."

"The peppermint?" Isabella asked. "Did you dilute it? You've got to be careful with that stuff, it's intense."

Larry laughed. "Your dick must be all cut up, Danny. Dr. Bronner's is concentrated; never use it as is." He turned back to his computer and clapped a hand on Isabella's thigh. "Come on, tell us what's good, Izzy!"

"Just go to Pornhub!" she said.

He typed it in and the homepage came up, a grid of videos. Each box was like a window in the face of a building, every room lit up, every neighbor a different kind of exposed and tangled.

His hand hovering over the mouse pad, Larry turned to me and asked, "What do you like?" It was too late, it was too strange; while I hadn't been paying attention, some part of me, the main part, had gotten much, much smaller. I was one of the minuscule people posed inside the little digital windows. From deep within one of those boxes, I answered, "I like everything."

Larry laughed again, looking at the screen. "You like everything?" He raised his eyebrows.

"That one!" Isabella pointed, bouncing a little on the bed. I wished she would put on clothes, but I hadn't, either. She could do whatever she wanted, I guessed. Larry was right–I should follow her lead. He clicked on the video. Two men were having sex with one woman.

"Oh yeah, that's what's up," Isabella said.

Larry shook his head. "I really don't like it when they have tattoos. You don't like that either, right, Danny?" he said. The girl on the screen had tattoos covering her back. I didn't have to look at Isabella to know she didn't have any tattoos anywhere.

"Right," I said. "I don't either."

⊣⊢

Larry hit the space bar as the video ended. "This is what I want you to do. Your boundaries are too tight, you're choking yourself—don't you feel that? Barely able to breathe, you're so uptight?" He was right; I did feel that way right then. "Have sex somewhere in public. It'll be good for you. It can be with anyone. It doesn't have to be Isabella, but you should try it. Do something you haven't done before."

Isabella crawled behind us and turned on the lamp; the three of us had been sitting in the dark around the glow of the laptop. I felt tired, beyond tired, the kind of tired you feel when you've been trapped on a long, crowded flight and can't get comfortable enough to sleep the whole time. This was exactly the kind of feeling Larry said he could help me with. When I was younger I'd read some Ken Kesey, and he talked about how in childhood our experience of the world is like a rainbow waterfall thundering from above directly into our open mouths. As we become adults, that waterfall diminishes to a gray trickle. I felt as if I had been desperately lapping for gray droplets; I wanted to unleash the water pressure again, and this was how. Having sex in public felt impossible to think about, but there wasn't anything so crazy about it, I knew that. What I was feeling must just be my fear, my prudishness. My brain thought it was protecting me, but really it wasn't. I had to get over myself, and the way to do that was to stop listening to the voice in my head that said no, and let Larry be in charge.

Larry snapped his computer shut. "Let's get out of here and have some dinner!" Isabella dug around on the other side of the bed and produced our clothes, and we quickly dressed before stepping through the bedroom door.

⊣⊢

As we made our way into the living room, it was like passing through some invisible barrier in reality. Iban, Santos, Talia, and Claudia were sitting around pleasantly chatting, and I knew, without being told, not to share what had just happened in the bedroom with anyone. It felt as if the last hour or so didn't exist out here. I could feel my newly shaved body, an unfamiliar sensation, the awareness of myself shifting naked inside my clothes.

"Hey, what's everyone doing! Where's dinner?" Larry shouted. His tone was totally different from how it'd been minutes ago. Now his voice filled the room, ringing everyone like a bunch of bells. All of them snapped to attention; Santos bounded across the room toward us. "I'm sorry! We didn't know if you wanted us to pick something up, or what, because you hadn't given us money for groceries or anything."

Isabella rolled her eyes, and Larry seemed to get taller, somehow. No one was asking what we had all been doing in the bedroom together. It was a secret, something that bonded me to Larry and Isabella, and there was a power in it, a privilege I could immediately sense. "Are you sure that's what you want to say, Santos?" With two fingers held stiff and hard, Larry poked Santos in the chest. Santos stumbled back. It was stunning how strong Larry could be.

"What? No, I didn't mean . . . I'm sorry," Santos coughed.

"You're sorry?" Larry advanced on him, and poked Santos again. "Why are you sorry? Because you assume I'm going to give you money, and I'm going to feed you? Where are your manners?" Another hard poke, this one pushing Santos down onto the couch. Santos's face looked like it was melting. "You need to remember that you're a guest in someone's house. In your girlfriend's father's house, right?"

Santos nodded, out of breath, disappearing into the couch. "Right." Larry answered his own question. I felt grateful it wasn't me, and at the same time, I believed Santos deserved it, for some reason Larry understood and I didn't. I was sure he was only acting angry, because it was what was best for Santos right now. I had to believe that. No one else seemed freaked out. Besides, Larry was a marine, and had told us over and over how violent and intense that training could be—anything that we experienced here in this cushy apartment in uptown Manhattan was a joke by comparison. In the marines, if someone was holding back the unit, endangering them, they got shot in the back and killed, that's what Larry said. He knew what he was doing. Larry sat down on the loveseat catty-corner to the couch, and just stared at Santos, glaring, while Santos looked down at the carpet. "Iz, do we have *anything* to eat?" Larry called into the kitchen, setting his jaw. His eyes looked like they could set Santos on fire.

Izzy was already rooting through the fridge. "No, not really, Larry! Just your Ding Dongs," she said. "There's some milk in the fridge."

Larry flipped open his laptop again. "Bring me a Ding Dong."

Isabella brought him the box, and he carefully unwrapped the cellophane, dropped two frozen chocolate pucks onto his plate, then leaned forward and plucked the cup of milk from the edge of the table where Isabella had placed it. Ice clinked in the milk, occasionally interrupting the white when it touched the glass. He looked at me and everything else vanished. "The trick, Danny, is you've got to keep the milk cold; it's the only way to eat Ding Dongs. It's always important to keep things cold; that's when their best qualities come out, when you can reveal what's best about them, isn't that right? In the restaurant we used to own, I built a whole room in the back, all marble surfaces, with a unique temperature control system. No one understood why I was going to the expense. It allowed me to keep everything at a very precise, very cool temperature. Do you know why marble?" I shook my head. "Marble stays very cold. Other types of counters will warm up the meat or fish, whatever you're working with, from the bottom. Didn't think of that, did you?" I shook my head again. He dunked a Ding Dong in the milk, held it momentarily, then took a bite over his plate. "Do you like Ding Dongs?" he asked me.

"I've never had them before," I said. "My mom didn't really buy sweets or anything like that because of the diabetes."

Larry exclaimed through another bite of chocolate and cream: "Izzy! Danny's never had Ding Dongs!"

"What!" Isabella yelled from the kitchen. "Can I get him one?"

In the corner, Santos was still disappearing. Larry, looking pleased, slurping milk, seemed as if he was taking everyone in for the first time. "Come on over here, Santy-os!" Larry called to him, and Santos came over and sat. "Izzy, we should have enough for everyone. Get out all the Ding Dongs!" The night refigured itself. Now it was celebratory, a sleepover, a playdate–it had been those things all along, no question.

Larry showed us how to dip a Ding Dong into cold milk, how long to wait, when to bite, how to savor the taste, and nothing existed beyond the threshold of the current truth, this side of the bedroom door, this reality.

When Larry decided the night was over, he sent Santos and me down to his driver, who had been waiting all night in the limo, idling nearby. The driver smiled through the mirror, his eyes watery with lack of sleep, and it was only then I realized how late it was. When he took the cash I handed to him through the partition, which Larry had slipped into my hand upstairs, I wondered how much this man knew about us, if he ever asked himself who we were, what we were doing, or if it was just easier not to ask those questions, to nod and start the car and take us back to Santos's parents' house in the Bronx, where I would sleep that night.

—||—

The following morning, I was nearly cool after a night of suffocating heat under the blanket on the floor of Santos's bedroom. I'd gotten accustomed to not having a bed—whether a conversation in the apartment had hurtled into the early morning and there was no couch for me to sleep on or I'd made some nest of blankets on a friend's floor, by now I could fall asleep in any situation. I'd tried to say something to that effect in front of Iban, and he'd scoffed, telling me that in Afghanistan he'd slept every night in the freezing desert on slanted, hard-packed sand and dirt with a rock for a pillow. To call a soft pile of blankets on carpet in a warm apartment in Manhattan with all my friends "difficult conditions to sleep in" was a fucking insult, he'd said, and Larry had nodded.

I felt intimidated by Iban the way one feels intimidated by an older sibling: He had a few years on me, he was handsome, it was obvious he could beat me up if he wanted to, and more and more the apartment bristled with voltage I recognized from boys' summer camp and the high school wrestling team—that you might have to prove you could take a beating or give one at any moment. This, too, was normal, something that happened, that had always happened among men, and it shouldn't make me scared. After one instance of Larry and Iban trading memories of the marines, Larry told us to hold out our fingers. "The mind has the power to control the body," he said. "Iban, you've seen the way your body transformed in the marines, not just as a result of physical training, but because of mental training, isn't that right?"

Iban grunted affirmatively, "Sir."

"When you embrace the masculine in yourself, your body begins to express those hormones. You can actually see it. Testosterone. Androstenedione. You've seen guys develop tits. Iban saw some of those guys coming into boot camp, right? If you're not choosing your masculinity, you become that. Danny doesn't believe me. Look at your fingertips."

I was still not sure I understood what he was talking about, but we looked. "See how rounded they are?" he said, pointing to our splayed hands. I looked at mine, then at Santos's. His nails were perfect, glossy and pale, his fingertips soft, whereas my nails were gnawed down so far each one was framed by flesh. They just looked like fingers to me. "You can track physical indicators," Larry said, and held out his own hands. His fingers were far thicker than any of ours, the skin darker, almost orange but burnt, and rougher looking. It was true—his fingers came to blunt, caveman tips, more squared than rounded off. They were pill bottles. They were shotgun shells. I looked back at Iban's fingers, then mine, then Santos's, and—almost like a Magic Eye picture—now I could see incremental differences in how the tips were curved, which must have corresponded to how manly we were. Iban's fingers were a little squarer than mine; Santos's and mine were similar, but I could squint at my fingertips and make them a little blunter than Santos's. I just hadn't been able to see it before.

—II—

I jolted on Santos's floor and realized I must have fallen back asleep. The sheer white curtains were floating into the room. Rubbing my eyes and sitting up on the blanket, I creakily said "Hey" to Santos, who was standing in front of his bureau, looking into the mirror. "What are you doing?" I asked him, as he leaned even closer to his reflection.

"Just cleaning up my eyebrows," he said, and I realized he was using tweezers.

"Really?" I said, "You pluck your eyebrows?" Santos had notably perfect eyebrows, so thick and rectangular that he had a reputation at school for them.

"Yeah, it's no big deal. You don't?"

Sitting on the floor, I blinked at him. "No, I definitely don't. When I was really little, like maybe fifth grade, I started getting hair on my arms, and kids called me an ape. And then I started getting hair in between my eyebrows and this kid Jeremy–whatever, it doesn't matter. I kind of thought that was why I couldn't date anyone in middle school. One day I literally tore that hair out with my fingers. You've got to understand this was a really big deal to me. I thought I knew the root cause to all my problems. I just never even considered the possibility of tweezing them."

He looked sideways through the mirror at me and shrugged. "That . . . is really crazy," he said. "You should just pluck them. Feel free, my tweezers are right here." Back in Slonim, when I'd heard people talk about how perfect and beautiful Santos's eyebrows were, I'd thought they were calling him feminine, and had felt bad for him. But now I wondered if it could be normal, acceptable, good even.

He shuffled off to the bathroom, and I approached the bureau, where the tweezers lay innocuously. I hunched into the mirror, brought them to my face, and began pulling out hairs. Santos came out of the bathroom and didn't say anything as he straightened his bed. As I tugged hairs out of my eyebrows, a kind of relief stirred in me, an unrecognizable feeling, the opposite of how I'd felt that day in the crowded hall full of middle schoolers rushing to their buses when Jeremy, the popular boy who'd just started dating the girl I liked, had pointed at me and yelled "Unibrow!" and everyone had turned to look. I'd run as quickly and as invisibly as possible to my dad's car and slumped down in the passenger seat. Making my fingers as blunt and hard as I could, I'd reached in between my eyes and begun pulling something out.

7

WHILE I CHANGED INTO a button-up shirt in the back room of the ice cream shop, I realized I'd never really bought a birthday present for someone before. I'd picked out gifts from the aisles of toy stores in grade school, sure, but those were more like the requisite ticket to attend some other kid's party, not an indicator of how well you knew or cared about another person, and my parents had always paid. Since Isabella, Santos, and Claudia had started talking about Talia's birthday, I'd decided I would buy her a teapot I'd seen on the top shelf in the fancier-than-normal corner bodega near the apartment. I'd finally gotten a paycheck from work, so I could make it uptown, cash the check, nab the pot, then make it back to the fancy French restaurant in midtown that Larry had chosen for dinner. The subway turnstile ticked, my MetroCard balance dwindled another $2.25, and a few minutes later I was hurtling uptown.

I arrived with the unwrapped, boxed teapot under my arm, forty dollars poorer, trying to catch my breath and air myself out after two stifling subway rides. The restaurant was dimly lit, and it took a second for my eyes to adjust so that I could see the waiters backing out through kitchen doors followed by clouds of steam, the plush burgundy booths and dark wood tables; even the air smelled expensive. I spotted Larry, Talia, Isabella, Santos, Claudia, and Iban sitting in a big circular booth in the corner. I was prepared to apologize for my lateness, but when I managed to reach them Talia jumped up and hugged me, pulling me down to sit next to her and her dad, and I was immediately enmeshed in a conversation they were all having about how much Talia had been through to get to this point. One arm behind my head, Larry snapped at the waiter, then pointed at the empty space in front of me. A menu and place setting appeared. I opened the menu and tried to nonchalantly search for something that wasn't too pricey. Larry might pay, but there was no way to really know until it happened, and even then, if he did, I would owe him. Better to not even think the thought.

He clapped my shoulder. "Why don't you pick us a wine, Danny?" he said. "Cheer up! It's a birthday."

I'd been frowning into the menu, I realized. I tried to unscrew the muscles around my mouth—not too quickly, not like it was fake, but just enough to match what he was asking for. "I don't know anything about wine," I said. I didn't want to pick something awful for Talia's birthday. Also, there were no prices.

Talia smiled next to me and pointed at a section on the list. "I like Malbecs."

"A Pinot Noir would be nice, Danny," Larry said.

I scanned down the menu, looking for something that didn't seem like it'd been named after European royalty, then pointed. "How about this?"

Talia laughed. "That's such a cute name! I like it, yes, let's order it," she said. Larry's face flickered, then returned to stone. When he wanted to, he could make it look as if it'd never made a single expression his whole life. He gestured to the waiter and ordered the bottle I'd chosen for the table: "Flowers."

—II—

We were partway through our entrées when Larry looked around and said, "So, Talia, what do you wish for on this birthday?"

I watched Talia look down at the table. She looked remarkably like her dad: There was this sort of sun-cooked glow that came off the hard edge of her jaw—a smaller version of Larry's own. It was what made both of their faces look a little unsettlingly wide, as if their mouths might unhinge at will. She said, "I wish for everyone to be happy. That's what I always wish. All of you have been through so much. Isabella has been through such hard times. But we're all together now. I want the world to be fixed. I want Ava back. I want justice to be meted out against Bernie and Teresa. I want everyone in the world to be better, to be happy. I really believe we can help them by doing good, important work. People like my dad can help them, if they would only listen, if they would only start to see the world the way it really is. I want to help more people think clearly, look at the world logically, and find clarity."

Larry was smiling, tears in his eyes. He cleared his throat. "Everyone should say something for Tal, who's sacrificed so much to get to this moment. My honeygirl, in her way, saved each of your lives. Let's hear what you all think of that."

Everyone knew what that meant, what Larry wanted to hear us say. We went around the circle, each person saying a different version of thanks to Talia for saving their lives, for sharing her home and her father with us. The table was like a clock ticking down to me. When I was a kid, my dad would bring me along to his Saturday business networking meetings, and occasionally I'd sub in for someone who hadn't shown up and make a speech about their company. I'm sure it was cute—the ten-year-old making jokes about how Jeff who ran the used-car lot had a promotion going this week, so tell your friends looking for cheap midsize sedans. I became good at ad-libbing.

I gulped a mouthful of Flowers, started to stand halfway up in my seat, then, finding that impossible, sat back down with one foot folded beneath me. I didn't want to sound like everyone else, parroting the same lines; I wanted to stand out, because I figured if I did, Larry might want to spend more time talking with me, and I might get more of that advice he'd promised. With everyone staring, I improvised.

"I grew up Jewish, you know, going to temple. But I never really prayed or anything. The closest thing I had to praying was making wishes, wishes like the one Talia just made, over birthday cakes, you know, eyes closed, blowing out little flames. It forces you to ask yourself what you want most in this world, to really know the answer. I wanted an answer I could say every time, so whoever or whatever was listening to those wishes would see them pile up, and maybe it'd be more likely to come true. So I started wishing just to be happy. That's all I wanted: to be happy. I'd wish it for every birthday, every shooting star, or whatever. I used to have trouble sleeping and when I'd wake up in the middle of the night, and I'd look out my bedroom window—there was this gigantic, ancient oak tree out there, so big it dwarfed the house, and I used to pray to that tree, really, to be happy. And then I hear Talia say that her wish is for everyone *else* to be happy. She, who's been through so much. It's blowing my mind right now. So I find myself wondering if the answer is to turn outward, to stop worrying so much about myself, and to start thinking about other people—their happiness, their clarity. How much does it speak to how evolved Talia is as a person, how beneficial her relationship with her dad has been, that she looks outward the way she does, wants to help and improve the people around her? Even when it makes her life harder. I want to be like that. I guess what I'm saying is that I feel so lucky to be here. What an unusual opportunity this is. I am so grateful to both of you, for letting us learn from you and from how you are. What a gift you've given all of us. Thank you."

I brought out the box containing the teapot, which I'd been keeping under the table. "Talia, this is for you. I know you love tea. I was thinking about how those leaves are all dried up, they look like nothing, and it takes boiling hot water to make them blossom with flavor. I think that's kind of like us. I hope you'll be patient with us, and we won't mess up your life too much, and ultimately we can help improve you and your dad's lives in return for everything you've done for us. Happy birthday, Tal."

Talia leaned in for a hug, murmuring "Thank you."

Under the table, I felt something squeeze my leg, and Isabella caught my eye before excusing herself for the bathroom. I waited a minute then excused myself as well, following her through the glow and chatter of the restaurant. When I arrived at the yellow vestibule outside the bathroom, Isabella was waiting there, and without saying anything, she led me through the door.

—⊩—

When Isabella and I returned to the table, dessert had come and gone and everyone had been sitting and chatting as the restaurant dragged past closing time. The bill was standing up untouched. Flushed and rumpled, I expected some acknowledgment of our absence, but none came. It was even darker in the restaurant than it had been when I first entered. Larry snatched the bill and held it out into the center of the table as if he were farsighted, though he talked frequently about the perfect acuity of his vision. "So, Danny, how are you going to pay for the wine you chose?" he asked me.

"Oh . . . yeah, of course," I said, digging the thin fold of my wallet out of my pocket. "How much did it turn out to be?"

He scanned the bill, then raised his eyebrows. "You picked a very fine wine for Talia's birthday. Very nice, didn't everyone think so? That was so nice of you, Danny. Seventy-five dollars for Flowers. Worth it, right? For Tal?"

"Oh, okay. I don't have . . ." I looked into my very empty wallet underneath the lip of the table. I ran my thumb over my debit card—between subway rides, train tickets out to New Jersey, meals in the city when I wasn't at Larry's, and Talia's birthday present, minimum wage part-time work at the ice cream shop had added up and whittled down to some balance I'd chosen to ignore, but I knew it was less than the cost of Flowers. Somewhere, far away, I could hear a phone ringing. Without a place to live, to buy groceries, a real job—I was burning money as fast as I made it. "I don't have cash. . . . I don't have it right now," I said.

"You don't have it right now?" Larry said, incredulous. "How are you going to pay for it then? I don't understand—what was your plan when you ordered the wine?"

I felt embarrassed. What had my plan been? Why didn't I say anything? "I didn't think, I guess." A phone kept ringing, muffled, as if in another room.

"You're going to have to see with the restaurant if they'll let you wash dishes for them. Or we could make some other arrangement." He looked around the table, his face deadly serious, as if someone else might be able to provide an answer for me. They all looked blank. Panic began to rise up in me. I didn't want to owe him any more than I already did, for staying at the apartment, for the food he'd bought. But what difference did it make at this point? Maybe I *could* wash dishes to pay for the wine. The panic felt like it was *hungry,* somehow, like it was a school of starving, carnivorous fish swimming up through my body and out the top of my head. No, *I'm* hungry, I realized, remembering that I'd left the table with Isabella after only a few bites of food. The phone was screaming now, it was on the counter in my parents' kitchen, it was wailing through dinner, after dinner, watching TV with my parents, right as I tried to leave for school; it was the phone I was never allowed to answer. The times I did, just to see, on the other end there was always a small, serious voice asking, *Do you know where Mommy or Daddy is?* and if I handed the phone to one of my parents they would put it to their ear, listen for a second, and then hang up.

When the waiter reached the table, Larry was holding out the bill, a few hundred-dollar bills hanging out the end. Larry was laughing silently, throwing his head back, pressing himself into the booth. It didn't look like real laughing; it looked the way a caricature laughs in a drawing. "You think I would leave you hanging, Danny? Please. I take care of you. I got him good, didn't I, Tal? That was funny," he said, squeezing Talia's side. "You'll get me back," he said, winking as he got up and edged out from behind the table. Everyone else followed.

Outside, the limo was waiting—a long, black snake always wrapped around whatever building we were in. I crawled in behind everyone else, the door sealed after me, and then we were in it again, the glamour that felt, somehow, deserved. Only natural that after Talia's birthday we would be in a stretch limo, all wearing nice clothes, her dad having treated his daughter and her friends to a fancy dinner. It was the adult version of a middle school birthday party at the mall—it made sense. As we began moving, Larry hefted his black bag onto the limo floor and unzipped it. It was rare for him to open the bag in full view, and I felt the collective desire to lean in. Iban, I noticed, was still sitting back as if he wasn't curious, his marine training, I thought, kicking in, so I felt caught between looking or not looking, and I tried to do both, sitting back against the seats while gazing down my nose at the yawning maw of the bag. Larry reached inside and pulled out letter-sized envelopes, thick and white, and tossed one to me across the length of the car. Then he passed more envelopes to his left and right. "Count them," he said.

I opened mine a little furtively, thinking it was some kind of present for all of us, some kind of reward. As I folded back the flap, I saw green. Inside the envelope was cash, hundred-dollar bills, enough to make the envelope bulge. Isabella was already counting, as if this was customary. "The trick is to count the bills, not to try to add up the total," she called out. Looking down at the envelope in my lap, I noticed a couple speckles of red on my shirt—tomato sauce, I realized after a second—and shifted in my seat, feeling a weird emptiness in me. Either it was hunger, or it was from having sex in a bathroom for the first time in my life. I had to start counting again, having lost track. Larry wasn't counting money, just watching us, smiling.

"Ten thousand," said Isabella.

"Ten thousand," said Santos.

"Ten thousand," said Iban.

Everyone concurred; their envelopes contained ten thousand dollars, as did mine. It was the most money I'd ever seen in one place, the most I'd ever touched. Larry held his backpack open and with the other hand beckoned, so we closed our envelopes and tossed them back. They were not, after all, for us. But I guessed, in a way, they were, because Larry was paying for the apartment, for our food, for everything. Still, I couldn't help but imagine what I could do if I had that kind of cash. I could take care of myself, for one thing. I started to wonder where the money had come from, how this limo was even being paid for, but then a wave of guilt washed over me: How could I be so selfish as to want this money for myself? Instead I should feel proud of Larry and Talia–look at how they'd rebuilt a life, look at how impressive he was, so soon after getting out of jail, and he was capable of taking care of a half dozen college kids. He was riding around in a limousine, and he could make an extraordinary birthday for his daughter who, not so long ago, was living in a homeless shelter.

—ı⊢—

I woke up the next morning to Isabella shaking my shoulder. "Come on, we've got to take care of the laundry."

The question "Why?" started to form in my mouth, but I swallowed it. Better to just go along. There was some kind of rush, so I quickly pulled on pants and followed her into the bedroom, where she'd gathered clothes and sheets into a couple of hampers. Larry was sitting on the stripped bed in a towel, his graying chest hair matted in tight curls.

"I need you to help Isabella take the laundry down while I meet with Cleo," he said.

"Fucking Cleo." Isabella groaned and rolled her eyes.

The laundry room was in the basement, 150 feet below the apartment. The elevator clunked to the bottom of the building and opened on an intestinal network of narrow, convoluted hallways made of gray-painted cinder blocks and exposed pipes–pipes which sustained the comfortable, private little worlds of the hundreds of occupants above. Isabella and I sorted through Larry's and Talia's clothes, taking up almost every machine, and then sat up on the white plastic table between machines while the clothes sloshed. We would be here for a while. The fact that we weren't allowed back into the apartment while Larry was talking with Cleo, whoever that was–not to mention the fact that it wasn't my business to ask who Cleo was–was all implied. I reached over and put my hand on Isabella's leg, and tried to pull her closer to me. The machines began to whir, throwing the clothes against their inner walls, sucking the liquid out of them. She turned away toward the machines and said, "We should probably switch these over to the dryers."

—ı⊢—

The elevator slid upward, fifteen floors of Isabella and I silently holding hampers of warm, dry laundry until it dinged open. Down the hall, to the right, the door with the "E" below the peephole. She slumped her basket against the door and knocked. We waited. Minutes passed.

"Should we knock again?" I asked. The lights in the hall were cheap and insufficient, like half the bulbs were missing.

"No," she said.

"Should we call or something?" I said, dropping my basket against the wall and feeling in my pocket for my phone.

"No, don't do that. He knows we're here. When he's ready for us, he'll get us."

I leaned against the wall and let myself slide to the floor. Sitting there, I felt deeply tired. Isabella was still waiting, stock-still. I wished I had brought any of my stuff with me, a book or something, but I'd assumed we would just be coming right back. I pressed my thumbs against the tips of my forefingers and watched the tips flatten out, then soften back. Isabella sighed loudly and said, "I'm going out."

I didn't know what to do with that information. "Going out? What should I do with the laundry?" I asked.

She was already standing in front of the elevator staring at the glowing red DOWN arrow. "I don't care," she said, stepping through the doors.

—II—

When Larry opened the apartment door, I had no sense how much time had passed, and he was letting out a woman I assumed was Cleo. She looked remarkably like my mom—tightly curled dark hair, worryingly thin—but she was paler. She looked as if she had once been terrified so badly that the blood had never returned to her face, her eyes frozen in a panicked goggle. She met my gaze for a moment, looked shocked, and then tried to sidle by me toward the elevator. I stepped out of her way.

Larry looked around the hall. "Where's Isabella?" he asked.

"She said she was going out," I said.

His look was a hand reaching into my chest. My heart hurt, suddenly. "And you just let her?" I started to stutter out an answer, but he interrupted me. "Come on, bring those in. I ask you to stay with her, you need to stay with her. You need to understand—everything I'm doing, I do for a reason."

I hefted up both the laundry hampers and followed him through the door. He was already on his phone, calling Iban, telling him to go look for Izzy. He flipped the phone shut and turned to me; I had followed him into the bedroom and dropped the laundry by the bed. "Come on," he said, pulling the entangled white intestines of the sheets out of the hamper. "Do this with me."

I went around to the other side of the king-sized bed, edging past the boxes and crawling over the corner of the mattress, being careful not to step on it with my shoes. He threw me one end of the fitted sheet. "I don't think you know what could happen to Izzy out there. There are things you can't comprehend about how a mind like hers works, how it forms with an upbringing like hers. That girl practically raised herself in a trailer in San Antonio. She would wake up before her mom—her obese, disabled mom who she shared a bed with—and make them breakfast, with roaches crawling everywhere. She'd eat her cereal with half-and-half because they wouldn't get anything else. You have no idea what that's like, Danny. You don't know how that feels, to live with."

He watched as I tucked the last corner under the mattress, and then threw me the flat sheet. "She's got this impulse, the same thing Tal developed, and of course Santos has got it. You've got it, too; you think you don't, but it's there. You have to be careful. You have to protect people like that. I've taken on that responsibility for you. I'm willing to do that for you, to keep you alive. Because you can't handle it right now, that much is obvious, right?"

I nodded. It was obvious we couldn't take care of ourselves, nor could we take care of each other. I'd just let Isabella go. My heart was pounding. He laid the duvet insert out on the bed and took one end of the cover. "Do you know the best way to put one of these on?" he asked me. "You've got to turn it inside out," he said, and reached his hand deep into its innards. I did the same, his eyes on me as I felt for the stitching on the corner seam, then reached through the sheet to grab the insert. "She could die out there, Danny. If I don't bring her back, she will die. You understand? That would be your fault, for letting her go. I'll get her back, I will, but I can't be one hundred percent sure. You don't want that on your conscience. I promise you, I *promise* you, you wouldn't survive it. You couldn't stand it. Your mind would discorporate. If one of you goes, if one of you feels responsible for it, then the rest of you will follow. You can't trust yourself; it's too much of a risk, you understand?"

We pulled the duvet cover over its filling, and I patted it down at the edges. We buttoned it up and then it was done, its insides still the same, but covered with something newly washed. "Claudia and Santos will be here any minute," he said. "Why don't you get breakfast started?"

Larry fell into his usual position in the living room, and I went into the kitchen. I was pulling out the eggs when I got a phone call from my dad, whose calls I had been ignoring for a few weeks. I held the phone to my ear, and as my dad was telling me about life back at home—they'd asked about me at the general store where I'd worked for a few summers, he was making a website for a new client, my mom was doing all right—I was looking through the mixing bowl, the globes of yolk floating in their albumen, before I dipped in a fork and began to break them. I poured the eggs into the biggest pan I could find and dragged the spatula across them, folding them on themselves. Talia, Claudia, and Santos were chatting in the living room.

Larry came in and patted me on the shoulder, nodding as if impressed. "Tal and I like them really wet; that's the proper way to make them. Good job, Danny," and he headed back into the living room. When my dad asked how things were going in New York, I said well, fine, you know, actually very good, Larry was taking care of all of us, really helping us all, like for example Isabella, who would be having a really hard time without him, who grew up without really a family at all, as I understood it, and was now being basically saved by him. "He's helping me, too, even though it's different," I told my dad. "He's helping me figure out things. How to manage my mind so that I can have clarity and how to feel good about the things I do every day, to be really deliberate and live according to principles. You know, I feel like I never really learned principles to live by, and he's teaching me that. It's kind of marine-like, the stuff he's teaching us, like we're going through a mini boot camp for the mind."

There was a pause on my phone; I heard my dad take a breath. "It sounds kind of like a cult, Dan. Sometimes, when you talk this way, it sounds like you're brainwashed or something."

I tried to turn my cough into a good-natured chuckle as I tipped the glistening eggs onto plates for Larry and Talia. "It's not," I said. "It's not that at all. Anyway I just finished making breakfast for everybody, so I've got to go!" I said and hung up. I scrubbed the pan in the sink, then brought Larry and Talia their eggs and told everyone else their food was in the kitchen.

Larry tapped out two orange pills with his coffee. "How was your dad?" he asked, a tiny wet egg curd dotting his lip.

"He's okay," I said. "I don't know, they're always kind of impossible to talk to."

Larry took a bite and then put his fork down. He looked around at everyone else. "Notice how he says 'they' even though he was just talking to his dad? Isn't that interesting?" Everyone nodded in unison; it was interesting. "Parenting is difficult. You dad doesn't know how to relate to you, Danny. Not like me and Tal," he said. "We're in sync. Sometimes we think the same thoughts. People can barely believe it. When Talia was born I would just hold her for hours and she would stare into my eyes. Hours. She didn't do that with anyone else. It was the same with Ava," he said, and then looked out the window hard, the flesh on the edge of his fist flattening against the glass table. He stood up, said, "I'm sorry, honeygirl," one hand on Talia's shoulder, the other holding the half-eaten plate of eggs, and then walked into the kitchen.

"We're going to get her back, honeyboy," Talia said. "We're going to get justice from Bernie and my mother and everyone else who dishonored us."

She looked at me. "Do you know how rare it is for sisters to be separated in a custody dispute? It's totally unprecedented. But here we are—the courts were willing to split up our family because with enough power and enough influence and enough corruption you can do anything. You know what's even more rare than separating sisters? Female child abusers. Mothers who hurt their daughters. Unheard of. That's why no one will believe us. We're going to save Ava from that monster. We have to."

The front door swung open and in came Isabella, trailed by Iban. She sat on the couch in silence as Iban went to confer with Larry about what had happened.

"Of course you will," I said to Talia, not able to make out what Larry and Iban were saying in the kitchen, but it sounded curt, like a soldier reporting back to a commanding officer. Then silence again, the sound of metal on metal, and Larry came out of the kitchen holding out the pan I'd used to cook the eggs. He didn't even acknowledge Isabella's return, the high boil of her sulk on the couch across the room, but instead darted at me, bringing the pan right in front of my face. I jolted back in my chair and it tipped, caught on the carpet, almost fell. The metal disk of the pan's surface flashed white then silver in the sun from the window. "Danny, why don't you make this easy and tell everyone what you did?" he said.

"What's going on? You mean letting Isabella leave earlier? We talked about that, though. I'm sorry, did I—"

"'Did I? Did I?'" he asked in an affected voice. "You know what you did. There's no reason to hide, Danny. No way to hide. I already know."

Was it a performance? A play I was meant to participate in? I looked around. Santos looked concerned, genuinely worried, but also a little angry at me already, his brow furrowed as he scratched his forehead. Claudia, next to him, leaned forward. "Just tell him, Dan! There's no reason to waste everyone's time. You know what it is, so let it out!"

"I'm sorry, I'm just really confused."

"Okay, you want to do it this way. What is that?" He sat down next to me and held the pan inches away from my face, pointing at its center.

"I don't see anyth–"

Suddenly his hand was on my thigh, squeezing hard. Through the glass surface of the table I could see his fingers clenching my jeans. It was just a hand, just human grip, but it felt like I'd gotten caught in some kind of industrial machinery, like my leg was being chewed off at the thigh. Blood pulsed at the back of my knee.

"It's ruined. Do you know how nice this pan is? How much it costs? That is a scratch. Scratches. All over." He clanked the pan on the table so hard the glass should have smashed, but didn't. I wondered if he knew, somehow, just how hard to hit the table–hard enough so it would scare me, soft enough that it wouldn't break. He ran his finger along the metal in a line, saying "Look. LOOK," each time vising my thigh harder with his hand.

It was me, now. How had it happened? I was on trial, the target of judgment. I'd thought I was somehow better, above the rest of them. When Larry had said people were sabotaging the apartment, it'd seemed absurd to me, something I could never imagine doing–why would Santos or Claudia or Iban do such a thing? But then they'd admit it, I'd watch them say they'd done it, and so it was hard to reject the possibility outright. I looked where Larry was pointing. The surface of the pan still reflected the sun, making the walls shimmer like the bottom of a dock. The surface was covered in tiny, thin scratches that caught the light. Everyone was silent, looking at Larry looking at me looking at the pan. "How'd you do it?" he asked. "Did you use a metal spatula? You scraped it on purpose, as hard as you could? What were you thinking about? Mommy and Daddy?" His hand tightened; snakes of pain shot out from it. I could feel the bone in my thigh. I shook my head. "How did you clean it, then?"

"I used a sponge and dish soap." From the couch, a disapproving puff of air came from Isabella. Claudia and Santos murmured something between them. Iban stood behind Larry like a mannequin, his thumbs hooked in his pockets. Everything was pain radiating outward from the hand on my thigh.

"You owe me for that pan, Danny," Larry said. His voice sounded almost sorry for me. "That's All-Clad from Williams Sonoma. Santos!" he yelled. "Get on your laptop and look up how much that pan costs. Tri-ply stainless steel. Make sure you find it. How much?"

Santos hunched over his computer, furiously looking around the screen, trying to stay out of the line of fire. "It looks like the pan is two hundred dollars." He was using his serious voice, I could hear it.

"Not the pan, Santos," Larry was yelling. "How much is the set?"

"Twelve hundred for the full set."

"From Williams Sonoma?" Larry asked. "That's not right. When I got them it was eighteen hundred. I don't forget things, do I, Danny?" I nodded my head like I knew what he was talking about; I had to. It felt difficult even to move my head. His eyes were locked on me. Somehow it felt like they were trapping me, turning my body to concrete. "I bought those pans for Talia. You knew that, didn't you? I'm trying to make us a home, and what happens, what upsets you so much that you have to ruin it? Why? Because you can't have what we have? A father who's trying to look out for you and take care of you?"

"No, I didn't–"

He grabbed my forearm and turned his hand against the surface of my skin, giving me what kids in grade school called an Indian burn, but worse, somehow, the worst I'd ever received, as if the bone itself was cracking, releasing acid into my bloodstream. He looked straight at me, his eyes crazy, green, the lids fluttering. "You feel that?" he said. "I know you can feel it, Danny. I have you now. You feel it? I don't use this on many people."

He twisted the hand more. Fire arced up my arm, got caught in my elbow–it was like every part of me was a funny bone ringing with hollow pain. Everyone else was pulled in toward us, magnetically, jealous of the unique attention I was receiving.

"Look into my eyes," he said. I tried to look away, but he squeezed even harder. "It feels like you could be trapped in them forever, doesn't it? I could do that if I wanted to. Make you crazy with just my eyes. You believe that? Actually crazy. I could make it so you never think about anything else. So you see these eyes in your sleep. I could come to you in your dreams. Never anything else, but just my eyes. Keep looking,

Danny. What do you see in them? Do you see yourself, curled up, lost, alone? Something striking you, over and over? Do you like this feeling? I could make you feel it forever. Feel it. Let the feeling overtake you. That's where you live forever now, because you won't tell me. I see you, Danny. I see you everywhere with these eyes, you understand? I know when you say something against me, when you doubt me, when you fear me. I *see* it. I see your fear. Tell everyone what happened. Why you felt the need to sabotage me."

I racked my brain. I had said something against him. Everything had been fine, and then suddenly it wasn't. The only thing that had happened was the phone call with my dad. If I told him, maybe he'd say I'd told my dad something that had led him to believe this was a cult—it couldn't have come from nowhere. And what if he came after my dad, made us both get on the phone or something? But I was already in trouble. He already knew, he said. So if I was honest, just totally open, then this would be over. "On the phone, my dad said what you were doing with us sounded like a cult. Us all living here and everything. I only told him good things, about how it was going, about how you were helping. He said it sounded like brainwashing. But he wasn't being serious, not really. I was telling him about you. I was only saying good stuff."

Larry nodded, but didn't let go. "I know, Danny. That's only part of it. What else?"

I felt like I was sprinting around my head, trying to find something that matched, a key that would let me out of this. I was sure that had been it. "I really don't know! I don't, I swear."

"I'll give you a hint. It has to do with Claudia."

I looked over at her, and her face was transformed. It was pleading, willing me to say or do something. I didn't know what.

"Danny, have you had any contact with Bernie Kerik, or the FBI, or been in touch with Teresa?"

"Your ex-wife? What? No, of course not!"

"But you've seen Claudia talk to them."

"I don't know, no, I mean, I don't think so. Not recently, that I know of."

"When did you see them?" I felt the pressure from his hand on my leg and his hand on my arm radiating toward the center of my body, closing in on my chest. The room was vibrating.

"I don't know . . . maybe at Slonim." I didn't know what I was saying. It was hard to think, to even know how to remember things. I thought this would end when I was open and honest, but now it was still going, and it felt like I'd entered some imaginary space. I could imagine Claudia talking to men in suits, men who could look like police, or FBI, or whatever I thought dirty cops might look like. I could picture her having a conversation outside of Slonim as I walked up the path, then the men leaving, rounding the corner, and her seeming especially awkward when I reached her at the door, squirrelly, trying to talk about anything else. I could just invent the image in my head, and it was as if I'd discovered it instead, lying there, perfectly matching what Larry wanted. And then it was as if it was real; a memory.

Larry looked around at everyone. "See? Danny knew exactly what he was hiding. Claudia, did you talk to them at Slonim?"

She nodded, said yes, she had, looking ashamed. So it was true, then, not imaginary. I had been hiding it, somehow, from myself. As Larry let go of my leg and hand, the blood rushed back to the parts of me that'd been cut off. "Was that so hard, Danny? I had to help you get there, through the door to the memory you were afraid of, that you'd put somewhere inaccessible. This is straightforward stuff, repressed memories, that you can read about in any psychology textbook. I know how to walk around in your head, whether or not you'll let me. But it's faster, and better for you, if you let me in. And the stuff with your dad, forget about that. So Dad said something that made you upset. He knows I'm helping you, but he still has some control, right? So how does he endeavor to hold on to that control? He spins you up, tries to undermine me, tries to sow seeds of doubt in your head. He's been doing that a long time, hasn't he? Ever since Slonim, even, he's been speaking against me, right? Did you repress that memory, too? That's why you didn't come talk to me earlier. And instead of coming to me about it, you felt trapped, and tried to lash out."

My own memories were hidden from me, and my sense of what memories I had, of what was even true, was unreliable compared with what he told me. I guess my dad had probably made me mistrust Larry, though I couldn't remember ever talking to my dad about him. I must have scratched the pan, too. The pan was scratched, which meant I must have scratched it. And because everything you did was a decision, as Larry had been saying since the beginning, I must have done it on purpose. He went on. "You know deep down that I'm helping you, but part of you wants to be unhappy—it wants the pain to continue. You feel that part inside you, right?"

I nodded. I did feel it. I had to, or else why was I here?

"That part of you doesn't want me to help. You have to stop listening to it. That part of you doesn't want me in there, cutting it out, doesn't want for you to have clarity. To get you to admit that you did something bad, that you expressed your pain outwardly by acting out, I have to show you something that's worse, that's more intense in the moment, to overpower that part of you. Danny, you're going to go study abroad, which Mommy and Daddy aren't even helping you with, are they? Right? You're going to get a job and do this all on your own? Then you'd better recognize how far you have to go. You're broken, and you need to accept it. Feel your arm. It's fine, right?"

I hinged my arm up and down at the elbow. It hurt a little. *It's fine.* "Yeah, it actually is," I said.

"You're all right, Danel. You made progress today. You hear that, Iz?" he said, looking over at her. "I gave him a new nickname. Danel, you like that?"

Isabella rolled it over in her mouth. "Danel. Oh yeah, that's his name," she said.

Larry slumped back into his seat as if exhausted from effort, but he was practically beaming. It was like some loose end, or a few of them, had been tied up. Claudia looked stunned, and I knew that she must be in much deeper trouble than I could understand, if she'd been talking to Larry's ex-wife somehow.

"People are so negative about the word 'brainwashing,'" Larry said.

"I don't see what's wrong with it. That is what I'm doing. I'm washing your brains. You should tell your dad *that*, Danel," he said, laughing, and Isabella laughed with him.

Santos piped up from across the room. "I would welcome some brainwashing!"

I kept looking at the frying pan where it sat on the glass table. My fingers burned and prickled, and my new name resounded in my head: almost the same as my real name, but with the "I" removed.

8

Don't cry
Don't raise your eye
It's only teenage wasteland

I WOKE UP AHEAD of everyone this time, finally. The bedroom door was still closed with Larry, Talia, and Isabella entombed behind it. I felt covered with grime. My stomach ached. I pulled the socks off my feet—it had begun to get a little cold at night—and leaned forward; there were little specks on the tops of my feet, like freckles. But I didn't have freckles. I wanted urgently to shower, to take this opportunity while Larry was still asleep. But what if he woke up while I was in the bathroom and wanted to use it, to sit in there and do work, critical, time-sensitive work for the government, and I was taking it up? What if I got out and he said my shower was taking too long—even six minutes was too long—and what if that meant I was intentionally doing something to sabotage him? I wanted permission to shower, I wanted him to come out and say it was okay, but I didn't know how to ask for something like that. I wanted him to just tell me to shower, so that I could. If I did it without him, he would know. I winced, then, at that thought, which might be negative toward Larry, and I wondered if that meant I would do something to damage his things, to lash out. Maybe I should tell him I'd had that thought, so that I wouldn't do anything to lash out. But that would mean a long conversation, an interrogation, about why I'd had the thought. And then it would be my fault nothing had gotten done, because I had caused the long conversation. So I wouldn't tell him, and I wouldn't shower, and I would try not to think anything else.

I was paralyzed on the couch until Larry came out of the bedroom toting his laptop, as if he had been sitting in there awhile, working. I resented him for not freeing me from this cycle of thought by coming out earlier. I had automatically, when the door began to open, rushed to turn on the morning playlist. Then to the kitchen, to grab the fifty-dollar-a-pound bag of Kona coffee beans Larry had told me to get at the Fairway on Eighty-sixth Street, saying it was the only good coffee, though later he would switch, briefly, to Jamaican Blue Mountain, which was somehow even more expensive. I poured the beans into the grinder and was about to grind them at the table, where Larry was sitting with his laptop, when he put the heavy glove of his hand over mine and said, "I'll do it."

I kept looking toward the bathroom, wanting to change out of my old clothes from the night before, not sure what I was hoping for—that Larry, in his clairvoyance, would know that I wanted to shower and would say something encouraging about how I should? At any moment he might say instead that he was going in there, or he might not say anything at all, and just go in there and close the door, and then there was no way of knowing how long it would be until I would see him again. Or it might be none of that, and something else altogether.

"What's your plan for going abroad?" he asked me.

"What do you mean?" I said.

"Your visa. Your passport. Do you have a passport? Your plane ticket? Where are you living? Do you need me to contact people I know overseas to set you up?"

"Oh, no, I have a place to stay. It's on campus." I had barely looked through the brochure when it had arrived back at Slonim, just checked off the cheapest housing option, "The Ziggurat," and sent it back.

Larry raised his eyebrows. "Those places can be terrible. You have a camera for when you're over there?"

"Not really, no. I have my phone."

"I'll get you a nice camera. Something that connects to your computer. Then we can Skype," he said. "What about the other stuff? How are you getting your visa?"

I didn't know I was supposed to handle any of that stuff. I had a passport somewhere. I didn't even know I needed a visa to study abroad; I'd figured it was just like going to school, but in a new place. I hadn't thought about any of it. I said as much to Larry. He stood up, saying, "Don't worry. I'll take care of it for you, Danny. You can help me with something, actually. I'm going to send you some things. I want you to look at them, and come up with a response." Then he walked into the bathroom and closed the door behind him, ending the possibility of a shower today.

I sat on the couch, opened my laptop, and refreshed my email. The message from Larry appeared: "Re: From the heart- do you see anything else in there- relax and look closely.-LVR." I opened the attachments, emails between Isabella and a Sarah Lawrence professor. As I did, Santos and Claudia walked in the front door—someone must have lent one of them a key. They sat down on either side of me. Santos asked what I was doing. I held the laptop screen in his direction, our new task for the day. "Larry wants us to look into this." They leaned in next to me, and I began scrolling through the emails. The messages laid out an entire situation I hadn't been cognizant of.

Apparently Isabella had been failing one of her classes. In a conference with her teacher, Isabella had opened up about how she had been abused as a kid, and she'd talked about how she was getting help from Larry. It looked like her teacher had offered to give her an incomplete in the class, giving her an option to retake it without failing. The teacher had said something about wishing that Isabella was receiving "professional help" for what she was going through, the implication being that Larry was not a professional.

As I kept reading, I got more and more confused about what exactly the problem was that Larry wanted us to address; there were emails between Isabella and her adviser in which Isabella claimed that the teacher had lied to her and had had conversations with Isabella's adviser behind her back, that somehow Isabella was being screwed over—

that she was, essentially, the victim of a conspiracy. In one email a meeting was being arranged between the teacher, Isabella, her adviser, and a school administrator, and Isabella had said that she wanted Larry to go in her place. I wondered if that had happened, or if it was forthcoming. Maybe that was why we were tasked with performing this analysis. I thought Claudia or Santos might have a better idea what was going on. The laptop felt hot on my lap and my finger ached from slowly, conscientiously scrolling so that they could both read along with me. I thought it best to sound vaguely offended in solidarity with Isabella, and let them fill in the gaps. "What the hell?" I said. "This is messed up."

"I can't believe Isabella's professor would do that to her," Claudia said. "What a liar!"

Santos still looked the way I felt. "It feels like they're just telling a completely different story than Isabella is. Maybe the way we help her is by really explaining her side of things, and simplifying everything?"

"Maybe let's make a timeline then, something that clarifies what happened from her perspective," I suggested.

Claudia and Santos pulled out their laptops. We sat like that, in a row, lit up by the glow of a shared document. It felt kind of thrilling, like we were in a war room, righteously defending our wronged friend against an unjust, unsympathetic system. The more we turned over the emails, the more each word Isabella's teacher had used became loaded—a deliberate attack, a deranged attempt to confuse and delude. This teacher was undoubtedly, we said to each other as we picked apart her sentences over the course of hours, insidious, conniving, a heartless academic, a twisted deviant even, who drew an extremely sensitive confession out of a vulnerable student on the threat of academic punishment. It was sadistic, practically, and this teacher got off on it. Totally dishonest, no doubt about it. It was all right there in our timeline, and in another document we'd made analyzing her language, and in yet another analyzing her character. We felt powerful, threatening, a monster with three heads, the body of a black leather couch, and a single, just purpose: to destroy the corruption at our school. More than that, we felt useful. Larry came out of the bathroom as if minutes had passed, rather than the entire day. He sat down at the table, unloading his laptop and backpack, and asked, "Well, what did you come up with?"

Claudia excitedly explained our documents and our breakdown of the whole situation. We had really devoted ourselves to this, she wanted him to see, really given it our all, but he looked more and more confused, then angry. He looked at me. "This isn't what I asked for, Danny," he said.

"What? I thought we were helping—" His eyes were burning into me again. I couldn't help but feel indignant; we'd really tried, honestly, to make sense of what had happened. Had he come out of the bathroom ready to be disappointed and upset? Was this an impossible task?

"What did I say I wanted?"

"You said you wanted a response but—"

"What did you give me?"

"Well, we tried to analyze the whole back-and-forth and look at it—"

"No, Danny." I watched his hand close into a fist. "What did you give me? Was it a response? Or was it a timeline and analysis and whatever the fuck this useless shit is? I did this in five minutes myself in there already. Five minutes, and the three of you spent all day. Completely worthless. Are you deliberately wasting my time? When I ask you to do something, I know exactly what I'm asking you to do, and you need to follow instructions. I asked you for a *response* for Izzy. But apparently none of you wanted to help her. I'll handle it myself. Apparently I'm the only one who cares." He closed his laptop and walked into the bedroom, leaving us stunned.

Santos was the first to collect himself. "Okay, I'll try to write something, a response, and maybe we all can edit it and make something really good quickly," he said, his laptop already out in front of him.

I had to go to work at the ice cream shop for an evening shift. I knew that saying I had to leave meant they would look at me like I was abandoning them. But the air beyond the door, unbreathed by all these people, called to me, and so I said it: "I'm sorry, guys, I've got work," and gathered up my things as quickly as I could. I wouldn't get a chance to shower. I needed to leave before Larry came back out and said I couldn't go, or delayed me in some way that made me late for work. They didn't even look up at me, absorbed in the task of fixing our failure. Then I was gone, through the door and out into the night.

⊣⊢

After my shift, I rattled back uptown. When I arrived, the hallway and living room were dark, and I was ready to collapse into the couch—it felt like a luxury anytime there was no one sitting on it and I could actually use it as a bed. I swallowed the thought when the bedroom door opened, and Larry, standing in the dim opening, told me to come in.

One way of dealing with a memory you can't bear is that you begin to build a box. The box is the same shape and has the same dimensions as the real room you're in when the memory is made. The box's walls overlay exactly upon the walls that are really there, made of wood and sheet metal and drywall, filled with plaster and rats and gypsum dust, the voices that echo up from downstairs, and the firebreaks to stop the whole place from burning all at once. The main difference is that in the real world there are doors to get in and out. In your head there is only more wall, so whatever happened is sealed up inside. Then the box and everything in it becomes very small, and you tuck it away on a shelf inside of you. You can put it to your ear like a seashell and hear something happening inside but it sounds very far away—a whisper of an echo of something that happened to someone who isn't you, but is a lot like you.

⊣⊢

I followed Larry into the bedroom, the clutter of it unchanged all summer even though he kept talking about how we would clean up, we had to clean up, and nothing got done. It was our fault—someone scratched a pan or dented a wall or stole a book and so the day was blown because of their sabotage, and their mind had to be fixed now, more than the apartment did. As we were walking into the box of the bedroom, he was saying, "The work you and Claudia and Santos did today actually turned out to be useful," and as the door shut behind me, I saw Isabella lying on the bed in her underwear again, this time not wearing a bra. It broke me, made me stupid then, to see her like that, with Larry walking in ahead of me like nothing was out of the ordinary. It was like a power line to my brain had been cut all the way through. Larry sat me down on the bed next to Isabella, and asked me to tell him about what had happened during Talia's birthday at the restaurant between us, as if it hadn't been his idea. When I told him, he shook his head. "According to Isabella, you've got some things to learn."

Isabella was smiling, lying back on the bed propped up on her elbows, and I couldn't help but fear that smile, that willingness, because of what it implied—what would happen if I were not as willing as she seemed to be. She rolled over so I couldn't see her face anymore, and Larry reached over to his laptop in the corner. The music that suddenly filled the room at an enormous volume was eerie: church music, voices echoing and vaulting over one another.

"These are Gregorian chants, Danny, from the thirteenth century. Can you believe that?" The music, the situation, the emptiness in my head, made it feel like he was speaking directly into my mind. "Sex should be beautiful, reverent. Not scary, the way you've treated it. You do a disservice to sex, to the person you're with, to yourself, by being scared of it. Look," he said, touching Isabella's ankle with his fingertips. "Not scary." He was barely touching her. His fingers reached her calf, the back of her knee, her upper thigh, and right before he reached where her thighs met, he switched to the other leg, then slowly, very lightly, returned to her ankle. "Sex, like everything in life, should be deliberate." He began to bring his fingers back up. "So that each action is in control, and nothing is random." As he reached the top of her thigh, this time he grabbed her flesh, and as he pulled her back toward him, curling her open, Isabella moaned.

"Now you," he said.

So I did, very lightly and slowly, with the leg that was near me, run my fingers up and down, and then eventually, when it felt right, grabbed her thigh and pulled it toward me, and she moaned, so it felt like I had done something right. This was easy, and clear, I thought, to just do what he said, and it would make her feel good. This was all it took, for everything to be simple, and not scary.

He nodded at me, and we kept going, very slowly. I was paying attention to him, trying to do it right, so when his fingers traced up her back, down along her arm, then back up to her neck, down her spine, I did the same. His hands looked funny, he was bent over her, and with the music I couldn't help but see it like a religious sculpture, like she was sick or worse and he, some kind of saint, might raise her with his touch, those thick fists uncurled like stone blossoms, scraping along her skin, barely in contact with the fuzz that raised up from her back to meet him. His fingers ran along the lip of her underwear, very lightly, and she shifted and quietly moaned, muffled by the duvet, so I followed him in parallel. I watched his finger hook under the elastic and run gently along the inside. I watched her skin indent, ever so slightly, under his finger.

The Gregorian chants made the whole room feel like a reverberating throat. If this was sex, then she and I had not been doing anything related to sex. The chorus in the background swelled and receded, like the ocean, or bile. I could feel her body tense and relax, in spite of how lightly he was touching her. It was the exasperation of it, the suspense, that was powerful—the not knowing when he was going to touch her in a real way, how things might change at any moment. I wanted someone to want me this badly.

"Danny, what you're engaging in is a perfectly natural submissive-dominant sexual dynamic. Of course, it's Izzy, the sub, the submissive, who has the ultimate power here. None of this happens without her choice. Isn't that right, Izzy?" Muffled, Isabella moaned again, and Larry said, "Now you have to give her more." He indicated with his head that I should go around to the other side of the bed, where Isabella's face was, and I did. "Take out your cock. For her. That's what she wants."

I wished it was over, all at once; I wondered how to get to the end of this situation, but there was no way around it, I was in too deep now. I should have walked out when I first saw her sitting on the bed shirtless, but it was too late even then. I moved my hand very slowly, deliberately, the way he'd taught me, and I touched her back, and as I did she lifted her head before I could do or say anything and she swallowed me. The music became catastrophic, apocalyptic, the kind of song that might drift out of the earth as it cracks open for the last time, when there's no one left to hear.

Larry pulled off his clothes, and in spite of the grip I was in, the choking, gasping sound Isabella was making, I saw his underwear, tighty-whities, almost neon in the dark, his body hanging over them, and there was a moment in which he seemed ridiculous, rotund, a fifty-year-old man in his underwear, and that was somehow even more terrifying, and then the bright triangle of underwear was gone, and it was just dark. He leaned forward and was inside her. I knew because of the sound she made, her mouth opening and then closing even tighter.

No time passed and all of time passed. There was no one to count it, and the music never changed. I wasn't thinking. I had stopped thinking a long time ago. The walls of the box had become solid, opaque, and then it was over, or it was for me. Isabella was on her back. At some point that had changed. She had been on top of me, and he on top of her, and then he was on top of both of us. Now it was over and he was telling me to leave, telling me I should feel good, when really as I passed through the door I didn't feel anything. Anything I felt, I left on the other side of the door, which was now a wall living inside of me. In the living room, I lay down on the couch and finally went to sleep, as if nothing had ever happened. It had, but I hadn't been there.

—II—

You believe you live a normal life. You do, you believe it. So anything that happens, you make fit. This is how I lived, and it became normal, and because it was normal, everything was normal, and it was normal like that over and over for what remained of that summer, and then I was with Larry and Cleo in the limo rushing to meet a man who would be able to expedite my visa, which meant instead of processing it in six months, which is how long it takes, this man would, for six hundred dollars and by some inexplicable means, process it in three days, which was how much time there was until I had to leave for England.

Instead of heading south on the FDR, the driver nosed inland, toward the park. I knew enough about Manhattan by now to know this was wrong, but said nothing, my knee bouncing nervously behind Larry's seat. Cleo was clutching her bag in her lap next to me, looking up through the window at the overcast sky. Once we were on the Central Park traverse it was clear that fall had come back to New York. The city was damp green and brown; it looked like a thinly applied watercolor on white paper. We stopped on the west side, and Cleo got out. She leaned back into the car, awkwardly past me and toward Larry, and began to say to him, "I'll take care of that thing, when–"

"Okay, Cleo," he said, not looking at her.

"Oh, yes, all right, I just will have it for you–"

"Okay. Cleo," Larry said again, each word a roadblock in the conversation, and so Cleo nodded like her spine was string and backed out of the car.

Larry was on his laptop in the front seat, and I sat directly behind him. "Don't listen to Cleo," he said.

I felt a little bold; I could tell she had done something wrong, and I wanted to twist the knife a little, to be as far on Larry's side as possible. "Yeah . . . what's her deal? She seemed pretty crazy."

"I've been helping her. She needs it, she really needs it. You think you've got issues with your family? Cleo's whole family, for her, they're like shadows bearing down on every side. She is constantly afraid, trying to protect herself. She didn't realize her husband was a con man, for one thing, and I helped her with that. Cleo does everything out of fear because she was born with a rare condition: As a newborn she had a layer of skin over her face, like a mask. It's called 'en caul.' Entirely covered. To her mother, she was a monster. Imagine the pain inside of you, to be rejected by your mother like that, from the very beginning, for your parents to be horrified by you. They did the surgery–the surgery for that is remarkable–and she's fine. But she's still traumatized from it, still feels ugly, disappointing, like she's a monster, like she has to hide. She was obsessed with getting treatments, surgery, spending inordinate amounts of money, because she thought of herself as monstrous. So I'm helping her with all that. She's an old friend of a friend, but let me tell you, Danny, she's a mess, and incredibly dishonest. She also owes me an inordinate amount of money for my work and she's always trying to sneak her way out of it."

"Wow, that's intense," I said. "It's really nice of you to help her."

"Some people find it almost impossible, Danny, to accept the truth. To act honorably. How can you ask for help from a friend, and then instead of thanking them, you hurt them? And then you try to find any possible way you can to avoid making things right? Some people are conquered by fear, and nothing can save them. I might be the only chance Cleo has, but unless she opens herself up to me and makes things right, I can't help her. The same way you have to, Danny. You're still not there, but I believe in you."

"I'm trying," I said, my gut twisting. "I'll keep trying in England." I didn't know if I meant it. It was almost impossible to imagine anything outside of the apartment, but when I thought about England, I knew that I felt something like relief, and I knew that I had to hide it. England was supposed to be more like a test, an unlucky burden, a risk for me, even. Larry had turned back to his laptop, and it was as if I didn't exist, so I pulled Talia's Bertrand Russell out of my pocket, which I'd been slowly reading all summer.

> If you are sailing in a ship on a fine day along a beautiful coast, you admire the coast and feel pleasure in it. This pleasure is one derived entirely from looking outward, and has nothing to do with any desperate need of your own. If, on the other hand, your ship is wrecked and you swim towards the coast, you acquire for it a new kind of love: it represents security against the waves, and its beauty or ugliness becomes an unimportant matter.

We arrived downtown, Larry handed me $600 in hundred-dollar bills out of his bag, and with that, I was able to have my visa expedited. Three days later, I was on a plane to England.

9

Dear Hailey,

I'm sitting on the bed I just made, on the second-to-top floor of a pyramid. I can hear the wind rushing somewhere and it sounds the way a distant waterfall sounds. From my window I can see a field stretching down to the edge of a lake. I sit out there and play ukulele some days. There's an epic swamp and forest beyond that, which if you walk through it far enough, you come upon a farm for only mini-horses. The other day I went to the enormous field in the other direction, which is dotted with trees which are very English looking, and very huge and old. I managed to climb one which should have been impossible to climb, and sat in its crook and read poetry as a storm started. I had just seen a rainbow moments before that. I'm watching birds play in the wind over the lake now.

I wish I could tell you the meaning of life, Hailey. But it seems like you're doing pretty well so far. I would say two pretty good shoes to put your existential feet in are do what makes you happy, and don't not have fun. I guess the trick is being clearheaded enough to really truly listen to ourselves, to strike our souls with a stone and hear it resonate. We want happy clear ringing golden

> notes; our bodies, our selves, we truly know when our insides sound like a dull thud or a swampy spludge.
>
> —Dan

I hit send on the Facebook message back to Hailey, who'd sent me a message out of the blue after I left for England, then closed my laptop and unplugged it from underneath my bed. It was four A.M. and I was on a five-minute break from my morning workout—the four hundred daily push-ups Larry had prescribed to me and Santos back at Slonim. I'd been in England a month, and if I was going to be here for a whole year, I had to prove to Larry that I was a man—disciplined, smart, aggressive, confident, dominating. Him, or his shadow. I had to prove I had at least enough of him in me that I could function as he would in the world. Every thought, every instant: deliberate, under control.

The dark would soon roll back from the lake beyond my window, revealing the gray behind it. I shared my room, the cheap option I'd checked off so flippantly a year earlier, with another American foreign exchange student from New York, named Ethan. The room was tucked into the side of a ziggurat made of concrete and glass that twinkled when the clouds briefly lapsed. I had learned nothing about the school before I arrived—just imagined England to be all spires, lawns, and cobblestones—so I was surprised to find that the University of East Anglia was in fact acres of poured, contiguous concrete, as if it had been formed all in one piece and just placed here in a field. Long concrete walkways led to sprawling concrete steps that descended to concrete plazas out of which jutted, seamlessly, concrete buildings. Our flat in the ziggurat was mostly one large room where Ethan lived and a niche near the door, no more than a closet with a bed and a sink, where I did. But the bed was a bed, not a couch, and it was mine. The little sink and the cabinets with empty space—not much, but some—were mine. The unfamiliarity of it, that was mine, too, the giant pane of glass and the view through it, the perpetually wet concrete ledge, and the lake, all of it. I'd covered the wall with a hundred taped-up postcard-sized pictures of book covers of Penguin Classics someone had given me before I left.

Under the hundred watchful faces of those books—postcards I never intended to send to anyone—I did push-ups alone in the morning dark. Even though a dozen other people lived on the hall, I felt as if my life was very small, and besides the pair of ducks that occasionally visited the ledge outside my window, I was alone in it.

I planted my hands in front of the sink and, pushing off the bed, flipped my feet into the air so they balanced against the cabinet, then, in a handstand, I began to lower myself carefully, pressing my whole body up and down. I had learned from experience I could only do about five of these full body presses. When I flipped back down, I looked in the mirror above the sink and saw one of my eyes was bright pink—a little bloody sunset in my eyeball, and it took a second to realize I had burst a blood vessel. Besides that, my forehead was an active landscape of new acne. My whole life I'd thought I'd dodged the worst consequences of puberty, but the moment I arrived in England, it arrived in full force. When I'd told Larry, he hadn't been surprised at all. My hormones were activated because he was ushering me through a puberty that had been stalled by repression, he said. And how could I doubt him—the evidence was on my face. I brushed my hair off my forehead, held it back against the top of my head, pulled it straight, then let it fall. Each individual strand landed on a spot. Maybe it was my hair, somehow, depositing grease.

I tiptoed into Ethan's room, where the curtains were drawn, and snatched his hair clippers from the desk. Ethan was an unconscious mound under the hospital-blue sheets we had both received upon arrival. Clippers in one hand and my towel in the other (also part of the standard sheet set), I tiptoed in my boxers and T-shirt down the hall to the bathroom. No one would be awake this early—the other people on the hall were mostly med students, and they partied in a way that was as unfathomable to me as it was constant, seemingly determined to condense all the alcohol they could drink into the narrow gaps between their classes, tests, and all-nighters in the library. Regardless, the idea of anyone seeing me using Ethan's clippers or making a mess was mortifying—the idea of them saying anything at all to me was mortifying—so I stepped into one of the toilet stalls and shut the door behind me.

As I brought the razor to my face, the stench of stale crotch sweat was undeniable. I held my breath—now it was too late—and brought the humming wasp's nest across my head. Black hair scattered over the toilet and the gray tile. I turned it off and touched a finger to the naked stripe I'd just made. *I was born with a head of hair, wasn't I?* I thought. *I decide if I want my head to be the blankest it's ever been.* I brought the razor up from the side this time, and it was surprisingly easy, the tines gently scraping my scalp until the hair was all gone and the toilet was matted black. I tried to clean up, but it felt like evidence was everywhere, the toilet, the tile floor, the walls of the stall, and it was on my hands, too, so when I tried to clean, I would just deposit more. Eventually, after wasting half a roll of toilet paper, I decided it was good enough to be unnoticeable, grabbed my towel, and hopped into the shower.

—ı⊢—

Back in the room, I crept into Ethan's area and left the clippers where I'd found them—he was still sleeping—then grabbed my notebook and got dressed. Through some exchange-student-sized hole in the UEA course registration system, I'd been allowed to register for creative writing classes that, for regular students, would require a series of applications and approvals, none of which I'd had to go through. Among those classes was one just titled "Dissertation," for which I'd meet with an adviser a few times over the semester. I was supposed to ultimately produce something like a book.

I thought I might as well head down to the lake and try to get started, but as I stood up, something hard clanged in my stomach. I realized it was hunger. Back at the apartment, I had gotten so used to waiting on Larry for the conversation to end or for him to finish whatever secret business he had in the bathroom, at which point he would produce from his black bag the money for groceries or takeout, or give us the go-ahead to start cooking. Everything was the result of his money, time, and effort, so to start cooking without him, or to order food and have it go cold, would be a grave insult. Food only happened when Larry was ready for it, in large part because he was generous enough to pay for all of us. But even if we were paying for ourselves, even when I was alone, as I was that morning, it felt rude, somehow, to eat without him.

My hunger is mine, I thought to myself, in a voice that sounded like it came from somewhere else. I wondered what that thought was supposed to mean. It felt like my thoughts had been louder and weirder lately—or like maybe I'd never been able to hear them before at all, and now here they were sometimes, sounding the way I imagine human voices sound to a fish inside its bowl. *What does it mean to have thoughts I don't recognize? Who is even wondering this right now?* I felt my breath getting shorter, a small stampede of heartbeats coursing their way up to my eyeballs. *You are not your mind.* Larry had told me that. I am not my mind. When I reminded myself of that, it shut everything down, somehow. My brain could think its own thoughts, but I was ultimately the one in charge. I shook my head and missed the satisfying flop of hair side to side. I caught myself in the mirror again as I left the room and shuddered. Now there was no hair to hide how catastrophic my forehead looked.

I padded down the hall, the chatter and the clanks of breakfast echo-

ing in somehow British tones from the kitchen the thirteen of us shared. The kitchen was thoroughly stainless steel, or some cheap facsimile, and sat in a corner of the ziggurat. Two mostly plexiglass walls overlooked a lake pocked with unfamiliar waterfowl. The lake was surrounded by walking paths ground in by what I liked to imagine were generations of English boots. I ducked into the kitchen and headed for the wall of cubbies where our belongings were stowed, but a group of my flatmates were standing in the way.

John, one of the medical students, whose diminutive size, tight curls, and perpetual ruddiness made him seem simultaneously young and old, like an overgrown cherub, was saying, "No, I swear it. Absolutely never."

Naomi, another medical student, sitting over at the blue-green cafeteria table, rolled her eyes. "Come off it, John."

Matt, as blond as Naomi but about twice as tall, was chopping something on the counter, and he put his knife down to turn the dial on the oven mounted on the wall. He looked in at the glowing red heating element as he said, "You've got to, sometimes."

"I swear! I don't wank at all, it's just the truth. I haven't wanked even once since I've been here." John had a cast on his leg and was leaning partially against my cubby, partially on a crutch. He'd broken his leg the week before, blackout drunk, trying to jump down all twenty or so of the concrete steps in the central campus plaza.

"Pardon me," I said, indicating my cubby behind him, and cringing a little at the way my voice and phrasing had altered since I'd been here. There was a chameleonic quality in me, I thought, a desire to blend into the background, and I could hear it when I suddenly said things like "Pardon" after only a month in England.

John hopped a bit to the side on his good leg. "You all right?" he said. "Nice haircut."

I nodded and grabbed a Cadbury fruit and nut milk chocolate bar out of my cubby. It wasn't breakfast, but at least it had the word "fruit" in it.

"Looks rather military-ish," Naomi said. Her hair was long and straight, and she'd also struck me as tiny, initially. It had taken me a while to realize that Ethan and I had been assigned to a first-year dorm, so they weren't small, just two years younger.

I tucked the chocolate bar into my jacket pocket. "Yeah, I was living in New York with a couple of marines before I came here. They said it's better this way. Less to worry about." I stepped past John out of the kitchen and down the stairs, which I took two at a time, something I'd noticed Ethan did when we walked around. I liked the brain-jarring feeling of it, changing how I did something that was so deeply learned. Then I was out on the grass, which was saturated and spongy.

It was warm—strangely warm for September. Birds I'd learned were magpies dotted the field, squalling with one another and occasionally batting their wings, coin flips of stark black and white. I squished past them on the soft grass to the lake's edge. I followed the path around the lake, crossing over the river where the water exited, and craned my neck to look. Farther down the river everything was impressionistic, willows swirling over grassy banks, overhung and laden with heat. This dissertation should be about my mom, I thought. I'd use the project as a means to open up, and then I could tell Larry I was making the most of my time here to find clarity.

I shielded my eyes from the sun and peered into the woods, and while I was trying to imagine what I would say about my mom, I kept thinking about the email, the inconceivable email, that I'd gotten from Claudia a couple days before, addressed to practically everyone we knew at school, including all of us who'd lived at Slonim, and the Sarah Lawrence faculty and administration. The subject line was "The Truth." It had been a wall of text, a typed-out version of the types of confessions I'd gotten accustomed to hearing at the apartment. But those, I had thought, were secret. Apparently not.

The story Claudia told in the email began at Slonim in the first few weeks Larry had started living with us. She said she'd spread rumors to almost everyone at Sarah Lawrence—all of the people to whom the email was addressed, our friends, teachers, Sarah Lawrence administrators—about Larry, saying he was a sexual deviant who was sleeping with college students and that he had tried to trick her into having a schizophrenic break. It had been the opposite, she now claimed; she *had been* having a schizophrenic break, and had blamed it on Larry.

The email went on for pages. She said she'd talked to Teresa, Larry's ex-wife. She'd talked to the police. She'd been at the center of the ongoing conspiracy against Larry, which he'd been aware of all along, and in spite of all that, he had deigned to help her. Now, it seemed, a necessary part of her recovery was to confess all this publicly, and so it was for her own sake that she was doing it. She was studying abroad, too, in Oxford—not that far from me—which meant that she'd made the confession from there, not even in Larry's actual presence.

When I initially read the email I'd felt sick. I couldn't remember Claudia doing or saying anything remotely like this back when we were at Slonim. Maybe she had told me, and I'd hidden that memory away from myself. On one of the brief occasions Larry and I had talked after I first came to England, he'd asked me to call Claudia, to remind her of that time I'd remembered seeing her talk to some people who seemed like law enforcement at Slonim. The memory itself had felt vague when I'd first remembered it at the apartment, but it got muddled up even more with the experience of Larry extracting the memory, and whenever I thought about the whole thing, it felt less like opening a can of worms and more like being buried alive inside of one. So I'd called Claudia, because Larry had asked me to, and hoped she wouldn't answer. When we did talk, I'd been too afraid to bring it up; I didn't want to be a part of it, but I didn't know why. The moment I'd hung up the phone, feeling like I'd failed at the task Larry had assigned me, I had let it all drift away, beyond the borders of this campus, and was glad to leave it there.

When I reached the other side of the lake, I cut into the forest. Ivy climbed halfway up every tree, then lost hold under its own weight, bending over backward into the empty air. This place was not, I had to admit to myself, as beautiful as I wanted it to be. The lake was small and marshy; the school was ugly and brutal looking. As I walked through the unfamiliar, ivy-coated forests, trying to transform something disappointing into something magical, I felt as if I were back in the woods where I grew up, pretending our house, barely obscured through a few hundred feet of woods, didn't exist at all, and that the muddy cliff I'd just slid down was insurmountable, that there was no way back, that I would have to find a way to live out here forever.

I would really let myself go in this dissertation, I thought, say whatever wanted to find its way onto the page, without restriction, and in that way it would come out unfiltered. I would find out what was holding me back from clarity, and push beyond it, winding up on the other side, if not an equal of Larry's, then something close enough that he wouldn't have to waste his time helping me anymore. I reached the farm on the far side of the forest where I had seen miniature horses the other day, but now it was empty. I leaned against the fence, took out my notebook, and wrote.

> You spend so long thinking about something you try not to think about, that when you see it in real life, you avert your eyes reflexively. Someone with a fear of horses walks by a field full of horses. When they try to recall the field, it's empty. I'm 3,525 miles away and suddenly I feel afraid. My memories are too strong for me. Something that in the distance appears small, close up turns out to be a mountain range, pulling me

closer until it fills my whole field of vision—a tumbledown rock wall stacked so tall it could at any moment bury me.

I closed my notebook and finished my circuit of the lake. I wouldn't think about what that piece of writing even meant, not yet, I wouldn't even remember that I'd written it. The bushy trees that hugged the banks looked as if they were moving, and when I came close, I realized that what I had thought were leaves fluttering in the wind were actually crowds of birds chittering, changing position on branches, jockeying with one another. I sat down underneath a willow and reached into my jacket pocket–I'd been carrying my jacket, which had turned out to be unnecessary in the heat–and felt the chocolate bar, soft in its wrapper.

I looked up at a sound like three muffled drumbeats in a row, progressively louder, and saw a swan fly past me. The ripples it left behind on the lake surface opened and closed, opened and closed. I wondered if I'd ever seen a swan fly before. I wasn't even sure if I knew that they flew at all. I'd always thought of them as glued to the water, as if there was no bottom to them. The Cadbury bar was just fruits and nuts and liquid chocolate swimming inside the wrapper, but I reached in with two fingers and scooped some into my mouth. I sat there, my notebook next to me nestled in the roots of the tree, dizzy in the heat as it neared noon, and ate the entire bar of chocolate that way. I wanted to sleep; I was so warm and hungry and all of a sudden dead-tired. I leaned back against the trunk, my bare head pushing into the bark.

What I had then was not quite a dream and not quite a memory. I was only half asleep while it happened–the lake, the school, the person or two who strolled by, the English lilt of their voices, I knew they were there, and at the same time I was beside a different pond in a different field, this one in New Jersey, and I was standing. I was familiar with this other grass, which was tall and gold and leaned in the wind, as well as with the little knoll that led down to the pond. Everything was warm, the light almost yellow. A car was on the side of the road, our car, and it wasn't quite parked but stopped at an awkward angle too far off the asphalt and into the field. I turned around and looked back at the pond. I had driven past this pond with my mom hundreds of times on the way to and from elementary school. I felt it now, the clench in my stomach when Mom drove, knowing what might go wrong at any moment—not wanting to think too hard about it, though, because that might make it happen—her head lolling on her neck, some lump there like she had swallowed a fist, the car drifting, not slowing down. Even after I got her leg off the gas, after we ground to a halt in the grass, she kept swallowing, drowning in air. And she was wet, her shirt clinging to her skin. I focused on the pond. It was idyllic, flecks of gold floated in the air, light glinted off the water. A small shack nearby was almost collapsed into itself. Sometimes I saw cows grazing here. I walked a few steps down the hill to get a closer look. Every time we drove past this pond I'd seen a swan in it. I thought the swan was stuck there, that it couldn't leave. Maybe its wings had been clipped, like a pet. If it could just fly away, why wouldn't it? Every time we drove past I looked for the swan, and it was always there. Now that we were stopped and I could look longer, I realized it was fake, painted plastic, an ornament. The car was still running. I needed to find a neighbor, someone with a phone, someone to call 911, someone to take me home.

—⊪—

I woke up feeling sticky and sick, and reached for my notebook, ripped off some paper, and used it to wipe my face and hands. Then I stood, my body stiff, and walked up the hill back toward the ziggurat. As I came into my room, Ethan was awake and dressed and eating cereal at his desk. "Whoa, I like the hair, man," he said. "A few of us are going to catch the bus into town to buy some groceries and stuff if you want to come."

My hands were still tacky from chocolate, which was the only food I'd had that day, as well as the only food I'd owned. I hadn't signed up for the meal plan, figuring it would be cheaper to just buy groceries and cook at home, not thinking about what it would mean to share a kitchen with a dozen people or, more important, where I would get the money to buy those groceries. Luckily, I'd finally gotten a British bank account set up with the bank on campus and my parents had just deposited $100. I had no idea how anything worked here, including the bus, so I agreed to join Ethan for the trip.

The bus that dropped us off in Norwich was a double-decker, not in the iconic red, but the same ugly pastel plastic as any bus back home. The money we used to pay for our tickets was all coins, thick and unfamiliar, but it was just money, after all. The reality of England, the fact that people lived in it, used it, that it had to be functional and practical, undermined its chances at living up to my imagination. Ethan had brought along his friend Fatima, another medical student, and she'd walked us through everything, laughing lightheartedly at my combination of wonder, ignorance, and disappointment. The high street where the bus dropped us off was all shops with giant banners in the windows advertising deals on frozen food and prepaid mobiles, everything in pounds. After informing me that "High Street" wasn't the name of the street we were on but was in fact a catchall term for this kind of commercial strip, Fatima ushered us down an alley toward the center of town.

We emerged on a square where people were milling about among the white-tented stalls of a market, which seemed to be a permanent fixture of the plaza. Larger stores lined the market, and numerous smaller shops were tucked away in every snaking alleyway. At the clink of a bell I turned to look as a door closed beneath big golden letters that read WATERSTONES, which to me could have been a charming, old world bookshop. As we entered the market, I wanted it to absorb us, I wanted to be overcome by vendors and prices and hands holding out fabrics. But in reality the market wasn't that expansive, and the stones under my feet weren't so much cobbled as they were paved together. One of the stands sold seeds and nuts and spices in baskets lined with cloth. I filled a plastic bag with linseed, an ingredient for a granola recipe I was thinking I'd make, and peered down the aisles past booths burgeoning with yarn balls, glass baubles, and gift wrap, spotting Ethan and Fatima at the other end. As I caught up with them, it sounded like Ethan had said he didn't like music.

"What? Like music? Like not any type of music?" Fatima's nose rumpled. We kept walking down another side street. It did feel satisfyingly medieval.

Ethan crossed his arms. "Yeah, I don't know, I never really got into it." His voice, nasal and so white, so American. I found it suddenly embarrassing, another human being speaking in my accent, a funhouse mirror of myself.

The three of us continued on to the grocery store, a giant box planted in the middle of a parking lot, just like back home. Ethan bought white sauce and pasta, his dinner every night, and I cobbled together the ingredients to make some slumgullion, a cheap goulash I'd found a recipe for online. As we walked the aisles, Fatima taught me about the British linguistic tendency for metonymy—extracting a syllable or two from a word and using it to symbolize the whole: "veg" for vegetables, "brolly" for umbrella. As she told me about getting my "five a day" and marveled at the fact that we didn't have squash back in the United States, a kind of concentrated juice apparently everyone drank in the U.K., I felt myself becoming marginally more comfortable and defined here, but in the negative. I thought I'd recognize myself *in* England, but instead I recognized myself *against* it. The things that separated me from a typical English person were the same things that made me an American. I had not thought of myself as coming from a culture of any kind. I hadn't really thought of myself as having, in any sense, defining characteristics.

—||—

One thing that objectively differentiated England from America was the drinking age. Sarah Lawrence had a "pub," but it was a joke on the students—it sold only limp sweet potato fries, sandwiches with cranberries in the bread, and sodas that, if you were fast and stealthy enough, you could steal from the fridge. At the University of East Anglia, the pub was real, with students working behind the bar serving pints to students who milled about on tacky, evidently student-mopped floors.

That night, I was sitting at the bar, trying on adulthood. As I sipped my drink, I thought I'd have to tell Larry that they didn't actually serve the beer here "warm as piss" as he'd warned. I felt a little nauseous for a moment, remembering that I hadn't called or texted him, or anyone else, since I'd arrived. It'd been a month, a little more even, and every day, the fear that he might call or email me, and that he might be mad I hadn't been in touch, was like a hard finger poking my gut. I had to correct myself. It wasn't fear of *him.* It would be bad to be scared of him. *I'm scared of myself.* I swallowed another mouthful of beer.

"What are you thinking about?"

It took me a second to register what was odd about the voice that had come out of the girl standing next to me. What was odd was that there was nothing odd about it—she was American. I shrugged, "Nothing. Why do you ask?"

"Oh shit! Where are you from?" she asked, clearly excited to meet another exchange student. It was happening—I was talking to someone at a bar. According to Larry, this should be the simplest thing in the world. I hated looking at her.

"Jersey," I said, looking at the couple inches of beer-stained bar that separated her hand from mine. "New Jersey. America. What about you?"

"I'm from Connecticut! Can I buy you another beer? Excuse me, pint." The shirt she was wearing, a loose white canvas-y thing that tied up over her chest, suddenly seemed irrefutably "Connecticut." *Why do I want so badly to be alone? What's wrong with me?* I nodded and let her buy me another.

"What are you studying?" she asked, as we moved to one of the plush vinyl couches lining the walls, which I thought must—or should—be hosed down each night.

I felt the cushion give beneath her, a gravity well opening up that drew us closer. "I have no idea. Poetry, mostly. I'm writing some kind of dissertation."

"Really?" She raised her eyebrows, looking impressed and confused, the way I also felt about what I was doing. "You're doing research on poetry or something?"

"No, no, I'm actually writing it. It's going to be experimental, I guess. I think it's about someone losing their mind. There are a lot of birds and trees, people transforming—I don't know, it's really weird. What do you do?"

She was looking down into her drink now, the straw in her mouth; I had no idea what she was drinking but it looked bloody. "I live over in Barton, where the international students live. It's weird that I haven't run into you before, but I guess it makes sense since you're living in the ziggurat. Me and a bunch of other Americans in Barton are watching the baseball game tonight. You should come."

I'd had no idea there were other American exchange students at UEA besides Ethan, much less that they all lived in one building together. I'd welcomed the loneliness afforded by being a rare species—resented Ethan, even, for making me more common—but now there was beer in my system, and being around recognizable-sounding people was appealing, so I said yes, of course yes, and once we finished our pints, I followed her outside. The alcohol had made me warm and wobbly, which helped against the cold night air. We were standing in the concrete square at the center of campus, from which steps rose up in every direction, a kind of inverted ziggurat, in fact. I wondered if that was by design. These were the same steps where John had jumped and broken his leg. I shrugged a little from the cold as we trudged up them, heading in a direction I'd never walked before. I couldn't tell if she was leaning into me a bit on purpose or if we were just both off-balance. Then she pushed her face into my arm, acting more drunk than, I thought, she surely was.

"My grandpa drew *The March of Progress,*" she said.

I walked on a little ahead of her, keeping a few feet between us. "What's that?"

"You know, the illustration you see everywhere of human evolution." She did the poses as she walked up the steps, starting with her knuckles brushing the ground then slowly gaining better and better posture. "From chimpanzees to Lucy to now. He painted it."

At the top of the steps I turned around and started walking backward. "That's pretty crazy. When you tell people that, do they treat you like a celebrity?"

"They can't keep their hands off me," she said.

We were on the other side of campus, on our way to a dorm I'd never heard of. I could envision the little TV, the baseball game, Americans crowded around, all pretending to get along or to care about one another, or maybe actually enjoying it—being there, being alive. I could see the TV screen switch off when it was over, the buzz as the image shrunk in the center like a deflating balloon, the implication of what came next, what she'd want from me, and I felt like that dot, receding. "I'd better go home," I said.

"What? What do you mean?"

"I just, you know. I don't want this."

"Don't want what? What do you think this is? We're going to watch the baseball game."

"Yeah, I don't know, sorry. I just have to go home. I don't like . . . baseball." I walked past her, not knowing if I was supposed to say goodbye somehow. I didn't even know this person. I was thinking so hard about how to get home from where we were that I barely registered her face, gaping at me as I brushed past. I couldn't ignore her voice, though, which followed me, echoing against the concrete, when she yelled "What the fuck?" at my back. I let the sound of it penetrate me, over and over again, as I trudged away into the night.

⊣⊢

Back in my room, where the light was warm, I settled into bed with my notebook. It wasn't right, I thought, how forward she was. I felt disgusted at something, at her, or at myself. What did she want from me? I started to breathe too fast, then couldn't stop thinking about my breathing. How much was I supposed to get in one breath? Is it possible to breathe too much oxygen? Can that kill you? I am alone. *I am alone, I am alone, I am alone. I'm always stuck in the same thoughts,* I thought. If I kept a diary, writing everything down every day, all these thoughts, I bet I'd go back and see the same fears and failures over and over again, and every time they'd seem new. *I'm trapped on a dangling spring, seeming to move upwards or downwards, but always spiraling in the same place. Larry is reaching out a hand, offering a way out of the cycle. This is the cycle. Take the hand.* I opened my laptop again.

It had been too long now, way too long since I'd been in touch with him. I'd been doing everything right except for that, the most important thing: staying in touch. That was the source of this weight on my chest, this panic–not guilt or fear, which it felt like, but lack–it was the absence of him in my life. If I just reminded myself what it was like, just let him back in, everything would be all right.

Hey Larry,

I tried calling you—my Skype freaked out and I had to restart the computer the first time, so I'm not sure if you got some sort of a weird call, and you didn't answer the second time. I haven't gotten an email from you so I wasn't sure what to do.

Anyway, this is what I've been thinking about in the past hour, what I think my problem is. When I first came out here to England, I had thoughts in the background of being happy to be out of the apartment, feeling like I was free to think my own thoughts, and basically those same sort of negative, unappreciative thoughts towards you I've had in the past. It feels painful, and painfully stupid, even typing out what those thoughts actually were, because they're unfounded and shitty to have and I feel like I should have been beyond having those thoughts, especially after my conversation with my dad. When I got Claudia's email, I also had skeptical feelings, which just makes no sense, but basically just letting this fantasy of you being manipulative rather than helpful, my very stupid resistance and self-manipulation, affect my understanding of anything that happens. I think that explains a lot of things—why I took so long to call you in the first place when I came here, and this most recent time. When you told me to tell Claudia the thing I vaguely remembered about the police, I called her hoping she wouldn't answer, then when I talked to her I made some excuse to myself to not mention it. I was not willing to commit to the fact of what happened, instead I was deciding to somehow frame you as a bad guy, and I cannot believe that was a logical path of thought for me. I really can't believe now that I'm thinking this out and typing it that I thought this. I'm really sorry, Larry. I can't believe I ever got into that way of thinking at all. It's incredible, and indescribable, how much you've helped me, and everyone, I don't know what happens when these thoughts come in. I feel embarrassed and frustrated. I also miss you guys, and I feel too distant and I really wish I could be back in that apartment, I can't imagine anything that would feel better to do with my time right now. Tell Iban I say hi, I'm sure we'll talk about how he's doing at some point. Get back to me soon, sorry again, and I really need to get that camera, I hate talking on my computer.

Dan

10

I WAS WOKEN UP, predawn, by explosions. In the moment of coming back from some dream—my dreams in those days were always fitful and fragmented, like torn sheets of paper being pieced back together—I couldn't tell if the muted booming that had cut through my sleep was Ethan playing video games all night again or the fireworks that had been making the horizon blush over the Norfolk countryside every night so far in November. Probably both. I'd thought Guy Fawkes Day was, as implied by the name, just one day, but it turned out to be an entire month. Norfolk was all rolling, empty hills, houses hundreds of years old made of flint dug out of the surrounding countryside, and my flatmates said the stereotype of this part of England was that the farmers fucked their pigs and had six fingers on each hand, so I guessed it was the kind of place where people had copious access to fireworks and not much to do but use them.

I swung out of bed and started my workout, two hours of push-ups between stints of washing dishes, an element I'd added out of exhaustion with the intractable grossness of my younger roommates. After my first set, I went down to the kitchen, where cold dawn light was just beginning to fill the room. I noticed a pool of blood on the floor, then traced the line of red up to the counter, where someone had left an uncooked steak in unwrapped plastic on the steel counter. I ignored that, not knowing what to do with it, and went to scrub the deep well of dishes like it was my job. Then back to the room for forty more push-ups, and so on, until I reached four hundred, and the day was almost ready to begin.

I had an assignment from my poetry workshop to write something inspired by a piece of art, so as the rest of the ziggurat woke up, I headed to the on-campus museum. The end of the semester was approaching, which meant returning to the United States for the winter holiday. I'd thought I wanted to stay here for the winter, but when I'd finally told Larry my plans, nervously explaining that I couldn't afford the ticket, he'd said I needed to come home, it would kill me if I didn't, and he would help me pay. Because he cared about me so much. I couldn't say no. Ultimately, he'd convinced me to convince my parents to pay for my ticket, which they had, but they insisted that in return I let them pick me up at the airport and that I come see them in New Jersey before going to New York.

The museum on the UEA campus looked like a gigantic marshmallow had been tipped over in a field, and it was connected to the campus by a long, thin walking bridge. From the bridge, I could see the lake, pale birds wheeling up and down, tracing some kind of vast, imperceptible pattern in the air. The sky was white, and a light snow had begun to fall. I felt sick. I stopped on the bridge and leaned against the glass railing, and wondered who was narrating all this, my thoughts. *I don't see the lake. I say to myself, "I see the lake." I don't feel nervous about the winter; I decide to feel nervous. Have my thoughts always been in words? In a voice like this? Whose voice is this, saying this? Can I turn it off?*

I tried to think without words, without articulating anything. I took a few steps on the bridge, flakes of snow flurrying around me. My tongue felt like the tongue of an enormous, heavy bell. I took another step and thought, *I am walking. Soon I will meet Claudia in London, then fly to see my brother for a weekend in Amsterdam—a flight he generously paid for, so even though I don't want to, I will go. Then back home, to my parents, and then to the apartment, which will be good, because I need to be there, to be better. This feeling I'm calling "nervous" is evidence of exactly that, that I need him to help me.* I craned my neck and stared into the bleary white sky, opened my mouth, and winced at the smudge of snow that landed in my eye. I tried pretending the snowflakes weren't falling down but were stationary, held there, and I was flying upward into them. My dissertation was due soon, at the end of the winter break. I took out my notebook and wrote:

> There is a feeling in the present moment, unadulterated by expectation or memory. That is what I attempt to describe to myself as I experience something. "This is what *really* happened—objectively." But during the describing, the reflection, there is also a feeling to *that* moment. Is there a way to actually just *experience* things, without *experiencing experiencing* them? I am always inside that transformation from experience to memory, and each new memory affects each new experience, and each new experience rewrites the entire history of myself, the whole catalog of my memories, falling around me like snow, never held in place, always melting the moment I touch them.

A week later, I arrived in London after a three-hour train ride, and as I walked around Hyde Park, the neighborhood where Claudia's aunt and uncle had a flat, the voice in my head kept talking. It was me, my voice, but sometimes it wasn't, or it was getting hard to know the difference. The trouble was that if I thought about the voice in my head, the voice in my head would be thinking about the voice in my head. As I sat by the Serpentine, a long, winding lake in the middle of the park, and watched the white English geese squabble over nothing, the voice that was me said, *No matter where you move around a body of water, the long line of the sunlight on its surface points at you. Because I'm trapped in a self, because I perceive the world through the sensory organs in this body, in this face, it will always feel as if everything points toward me. I have to try to become less self-centric. I have to worry less about myself, and then I will be happy.* I tried to write that down, but it began to rain. I bought a croissant at a restaurant by the lake with a covered patio just to have a place to sit out of the shower. Two birds landed on the railing in front of me and were silhouetted by the sun—they looked like notes on a sheet of music. Then Claudia texted me that she was home and I should come over, so I started to walk.

The streets along the park were lined with modern glass structures pushed right up against beautifully wrought stone buildings that were probably older, I figured, than any buildings I'd ever seen. *Claudia's aunt and uncle must be loaded,* I thought as I passed the Royal Albert Hall, a giant red nipple of a building, somehow ugly and beautiful at once. I wanted to cross the street to look at it more closely, but didn't know what was allowed. The street was painted with white zigzags that meant nothing to me, and I imagined myself being arrested for jaywalking by a whistle-blowing bobby.

Maybe it's because I've felt so lonely, lately, that this voice has appeared. Even when I'm with people, there's that alone feeling, that always unbridgeable distance between myself and others. So maybe that is the answer to all this. It's this self-obsessive thing, this always thinking thing. If I stopped thinking about myself so much, I'd stop feeling lonely, because there would be no me *to be lonely. To be alone, you have to* be. *It's like Talia said when we talked about what we used to wish for on birthdays and stuff. She always wished for everyone else to be happy.*

Maybe you start being happy when you stop wanting to be. Maybe happiness is like this, living somehow in the past and the present, and even the future, all at once—like the version of myself back then, looking out my bedroom window, wishing on a tree for happiness, as if he is imagining this future, right now. At the same time, some version of me in the actual future is looking back, cataloging this as the moment everything changed, the series of thoughts that led to me becoming whole, fully myself, and that version of me is sure of himself, and can understand this within a broader context, so that as he looks back on this, he knows what it all meant.

I arrived where Claudia said we'd meet, at a brick townhouse in a row of other brick townhouses with a glossy black door at the top of a short flight of steps. Claudia opened the door halfway through my knock and hugged me across the threshold. She rubbed my shaved head saying, "It's so much better! You look like you could be a marine." I came in and dropped my bag, trying to ascertain what made an English apartment different from an American one, as well as what wealth looked like in London. She took me to the back room and offered me tea while poking through cupboards, looking for what she had offered on the presumption it would exist, this being England. While she boiled water we talked about Oxford, where she'd been studying abroad while I was in Norwich. She was eager to tell me about her philosophy classes, how she met one-on-one with her professors in what were called "tutorials," similar to Sarah Lawrence's conferences but somehow more magical, how she in many cases had more clarity than her Oxford professors did. It helped that she talked to Larry and Talia regularly even while abroad. She didn't say anything about how sparsely I'd been in touch, nor about the email she'd sent.

"We should Skype with them!" she said. I enthusiastically nodded. *Why would I not want to see them?* I stopped nodding because I thought I'd been nodding just long enough to show I really meant it. My insides felt vacuum sealed. All I'd been doing for months was working out and studying, rigidly controlling every choice I made, every thought a squared-off block in the wall I was building in my head. *Claudia is getting better—look at her. She is happy; she has clarity. She let them in, trusts them.* Then there was nothing, just silence in my head. What had I just been thinking about? I tried to recall, but it was still silent as I followed Claudia into the bedroom at the back of the flat. We sat cross-legged on the bed, and she opened Skype. The silence was replaced by the bubble-blowing-and-popping sound of the call connecting. Then Larry's face came on the screen, fish-eye close. When he moved the laptop back, Isabella was next to him. They were in the bedroom, also sitting on a bed.

"Claudia!" he said, and I'd forgotten exactly how his voice sounded, like a bulldog barking at you and licking you and trapping you in its jaws all at once. "Izzy here wants to know how your sex life is out there."

"Yeah, Clauds. You getting all kinds of jolly old English D?" Isabella snickered at her cockney accent.

Claudia laughed. Pretending bashfulness, her voice up half an octave, she moved and gestured like she was an entirely different person, a much more stereotypically feminine person, and we were gossiping at the mall. "Well, you guys, there is this one guy in England, but like . . . I don't know if anything is going to happen."

Isabella rolled her eyes. "Girl, you've got to make it happen."

Larry leaned into the camera. "Claudia, you're looking good! Danny, isn't she looking good?"

I said, "Yeah, totally."

"Claudia did a very good thing," Larry said, "by being open and honest with everyone in her email, and it's really shown. Aren't you feeling way better, lighter, more beautiful, Claud?" Claudia bounced on the bed saying yes, yes she did. "Her body has really changed, like magic. Isn't that right? Show us, Claudia," Larry said. The wall in my head cracked, some window had been opened, oh god, we were in it, the room—we'd entered it through another threshold, one I hadn't been aware of. Claudia was here, part of it now. She pulled up her shirt at the camera like it was part of the fun. She was so willing. *I should be more willing, like her.* Larry and Isabella were expressing approval, how good she looked, exactly as Larry had said she would, and I had this acne, this evidence of my subversion, so Larry must know, he must just be waiting to address me, and meanwhile what was I supposed to do? Pretend he didn't know? I had to just agree, blend in, try to remain unimportant. But wherever I looked it was happening. Her, sitting there in real life, shirt held up just below her neck, or on the screen, smaller, in a little box, with Larry and Isabella goggling, literally applauding. I thought what I was supposed to do was look at her, and approve too, so I did.

"Danny loves it–look at him!" Larry said. Isabella was laughing. He went on, "The two of you should have fun tonight. You're traveling together, you're both young; if you don't have sex somewhere out there in London I'd be very disappointed in you. Right, Isabella? That's what it's all about, having fun. Tell me how it goes. We've got to go take care of something right now, but I'll be checking in again very soon." Isabella was nodding as the window closed with the sound of another bubble popping. Claudia's shirt was back down.

—I—

At night, when you are stalking the street, looking for a place to do something you know is socially unsanctioned, every place becomes the same–threatening and strange. However, from any other perspective, it is you and your friend, the ones trying to find an alley or a fence to hop, a place dark and not visible from the street, a place where you can safely have sex at the behest of another friend's dad, who are in fact threatening and strange. Stupid of me, prudish even, I realized now, to think this would just be a sleepover in England, a hangout. We had to be alive, we had to have fun, we were young and I was the one being a wet blanket, so I was following her down the street, looking for a place private enough. I hoped no such place would materialize, and we could go home and say we tried, really did honestly put in a good effort, and that would be that.

We turned a corner, and there across the street was a wrought iron fence. Beyond that, the darkness deepened in the way it does over a field at night. *This is what I would want to be doing if I were healthy.* We giggled nervously at each other as we crossed the street, kind of excited just by the thrill of it, and I was thinking maybe we won't actually do it, even now. Claudia and I paced around the edge of the fence, trying to sense the presence of guards, overprotective neighbors, or ravenous, barking dogs, but there were none.

If there was one thing I'd learned in England, and in Manhattan, and at Sarah Lawrence, too, it was that if you didn't give anyone a reason to inquire about what you were doing—what was going on, what was wrong, why you were skulking about, why you looked panicked like that—then they wouldn't question you. Easier to go on with their day, to stay within the bounds of their property, their commute, their job, their life. According to Larry, there were things happening all around me, all the time, that I didn't see. Mostly to do with sex—people fucking in public; people flirting, trying to seduce one another. He'd told me how our female roommates, Raven even, had constantly tried to get him into bed when he'd lived with us. I hadn't noticed any of this, so I must have been living with my eyes closed, as he said. Now I was part of it—the unseen, the real world that hid in the cracks of what I'd thought of as normal society.

Now that Claudia and I had found a place, we would have no excuse not to do it. We couldn't fly home to the apartment and admit that at the last minute we hadn't had enough faith in Larry to get over ourselves, not to mention a measly bit of wrought iron. And we definitely couldn't lie. I couldn't even propose the idea to Claudia, because she would tell on me and relish the chance to be in Larry's good graces. The fence wasn't all that high, so I gave Claudia a boost, heard the crunch of gravel as she landed on the other side, and then scrambled over myself.

On the other side, a football pitch yawned before us. It was eerie to go from the shrugging blocks of London to this openness, the trimmed grass batting this way and that in the wind. It was suddenly much colder, and Claudia and I walked shoulder to shoulder. We'd always been close but never close enough as friends to embrace exactly—not, at least, like this, in a way that felt sort of romantic, arms wrapped around each other against the cold as we walked across the empty field and then stopped in its center. There was a circle painted there, like a target, and we lay down in it, in the soft, freezing grass, and held each other. Maybe this was enough.

Her head on my arm, Claudia shifted, and then I felt her awkwardly kiss my neck. *It's happening,* the voice said. I let the silence in my head leak down my jaw, reach the spot where she was kissing me, take away my impulse to recoil, to freeze up, to run away, and leave behind nothing. She was laughing, so I was laughing, too, and sex had always been pretend anyway, a show to perform, so what was the difference, it was just stage fright I was feeling again, and I kissed her. It all felt hard and cold, like two skulls kissing each other, but I was finding it easier, once I admitted it was just an act, a choice—not just to do it, but to not feel anything about it. I lay in the grass and Claudia sat up, straddling her legs over me. This must be how Larry did it, what he had meant all along. I could feel it, like he had promised, fear, weakness, sadness, they all became nothing more than words, meaningless, an enormous pile I'd built inside myself, and now they were leaving my body, leaving nothing behind.

—II—

The next morning I hurried to the tube, which took me to Gatwick Airport, where I'd take a plane to meet my brother in Amsterdam. He was there for a business trip and had insisted I let him buy me a ticket for the weekend before I went back home. I had to go somewhere in Europe other than England while I was here, he said. My brother was my only sibling, and he was also twelve years older than me. When I told people this, I would watch them realize that I'd been, surely, a mistake, and often I'd say something tongue in cheek about how my parents called me a "miracle baby." Sometimes I'd roll my eyes. Less often, I'd explain that my mom had been so sick that doctors hadn't thought it was possible for her to get pregnant, and that when she did, they recommended she not go through with it—with me. She liked to tell the story of how she held the positive pregnancy test in her hand, staring at the symbol that meant yes, I *was;* how she leaned against the bathroom door, my dad in their bed on the other side, unaware that this was even possible; and how, for what felt like an eternity—what could be, for all intents and purposes, a lifetime—she couldn't decide whether or not to tell him. For those few minutes my very existence balanced on a razor's edge.

Immediately when I arrived at the airport, I realized I'd forgotten my passport—it just hadn't occurred to me that I would be flying between countries. I felt like an idiot, and called my brother, who said he would buy me a ticket for the next morning. So I took the train back to Norwich, the bus to campus, draining the meager savings I'd scrounged together for this trip, grabbed my passport, said "Hi" to the flatmates I'd passed on my way in, laughing as I rushed out again, then back to London, then finally, finally, I was in line for my flight. I was rummaging through my toiletry bag, in which I thought I'd stowed my headphones for some reason, when my thumb went numb and an odd ache traveled up my knuckle. I knew I was bleeding before I even saw it, like my brain dropped into the bag where my thumb could be, for a moment, still whole. I pulled my hand out of the bag, and as I looked at my thumb, I felt a distant interest in the deep slice that mouthed open when I flexed, when I manipulated the digit, and the tiny curtain of red already running down my hand. I had touched, I realized, the safety razor I'd bought for myself at Larry's behest, which must have come loose in my toiletry bag.

I looked up and down the line of people, but no one seemed to notice. I stepped forward in unison with the person ahead of me toward the gate and the beeps of accepted boarding passes, legally recognizable identities. *I have to put pressure on it,* my head said, and wanting to keep the other hand free for my boarding pass, I pressed the forefinger of the same hand down on the split-open thumb, with the other three fingers sticking out. Blood was dripping onto the floor, so I hid my hand inside my backpack. I got through the gate that way, figuring they would have a Band-Aid on the plane, and as I boarded, I revealed my hand to the flight attendant.

"Oh my god, your hand," the flight attendant said, looking at the wound, then back at the line that stretched behind me up the Jetway. "I'm so sorry, I don't think we have anything on board, but I'll check for you."

I shuffled to my seat, and before takeoff the flight attendant came back and confirmed there was no first-aid kit on the plane. Did I need to get off the plane? I shook my head no. I couldn't imagine how my brother would react if I screwed this up further, and I'd spent the last of my meager funds on all these bus and train trips. This had to be it. It felt like major sections of my brain had shut down at some point, without me noticing—or maybe the parts of my brain in charge of noticing were the ones that had shut down. For the next couple of hours, I sat in a plane to Amsterdam to meet my brother, keeping pressure on the wound until the blood coagulated and my hand was glued into an A-OK position. When I arrived at the Amsterdam airport, I would take the train from the airport in the wrong direction, get off in the Dutch countryside, and nervously approach a confusingly beautiful Dutch person, who would explain to me that I had to turn around, buy another ticket, and go back the other way, which I did, now completely out of money, until finally I arrived in the city.

⊣⊢

In my brother's hotel room, I pulled my fingers apart, and the blood began to flow again. He'd let me in to drop off my bags, then had to go to a business meeting, so I had the city to myself. He'd also taken the hotel room key, of which there was only one—I guessed it was some arrangement with his work where he was supposed to be the only one staying in the room—so when I left, I'd be locked out. I didn't have any money, so I wouldn't be able to eat until he got back from work that evening. On a small glass table near the TV, there was a mountainous piece of cheese, almost a quarter wheel, which I guessed my brother had gotten that morning while he waited for me to arrive, probably thinking what an immature mess I was. The hotel room was modern and claustrophobic. I looked around for something to cut the cheese with but found nothing. There were two water glasses covered with little paper doilies next to the bathroom sink. I used my non-dominant, not-bleeding hand to scrape the lip of the glass against the hard cheese, carving out crumbled crescents. I ate until I felt sick, shaving away places I'd used my other hand to keep the block steady to hide the red prints.

Once my finger stopped bleeding, I walked around the city, admiring the narrow leaning houses reflected in the canals. Eventually, I discovered that Amsterdam was smaller than I'd imagined, and I'd walked pretty much everywhere, getting more and more tired from the cheese and the hunger underneath it, not to mention my inability to stop or sit anywhere because I didn't have money to buy a coffee. Eventually, my brother called me—he was back at the hotel and could let me in—and when I walked into the room, he was changing out of his work suit into jeans. "Hey, man! How was your day? Let me take you out tonight." I wondered how much my legs looked like his, or would in twelve years, the skin pale from being trapped in slacks all day, I guessed, and the black hair, which on my legs was more of a suggestion, closer to Velcro. Seeing him always felt like looking into a mirror and having trouble being able to recognize the person reflected—it threw me off balance.

"I'm kind of tired," I said. I was sitting on the only bed. I couldn't remember if we'd ever shared one before.

He ignored me, stuffing his wallet into his pocket. "I'd planned for us to have more time, but since you came a day late, we've only got tonight. Come on, we'll go to the red-light district and walk around."

—⊪—

I didn't expect it to actually be so red. The red light behind each window rolled out over the street and then sank into the black water of the canals. My brother led me through crowds of milling tourists, the laughing groups of college-aged boys, *my age,* I realized, and occasionally we would turn down stretches of narrow alleyway where the lower-rent, more niche prostitutes swayed in their picture-frame windows. Occasionally we stood and looked, and I wondered if the red light was absorbing the flush rushing to my face, if it made the acne on my forehead blend in. My brother pulled me farther along, as if we had somewhere particular to be. We had gotten drinks and street food, and he'd paid for everything, which made me feel younger, and beholden. At least I wasn't hungry anymore.

He walked ahead, a version of my future, lit red. After a few more turns, we stopped again, and the woman behind the glass in front of us beckoned. Through the light, between her legs, I could see a room. I hadn't thought about it, but of course there was a room—and in it was a bed, and on the bed was a towel. The grid of windows, the people inside, the rooms—boxes into which you could disappear. It all felt so familiar; I couldn't figure out why. I was afraid my brother thought I was a virgin, and he was going to try to pay for me to have sex. We stood for what seemed like a long time, and I felt awkward for the woman in the window, who had to keep writhing. I stared at the glowing ruby space between the woman's legs, which came together and apart as she moved, her thighs blinking, revealing and then hiding the bed, the towel, the red. Open, close. Open, close. On, off. On, off. I wanted a way out of this life, out of this *I.*

"You want another drink?" my brother asked. He had walked a little ways down the alley, and was beckoning.

I followed him to a bar, which was like any other bar late on a weekend, burgeoning and loud. I stood up against the wall; my brother was snaking his way back from the bar, holding two beers above the crowd. At the same moment he arrived and handed me my drink, two men wearing business suits came up to us.

"Excuse me," one of them said. He had a thick German accent. "You are Jewish?"

I felt immediately a kind of fear and confusion I wasn't used to. Most of our family had died in the Holocaust, in Belarus and Germany and Poland, and we were the remnants of the few who'd crossed to America. Now I was back on the wrong side of the ocean. My mom had warned me about anti-Semitism in Europe, but I'd brushed her off. That didn't happen anymore, surely. Without thinking, I told the men yes, we were Jewish. "Ah, that's what we thought," the other German businessman said. "We just wanted to say how we are sorry."

They were standing there, expectant. "Excuse me?" I said.

The second man seemed prepared for this. He leaned toward me and dipped his head, a shallow bow, as much prostration as the crowded bar would allow. "We are German," he said, by way of explanation.

"Oh. That's okay," I said. It came out automatically, the forgiveness. I didn't know what to do, or who I was speaking for. We all stood there awkwardly. Then I turned back to my brother, and the men dissolved into the crowd.

"That was crazy," my brother said, and we forgot about it, spending the rest of the night talking about our parents, and what I would do when I went home.

11

YOU DON'T HAVE ANY idea how this works, Danel. You come to a place like this, Ralph Lauren, Bergdorf, Louis Vuitton, and they understand how to take care of you. Look, sit in this chair. We used to come to the Ralph Lauren women's store here all the time and I'd sit right there, they bring you a scotch, and I'd watch Talia try on clothes. I'd give her everything she wanted. That's what a father does. Takes care of his baby. Teresa didn't understand. Look at this one. This sweater. Feel it. Have you ever seen a color like that? In high, luxury fashion–you wouldn't know this–it's not about design. It's about color. That's what you don't realize. Every year, they're coming out with new colors. Really look into it, deep into it, the color, Danny, yeah, get close. Have you ever seen a color like that? No, that's not the one for Tal this year. Come over here.

I want you to hold on to my bag, can you do that? Do not open it and stay in my sight. Good. Teresa didn't understand that when you're married, and you have kids, the relationship between parent and child supersedes the relationship between the couple. That's natural. Once Talia was born, she was my whole world. Teresa couldn't stand it. Isn't this beautiful? This store. This is how life should be. How your life should be, too. This is what I'm trying to give you. Elegance, beauty. Look at this shelf. Every detail considered. Look at the grain of that wood. You're used to ignoring everything, right? Details like that. I want to wake you up, Danny, and you're close, you are. I can see it in you, you've been awake to these aspects of reality, but then something changed in the last few years, didn't it? I bet you wonder what that was. I know, and I could tell you, but you have to find it for yourself. That's the only way it works. Come here. Stop following me around, I swear you're like a tumor sometimes. Come on. Talia would like this one. Do you know what you call that color? That's right, cerulean, exactly. Very good, Danny. Here's what I want you to think about–can you tell me what the difference is between an adult and a child?

We need to fix that mumbling problem of yours. Either say something or don't. There isn't one. You thought there was, didn't you? That's what's been so important to me as a parent, to treat my daughters as adults. This one is perfect. Exactly what she needs right now. How do I know? You wouldn't even be able to comprehend the millions, literally millions, of tiny decisions that go into choosing something like this and understanding how it will affect someone. You'll see. Come with me back downstairs, bring my bag.

So many people make the mistake of treating kids as kids, as if they're some fundamentally different being, as if their ability to form thoughts, to understand things, to be conscious, to be responsible, is different or limited. They have it all, already, inside them, it's all right there–it's them we should be learning from. They're like the history of human society itself–all the knowledge we've ever had has always been contained inside us. There's no difference between you and a person a thousand years ago, the same way there's no difference between an adult and a child. And in the same way, there's no reason that person a thousand years ago couldn't, with the right combination of circumstances, become as advanced as we are now. I could teach you to become as advanced as humans will be a thousand years from today. The concern our society has with age is a puritanical construct. But, more importantly, we traumatize our children by treating them for the first half of their lives like they are crippled, broken versions of adults. Like they don't have preferences and are unable to make choices. Thank you, we'll take this one. Cash. Let me ask you: What makes an adult, Danel? You know this one. That's right, preferences. I brought Talia to this store when she was very young, ten or twelve, and she wanted a sweater, just like these. Cashmere, knit, all of it, and you saw how much these cost, right? Thousands of dollars. For a sweater. Her mom flipped. Why? Because she thought Talia didn't deserve it. Because, she said, a little girl would ruin something so nice, or have no use for it. But let me ask you this: Why wouldn't I want my honeygirl to have something beautiful like this? She was expressing herself, her preferences, her adulthood, her personhood, and her mom couldn't understand that at all. If I didn't get Tal the sweater, I was saying this thing mattered more than she did, that she was worth less than a few thousand dollars. On the other hand, if I got it for her, and Talia ruined the sweater, well then I would sure as hell make sure she knows I care more about her than I do about a thing, no matter how much it's worth. Did your parents make you feel that way, or did you constantly feel as if things might be more valuable to your parents than you were? Exactly, that's what I thought. Don't I know things, Danny? Besides, I trusted her. Ever since then, I got Tal one of these sweaters every single year for Christmas, just like we are now. She never ruined a single one of them. Of course she didn't. Teresa hated that.

Come across the street with me, Danny, you might as well see the men's store. I can't believe you've never been here. Your parents never took you here, shopping on Fifth Avenue, not even once? Yes, the women's and men's stores are separate, whole buildings on either side of Fifth Avenue. Why would that be surprising to you? It makes sense, doesn't it? It does look like Paris, that's right. I spent some undercover time there, actually, I'll have to tell you about that sometime. Let's cross. Teresa couldn't stand how I took care of Talia. When Talia would come in the house crying with her shins skinned because she'd fallen down on the sidewalk, you know how I'd make her feel better? I'd say, show me where that sidewalk is that hurt you so I can beat it up. And she knew I would. I would actually do it, to protect her. I'd punch the ground for her, you see? Her mom would blame her, would tell her she should be more responsible, would worry about the clothes getting scuffed up. Like that's any way to treat a child.

Come upstairs. I really want you to admire the craftsmanship here.

You are living inside a sliver of life, taking in one percent of everything. Open your eyes, Danny, think about how things work, the choices that have been made, how richly imbued every single aspect of the world is with meaning. Why is Ralph Lauren so successful? Every choice, no matter how small, has been made deliberately and with care. I am teaching you to be like that. You could be as successful as Ralph Lauren, but in any field you want, if you listened to me.

We have to cut to the inside of everything. I have to show you how it works. Look at the dark hardwood of these floors, the columns, and how that disappears into the white, vaulted ceiling. What does that make you think of? Right, it is kind of like a cathedral, exactly. At the same time it is like the inside of a very elegant closet. So what does that tell you? That what you put on your body, what you acquire here, is holy. Man is made in God's image, but man determines what God's image is. You see? It's very rare for a mother to be abusive like Teresa was, did you know that? Don't nod like that, Danny, you didn't know that. But it's more common than people think, it just goes unreported, under the surface. My own mother was abusive, terribly abusive. Do you know what a cat-o'-nine-tails is? She used to whip me with one of those. But I got her. When I was old enough, I walked out of that house—my dad had divorced her by then, and he was waiting by the car on the curb—and I turned around on the stoop and punched her right in her fucking face. That's right. And Talia did something just like that, in a way, when she refused her mother's custody. You never did anything like that in your life, did you, Danny? Wouldn't you like to be a person who could do something like that, before it's too late?

Look at this sweater. This color's called cantaloupe. Do you like it? What do you mean "neon-y"? Danny, don't make me hit you. You're too afraid to wear bright colors. Learn to exist. Look at me, I'm wearing pink. I'm not afraid to be a man who wears an expressive color. I am who I am, I have my preferences, and you would never question me, would you? That's right. You better not. I'm kidding, Danny, calm down, I'm not going to hit you in Ralph Lauren. Give me my bag back. You have to start expressing your preferences if you're going to move forward. You like this sweater, don't you? I'm going to get it for you. No, don't worry about it. Try it on. See, I told you, the cantaloupe looks great. No one else in the apartment is afraid to wear bright colors, you notice that? Tal and me have been wearing color since she was born. You should let yourself shine to the world. Why do you feel the need to hide? Stop mumbling, Danel. Feel that. You've never owned cashmere before, have you? Most cashmere you see in stores isn't even really cashmere. This is the real thing. It feels like something else entirely, doesn't it? Like a material that doesn't even exist. That's yours now. Think about how that feels. That it's yours and I'm giving that to you. You have to learn gratitude, too, if you want to be happy. I'm giving you the thing I would only give my daughter every year. Keep it on, wear it.

It's good that they broke up, Santos and Talia. Good for both of them. You didn't see how that went down. Scary, scary stuff, Santos. Talia's like me, she's going to have a tendency to want to help people, a compulsion almost, because she knows how extremely high-functioning and capable her mind is. She knows that she can help. The difference is that she can't understand a mind like Santos's. She doesn't have the training. She can't relate, you see. Thank you. No, that'll be cash. Thank you very much. I felt the way she does now, once, unable to understand why people think the way they do, act the way they do. It seemed chaotic, nonsensical, until I trained myself deliberately to understand the illogic of so many human minds. That's what I'm giving Tal now—training, so that she's able to understand and help the way she wants to. I'm doing everything, letting my life get put on hold, my things get broken, my plans for a life with Tal get sabotaged. We have to protect her, Danny. Come on, let's head back. You got that stuff? I'm calling the driver. Oh yes, Tal saw the darkness in him. She just didn't know the extent of it.

Put those things on the seat. No, I never take the subway. My body is so sensitive I can feel it the second I'm there, all the viral infections in the air, the mold spores. I can smell it. It's one of the most dangerous things you can do, take the subway. Talia's unbelievably smart, her mind works on a level that you couldn't possibly comprehend. That's right, you are lucky to be exposed to her, to have gotten to meet her. Look at this place, over here on my side. Have you been here? What do you mean you've never been tanning? No, Danny, I don't go to "get tan." That's a good one. The UV light kills all the germs and microbes off your skin, that's why you go to a tanning salon. No one realizes that. Tal and I used to do that all the time, before you all showed up.

Say hi to the doorman, Danny. Jesus, be a decent human being for once. Sorry about him, guys. Here you go, take that. You keeping an eye out for me? That's all right, keep it, it's no problem. Danny, hit fifteen. One thing I'll teach you right now that you'll do well to remember, is you always take care of the doormen and they'll take care of you. They're my eyes and ears. Same thing with the homeless people all up and down the block here. They give me updates. I know every single thing that's happening in a ten-block radius. This is the kind of thing you don't think about. Every time you and Izzy go to buy groceries, I know every single thing that happened, everything you talked about. Hold the door for me, Danny, come on.

You can just put that on the workbench, Danny. That's fine. Come sit down with me. I know you're tired, of course you are. All of that's intentional. You're only here on your winter break for a short period, so we have to take as much advantage of the time as we can, to mold you, to help you. I have to keep you up because it makes you like a raw nerve, which means that I can work on you, make changes in your brain, at an accelerated rate. That's right, I'm sure you found the conversation with Santos last night pretty surprising. No, it was exactly what I expected, none of what he said was a surprise to me, it was just a matter of getting him there. He's quite dangerous, in fact, and I've always known that. It was reaching the point where it was necessary to protect honeygirl from him. She'd normally be able to recognize that on her own, but his mind, he's very tricky, very insidious. I just made him face what was already inside himself, what he had been hiding from all of us. Make us some coffee, Danny, if you're tired.

The tree looks good, right? You didn't do Christmas growing up, did you? No. Just Hanukkah, that's right. Have I told you I converted to Judaism in prison? Don't nod at me like that, Danel, I know I told you. I studied every religion, I'm fluent in all the ideologies, and let me tell you, Judaism is the wisest one, the closest to an accurate understanding of how the world and the human mind works. Yeah, you're probably thinking that wasn't too popular in jail, well, I didn't care what was popular, did I? No one would dare mess with me. By the time I was leaving, me and my other Jewish guys were the most powerful group in there. So are you going to help me with some of this woodworking? Good. You and Santos are going to build a floating shelf for the printer. It's going to be beautiful. Come look at this wood. This is called zebrawood. I bet you can't tell why. It's an exquisite, rare hardwood. Run your finger along it, there. See the grain in it? Really look, Danny. Here, okay, grab that sander over there. No, that's a planer. The sander. That one, there. I know, it's nice, right? Felder is the only brand to use for this stuff. I have some Hilti, the red ones, for other jobs. But here, look, give me the sandpaper. That's right, all of it. We have to start low, one hundred grit, coarse, and be very gentle. Here, you take it. No, don't apply any pressure, just let the machine do it, let it run across the surface. Good, now let's take it up. Again, same thing. Keep going now, do the four hundred. That's very good. See how the grain is rising? Can you believe that? Just wait until we go up into the thousands and we start wet sanding. That's right, you should be excited. Listen, Danny, this is the kind of stuff you need to be doing. What are you doing at that school in England? And what is writing going to do for you? Did you know that furniture made out of wood like this sells for thousands of dollars? That's right. Here we go, I'm going to wet it for you. Try the two thousand now. Good, remember, only the lightest pressure. If you stick with me, and work on this, you could be making a six-figure salary, just from woodworking. Three thousand now, we're polishing. Watch it, watch it change. You can help your friends, and you can help Tal. That's what you want, isn't it? Here's the four thousand; let me take over now. That's exactly right, it does look like its glowing, doesn't it? It's not possible for Talia to date just anyone, you should have put that together by now. They need to have clarity, to have total management of their mind, to be her equal, though of course no one will ever be her equal, but to be close, in order to ever be in a relationship with her. Let's go up to ten thousand. Keep it wet, very gentle now. You're a good guy, Danny, but you have so much work to do until you're able to manage your mind. I want to give that gift to you, but you have to be ready to receive it. Okay, stop there. Grab that rag and wipe it down with the mineral spirits. Good. Do you see that? If you wear it down enough, gently, and you don't skip any steps, it's like there's a light inside the wood that comes out, like the sunlight that the tree absorbed when it was alive is still there, inside the wood, waiting to be released. Think about that, Danny.

If you're going to go back to England at the end of this break, I want you to help me while you're here, can you do that? We're going to clean this whole place up together and if you actually listen to me, it'll happen fast, right? This apartment is out of control and I need to put a pause on all of you for now so that I can get it in order. When Iban comes over later, you go with him and take everything that we don't need up to storage. Yes, everything. You'll know what. And try to keep Iban in line. Then after that, tonight, I'll help you make your shelf. What? Yes, you'll get a full night's sleep, don't make that face. What did I tell you? You're whining to me, and I don't have time for that. You need to trust, Danel. The most important thing is that you make your own choices—to do what's right. Not for me, for you.

12

ETHAN AND I WERE sitting on opposite sides of our room on our computers. The sky looked like the drop ceiling in an office, as it had since I'd come back to England for the spring semester. Every day there was intermittent rain, and more and more cracks of blue sky appeared as spring began in earnest. I was reading my email, checking for messages from Larry, which had been sparse. I assumed things were too busy in the apartment for him to stay in touch. Instead, I'd been emailing back and forth with Talia. Over winter break, right before I came back to England, things had gotten borderline romantic with her. I kicked myself mentally for having just about no control over anything I did. Thankfully nothing had materialized. What would have become of me? I thought of Santos, moping around, melting into himself until he'd become sort of detestable.

Ethan called me over; he wanted to show me something on his computer. "One sec!" I yelled. I was reading through the new email I'd just gotten from Talia, which was many pages long. She'd had a contentious conference with her psych teacher because she'd compared her sister being taken away by the courts to what happened to families at Auschwitz. The teacher, Marvin, who was Jewish, had taken umbrage and in the course of doing so, he had crossed Talia. I knew what it meant to be Talia's enemy. It meant becoming an enemy of the Ray family. It meant a whole team of people devoted to your downfall. I didn't envy his position.

> When I came back from that conversation, I received an "apology" email from Marvin for his behavior toward me today in conference. His behavior was in fact rather insensitive (he abruptly stopped me mid-sentence to ask what relevance I saw in my mention of an instance when my sister was taken from my father by the court, later cited for bias by the appellate court and referred to in psychological terms as "emotional stripping" by a psychiatrist, with regards to the book we had read describing the experience of Auschwitz) . . . but perhaps he is unaware of why it might have been in fact insensitive. Now it becomes my task to inform him. On top of that, he claimed to me that there is no empirical language to account for the methods so notoriously described by firsthand and historical accounts of the Holocaust, and all the psychological warfare to attack the Jewish identity before they even were taken to the death camps, or the gas chambers. I researched it today, as this claim also made it my task to look into such a questionable assertion as his and to report my findings to him if they might alleviate any ignorance he conveyed to me on the topic by saying the sort of language I was looking for does not exist. As it turns out, the psychology of psychological warfare methods is considered a science, and it is a science our government has been pouring federal dollars into ever since they got the term "psychological warfare" from—guess who?—the Third Reich. Yes, this phrase (and the field of empirical study to which it refers) comes from a German word coined by the Nazis themselves—in their own attacks on the Jewish identity. These are the psychological attacks I was referring to.

Ethan called out again, "I'm finally finished with the tree!" and I didn't answer. It looked like the teacher had suggested Talia might want to leave the class, which had only made her dig in her heels. I was trying to come up with a way to respond that was encouraging and that showed I was paying attention and had no doubts that Talia was completely right. I didn't entirely understand the argument, which I figured meant she must be right, because it was above my head. Most important, supporting Talia meant supporting her dad. Pages into the email, she was talking about how her dad had saved her by confronting her in Bronxville about the impulse to take her own life. It wasn't difficult to imagine that exchange; I'd seen it happen for every one of us, the people who'd followed Talia from Slonim to the apartment in Manhattan, including myself. I wondered if the rest of the people who'd lived at Slonim—Gabe, Max, Juli Anna, Raven—had also harbored suicidal impulses, and had been too far gone to accept Larry's aid.

I closed my laptop and walked around the wall to see what Ethan was talking about. He'd been playing a game on his computer in which the world was composed of blocks. The borders stretched infinitely in every direction. If you wanted, you could travel unending distances over hills made of dirt blocks and grass blocks dotted with trees made of tree blocks and leaf blocks. You could combine these simple blocks to make more complex blocks, and then combine those complex blocks further to make even more complex blocks, which is how you could, for example, get from bamboo to paper to a map that would fill itself in as you explored. Ethan was not attempting to make anything more complex than what was already available in the world. He was building a tree out of trees, what must have been tens of thousands of tree blocks, deconstructing every tree in the world and then recombining them into one massive tree that towered above the surface, so big that when he looked up its trunk, it disappeared into nothingness.

I left Ethan to his tree and sat back on my bed, my legs poking out over the edge, and opened my email again. There was a hush outside beneath the low clouds, and past the lake a glow on the ground from the sprouting bluebells. A new email with no subject had popped into my in-box while I was gone. It was from Paige Crandall, the head of student housing at Sarah Lawrence. I opened it and read, and as I did, started feeling like I might throw up. The email said that I wouldn't get housing in the fall. I hadn't been present at the housing lottery, it said. I stared across my room at the mirror. I could see only my own eyes and my shaved head, surrounded by the background of book covers. *How was I supposed to go to the housing lottery if I'm studying abroad?* I searched through my email to see if I had received any kind of notice, and found nothing. The panic kept rising inside me before being choked back by emptiness. *This is the world deciding how things are supposed to be. Or maybe it's somehow Larry guiding them.* The only place I could afford to live while still going to school was Larry's apartment.

Suddenly I felt a well of homesickness. I tried to remember what it felt like to hang out with Raven, Max, and Gabe, to have a day with no big objective, no plan that went awry, no pressure to realize my potential at all times, and I just couldn't do it. I pulled up Facebook and started looking through old photos. Our living room at Hill House, the walls covered with drawings we asked anyone who came over to make. Another of just my back, which Claudia had drawn all over. Another of Gabe, Santos, and I pushed up against one another, sandwiched into a wall, pointing at the camera, at me, sitting here, on the other side of time and space, unable to reach out to them even if I wanted to. They wouldn't understand anything happening in my life. How would I explain it? They didn't want anything to do with it, anyway. I didn't want to have to try to answer or avoid any questions. I especially didn't want to risk doing or saying something wrong that I'd have to explain to Larry later.

I closed the email and clicked back to Talia's message. Further down, she was talking about her time at Sarah Lawrence, having escaped the terror of her mom, the courts, and the shelters, finally getting to live her own free life. "It's like when I used to hang out in my room at home, reading and listening to music and chatting with friends here and there," she wrote. "It's just beautiful and amazing that I even have the same dolls on my bed. My life feels like it's real again. . . . I'm a member of society again, I live in peace, not in fear, and I sometimes even have to try to remember how my days were when I walked around grasping for connections and mustering all of my willpower to just stay grounded . . . until hopefully somehow I could be freed of the terror and isolation I was thrust into."

I sat back in the bed, and I hated myself. *Why do I feel so terrible?* I just wanted to sleep, but I had work to do. I packed up my things to head to the library. As I got up, I caught my eyes in the mirror again. For a moment I saw something inscrutable behind them, a person I almost recognized, and then I blinked. Whatever I had seen was gone.

—⊣⊢—

I walked to the library along the concrete gangways, avoiding puddles of rainwater that revealed the surface's depressions and imperfections. It wasn't that I didn't want to go back and live with Larry again. *I do want to–I had to want to–I want to help, to pay him back for everything he's done for me. I wouldn't even be here at all if he hadn't paid for my visa.* I carded into the library through the turnstiles, then headed downstairs. The library had been, perhaps, the biggest disappointment of all. I'd hoped for vaulted ceilings painted with clouds and cherubs and bookshelves towering through multiple floors with librarians rolling past on ladders. Instead, the UEA library felt more like an open-plan office crossed with a middle school cafeteria–laminate tables with bright orange and yellow plastic seats around which medical students crowded, cramming for exams, which seemed to be constant and relentless.

I headed downstairs, where they kept the oversized esoteric books, and where no one else ever really seemed to go. The basement was dim and the deep storage shelves had gigantic wheels on the sides that you could spin to slide the bookshelves together or apart, revealing new rows of books. I sat on the floor next to the oversized editions of Goethe printed in gothic German script, and opened my Shakespeare to read for class.

Minutes passed and I realized I'd been reading the same paragraph over and over again. I kept thinking about the housing at Sarah Lawrence. I wouldn't have the housing on campus that was included in my tuition–almost all of which was paid for by financial aid–and I certainly couldn't ask my parents to pay for me to rent a place off campus. I looked back down at my collection of Shakespeare. Why didn't I want to go back? *I'm afraid.* No, I'm not. I couldn't be, because of what would happen if I felt that way. Or no, it was that there was nothing to be afraid of. It was that I didn't feel that way at all. I tried to read the play I'd been assigned for class, tried to push everything else aside so that nothing but the words, barely distinguishable in the dim light from the empty page around them, would fill my mind, and I promptly fell asleep.

⊣⊢

I was back in the apartment in New York. It was winter break again, before I'd left the apartment to come back to England. Larry was sitting across from me in the living room, and his friend Lee, whom I'd met the first time I ever met Larry, was next to me. This apartment, I'd learned, was actually Lee's. Somehow Larry had convinced Lee to let all of us stay here while Lee found somewhere else to go. An amazing feat, I'd thought, to convince someone to move out of their own house. Larry and Lee were talking about where they'd met—prison.

"I could get anything I wanted, couldn't I?"

"Yes, Larry," Lee said, nodding.

"Guys in there knew instantly what I was capable of. I moved so quickly it terrified some of them. They'd never seen anything like it."

"That's right."

"If another guy ever went against me, he knew I wouldn't just hurt him, would I, Lee? I wouldn't just beat him up. That would be too easy."

"No, Larry." Lee looked awkward, leaning forward, forearms on his knees, hands bridged. He was somehow too big for his gray suit, and the suit was also too big for him. Both men seemed titanic, while I was shrinking into the couch. Lee had gone to prison for some kind of Internet fraud; I didn't know much more than that.

"I'd be much more precise than that, much more effective." There was a gleam in Larry's eye. "Tell him what I'd do, Lee."

"The vas deferens." He made a snipping gesture with his fingers. "He'd cut it."

"That's exactly correct. Danel, do you know what that is? That's the vessel running along the underside of your cock. One snip, delicate, deliberate, and you can never get hard again. How would you like that?"

I hadn't realized I'd been looking at my hands, pushing the ends of my fingertips into one another, flattening them. I looked up. "I wouldn't," I said. The scene began to change, merge, and now it was just me and Larry in the room. Through the window, I could see it snowing. There were wood planks piled around the room for carpentry projects, buckets of paint all over the place, a workbench in the living room, and a sound like a jackhammer making the windows rattle in their frames. Plastic was hanging everywhere so the room looked like the den of a giant spider. Larry was wearing a mask and goggles, holding what looked like a chrome hypodermic needle with a long rubber tube coming out of the back, which was attached on the other end to a compressor. The needle produced a mist that slowly coated the hallway walls with a color like the inside of a body. I was standing on a ladder, waiting for Larry to tell me what was next, feeling heavier and heavier, and then I began to fall.

I landed in the apartment again, but now there was a Christmas tree in the corner all lit up with big multicolored Charlie Brown bulbs. We were giving one another presents. Larry and Iban were talking about their time in the military, and Larry was describing the satisfaction of shooting someone in the head with a sniper round, the high that comes from your first "pink mist." I unwrapped my present from Santos, which was *Meditations* by Marcus Aurelius.

Dan,

Here is to gaining and forever treasuring <u>clarity</u>.

Your friend,
Santos

P.S.
I am honored that we could go on this journey at the same time and I am forever honored and grateful for your friendship. You are a great man and a best friend. Thank you.

Larry saw it and clapped Iban on the back. "You ever read that during basic training? Danel, flip to book three, number five. What does it say there?"

I looked down. Though the words were blurry and seemed to move on the page, I heard myself saying them. "'How to act: Never under compulsion, out of selfishness, without forethought, with misgivings. Don't gussy up your thoughts. No surplus words–'"

"No, no, not there. The end, Danny, the last one. Look at what it says. 'Straight, not straightened,' right?"

I looked down again. I knew it said 'To stand up straight–not straightened,' which wasn't exactly the same, but it wasn't worth what would happen if I read it out exactly as written.

"Yeah, exactly," I said.

"Now what do you think that means? Iban?"

Iban sat up straighter. "I think it means that one has control over one's own life. That if one is deliberate, thoughtful, and direct, they can achieve any objective."

Larry smiled and looked at me. For a second, I was in both places at once, and he was looking at the version of me asleep on the library floor. "That's exactly right, Iban," he said. "But it has a deeper meaning, layered into the grammar, which you wouldn't understand unless you could read the original Greek. Your house burns down. You decide how you react, right? But you don't decide whether it is fundamentally good or bad, because it isn't up to you. It's neither. It just is the way it is, *a priori,* not made that way, not acted upon. Straight, not straightened. You can't change anything outside yourself. That is what is different about me. I can make things good or bad for you. I can tap into that part of you, that judgment part, and make adjustments. I can help you learn how to do that for yourself, too. How about this for a quote–you better know this one, Danel, big poet, right? 'Nothing is good or bad, but thinking makes it so.' What's that from?"

—||—

I woke up on the floor of the library basement. The walls were closing in on me. I tried to shake off the dream, thinking I must still be half asleep, but the walls kept closing, the far shelf was starting to push my feet, and I realized someone was turning the wheel. "Hey!" I shouted hoarsely. The shelves stopped moving. I tucked Shakespeare under my arm and stumbled out of the aisle, but no one was there.

13

I WAS SITTING IN Larry's new car idling on Ninety-third Street at eight A.M., waiting for a parking spot to open up. I'd made a big deal in my head about coming back to the apartment, freaked myself out, gotten "spun up," as Larry would say. I had to try to see things more clearly. The Marcus Aurelius book Santos gave me was helping. Just this morning, before running down to move the car before alternate side parking came into effect, I'd read:

> You need to get used to winnowing your thoughts, so that if someone says, "What are you thinking about?" you can respond at once (and truthfully) that you are thinking this or thinking that. And it would be obvious at once from your answer that your thoughts were straightforward and considerate ones—the thoughts of an unselfish person, one unconcerned with pleasure and with sensual indulgence generally, with squabbling, with slander and envy, or anything else you'd be ashamed to be caught thinking.

I could fix myself by controlling the inside of my head. It was my thoughts that were making me so stressed out. What else did it mean to be "present" or "grounded," other than knowing what was in your head, every moment? Wasn't anxiety just a fear of the unknown? All I needed to do was manage my mind so that every thought I had was a good one. Nothing random, nothing malignant.

I put the hazards on and leaned my seat back. Larry had leased the white SUV under someone else's name. Iban's, I thought. The conspiracy against Larry orchestrated by Bernie Kerik and Larry's ex-wife, Teresa, made it impossible for him to get his ID reissued after getting out of jail, so that made things as straightforward as leasing a car impossible. Not to mention that the people who were conspiring against him made it potentially dangerous for him to foray outside. These were the kinds of injustices we were able to rectify, by offering up our identities for a car lease, or going out to buy the groceries. Since I'd come back from England and moved into the apartment again, I'd noticed that Larry didn't leave the apartment at all anymore, just worked in the bathroom all day for the Defense Intelligence Agency, and then all night on woodworking and renovations. At least the place was somewhat clean now, as in disinfected, ever since Claudia's mom had insisted on coming over the other day. Right before she'd showed up Larry had us wiping down every surface with Simple Green, which he said was what they used in the marines. We should use so much, he'd said, that Claudia's mom should be able to smell it when she came over. Then she would associate the place with cleanliness, and subconsciously understand that it was all under control. It didn't matter that she had to step over piles of wood and around a worktable to get to the couch.

Street sweeping would be over at nine, at which point cars would descend on the empty parking spots like flies. In the meantime, I could get some sleep. I lay there, half reclined, listening to the vague sounds of construction that drifted through the car windows from the always unfinished city. Last night, Felicia, Santos's older sister, had helped with the woodworking project that had kept us up through the night. She was a doctor finishing her residency in California. When I got back from England, she was living at the apartment. I'd been too afraid to ask how she got there, but I slowly pieced it together.

Santos had put Larry in touch with her because she'd been having some kind of breakdown. Then, shockingly, it had turned out that she, too, was involved with the conspiracy against Larry. He'd gotten on the phone with her and, after talking to Larry for hours, she'd revealed everything. Ominous people had been watching her, just as Larry had suspected. They'd been in contact with her even, and these people turned out to be connected to Bernie Kerik. They were coming after her now, because she didn't want to be involved anymore. The only way she would be safe was if she was in Larry's care—he was the only one who really understood what was going on. Besides that, she was suicidal. She had been her whole life, it turned out. Felicia flew cross-country from California to New York, the city where she'd grown up and where her parents still lived, and moved into the apartment with Larry. Whether or not it was true was irrelevant; the fact that Larry had gotten her to give up everything and come here—someone who was about to be a doctor—that alone confirmed his abilities. If he was able to do that, then everything else must be real as well.

I decided to try driving the car around the block again just in case I got in trouble for idling on the street, or got in trouble with Larry for not trying to find a spot quickly. There were things to do upstairs; dawdling would be intentional sabotage. We were finally going to clean up the crates of clothes and knickknacks and memorabilia, the history of Talia and Larry's life before we came into the picture, and take them to Larry's storage unit. I couldn't believe this hadn't happened the whole time I'd been gone in England, but that just went to show how obstructive everyone who was staying in the apartment had been in my absence. Larry had told me all about it when I'd gotten back. Up in the apartment, the boxes and crates full of clothes and keepsakes were getting overrun by tools, workbenches, cans of paint ("Bermuda Sunrise"—a putrescent, fleshy pink Talia had chosen), and white primer; smaller cans of mineral spirits, mineral oil, and paint thinner; the air compressor connected to the high-volume low-pressure paint sprayer and its briefcase of delicate, expensive needles; HVAC ventilation systems; long, flat stacks of exotic hardwood; garbage bags full of drywall from the wall between the kitchen and living room, which Larry had knocked out to make a pass-through; blue painter's tape in rolls of various widths, the widest of which Larry had explained were surprisingly expensive; and stacks of plastic, ready to be draped between rooms, shrouds to keep the pink mist from traveling, which it did regardless.

As I pulled around the corner on Ninety-sixth Street, I saw a spot and beelined for it. I adjusted my seat back, which I realized had been reclined the whole time. I thought about calling my parents, but what would I say? *I'm going to keep living at Larry's all summer, and in the fall, I'll commute up to school in Bronxville. No, I don't have a job, I'm helping Larry. I owe him for all the help he's given me. Trust me.* It all made sense. They just didn't see things clearly, the way I was learning to.

⊣⊢

Felicia let me into the apartment, and I stepped past her through the translucent plastic hanging over the door. She fell back onto the couch and pulled her laptop onto her lap. The hoodie she was wearing engulfed her—it looked like she was floating in a pool of gray with only her face breaking the surface. The other chairs were stacked with boxes, paint trays, shims, and paint stirrers, except one, which was clear. I couldn't take the only chair and leave nowhere for Larry to sit when he came out of the bathroom or the bedroom, whichever door he was currently behind. There were a few spots of unoccupied space on the living room carpet, so I sat down between stacked cans of paint and the HVAC air filter, a tall white box on four wheels built for a woodshop, which Larry said we were going to hang from the ceiling by the chains coiled in the corner.

The bedroom door opened after a few minutes and Larry came out, followed by Isabella and Talia. He was wearing nothing but his briefs, which had been the case more and more since I'd come back. If he was wearing his polo and nice, pressed jeans, plus the neon-yellow running shoes he'd taken to wearing at all times outside the apartment, it meant he was meeting someone. For a while now, we'd all been wearing nearly the same getup whenever we went anywhere outside the apartment. Bright colors meant you were secure in your masculinity or your femininity, that you had nothing to hide. In the apartment, though, Larry was often dressed as he was now, in nothing but tighty-whities, sinking into the chair, the gray curls of hair on his chest a little matted. For a second I could see the hairs up close, right above me, inches from my face, moving back and forth, a drop of sweat forming among them—I closed my eyes tight, then opened them again, and I was back in the room. As Larry sat in the open chair, he looked around, searching for a spot to put his backpack down. "Let's move some of this shit out of the way, Danny, come on! Make space for Talia and Isabella. What are you doing, just sitting here?"

My eyes snapped open. "I'm sorry, I'm sorry, Larry," I said, rushing to try to move some of the clutter on top of other clutter. I picked up a can of paint in each hand and set them down on the long planks of wood stacked up below the window.

"What the fuck are you doing?" he yelled. "Do you know how expensive that wood is? Come on, Danny, where's your head at? What's going on with you?"

"I don't know!" I tried taking some of the paint trays off one of the chairs, and held the pile in my hand, paralyzed. "I don't know!" I said again, my breath short.

"Danny, you're spinning out. Clearly you know there's something on your mind that you're not sharing with me. Take a breath. Put those down."

Isabella and Talia were watching through the blown-out wall, the cut and twisted metal studs hanging at odd angles with clinging hunks of broken drywall. The drywall was why we needed the air filter, Larry had said. It released gypsum dust into the air, which could give you a respiratory illness. Felicia was sitting up on the couch, watching me put the paint trays coated in dried white primer back onto the chairs that circled the glass table.

"Come over here, Danny, I want you to look at this." I followed him into the kitchen, stepping carefully over tools and around the dovetailing jig. "Open the oven," he said. The oven was new—restaurant quality, Larry had explained proudly when he had it brought into the apartment. A yellow tube snaked out the back, full of gas, I knew, because

Larry had been so worried when he was installing it that one of us would try to sabotage him by causing a gas leak. "Get down there and open the door," he said.

I opened it. There was nothing inside, just a gleaming, brand-new oven. The metal was almost bluish. "Get your head out of there. Close it again. You see? Do you want to explain this to me?" I was looking up at him, confused. "Danny, I want you to figure out what the hell you did while I get dressed."

The hard tile was hurting my knees, but I knew I couldn't move. He went into the bedroom. I tried to formulate a response. After a minute, when he came back out wearing pants and a polo, I blurted, "I'm sorry, Larry, I don't know what's wrong, but I'm sure whatever it was, I can fix it or make up for it."

"You hear this?" he yelled into the living room. "Felicia, I want to make sure you're hearing this. Come here and try this oven door." Now they were both standing over me. She opened the oven door and then closed it. "It's bent, right?" Larry asked her.

"Yeah, it's bent," she said.

"So either you're calling me a liar, Danny, or you bent my oven door on purpose. Which is it?"

I thought, for a second, that maybe this was the lesson. I hadn't actually bent the oven door, and he knew that. So the only logical conclusion was that I needed to learn to be yelled at. I needed to build experience in stressful situations like this to prepare for the world. It was like how Larry and Iban had described drill instructors, how they treat you in boot camp so that you'll be able to endure much worse in the field. "Pain is weakness leaving the body," the marines said. I had to learn to take this kind of confrontation, to be a man in the face of it.

"No, sir. Neither, sir. You're not a liar, but I also didn't bend it. I swear."

"Neither, huh? You think you're smarter than me, don't you? See, I know you don't believe I am who I say I am, Danny. It doesn't make a difference if I prove it to you over and over. Something is broken in you that makes it impossible for you to believe. But that doesn't matter to me, does it? Because it's true. *I* know it's true. *I* know what's real. So let's find out if you know better than I do." He pulled a knife out from the drawer. The knives were all wrapped in paper towels and sealed with painter's tape in a kind of sheath to protect the ceramic blades. Larry had said that ceramic knives were the sharpest—sharp enough to cut through bone—but brittle, so they might snap inside. I couldn't make out what he'd chosen—something big—a chef's knife or a cleaver. He slid the paper towel off the knife and left it on the counter. The unsheathed blade caught the light from the window behind me and seemed to cut through it. "Izzy, go line the tub with plastic for me, would you?" he yelled.

"Okay!" I heard her chirp back, then the rustle as she collected painter's plastic from one of the piles and walked into the bathroom.

"Don't look at her. Look at me," he said. "Now, you say you didn't break my oven. Is that true? I know what happened, Danny. I want you to try out telling the truth, for once." The knife was hovering in the air above me. I didn't doubt that he would do it. I could hear Isabella taking boxes out of the bathtub, clearing a space. I started to cry.

"Yes, I did. I must have. I'm sorry, I'm sorry, I didn't mean to."

"You did though, Danny! You did! That's what you have to understand. You did mean to. You know that! I want to help you, so tell me why you did it."

I racked my brain. If I did it, and I did it on purpose, then I must have done it for a reason. What had I been thinking about that might have made me upset enough to do something like that?

"I was thinking about my parents. . . ."

I could hear plastic rustling in the bathroom, the stretch and rip of pieces of tape fastening the plastic to the edges of the tub, preparing it for me. Larry's eyes almost looked hungry, and with the knife in his hand, it felt like he was about to cook me. "What about your parents?"

I closed my eyes, hot tears squeezing out from under cold lids. In the darkness I saw a knife made of light cut through layers and layers of plastic, which opened like the pages of a book, and then underneath the pink flesh, my flesh, and then finally nothing. I was really sobbing now, shaking, and almost fell from my knees to the floor. I reached out to support myself and grabbed something metal.

"Look, he's trying to do it again, bending my oven. Let go of the handle." He put the knife down on the counter and I felt him grab my wrist, hoist me up, and now he was holding my limp body against his. "What is it, Danny?" he said forcefully into my skull.

What I said came as if from nowhere—I heard myself saying it from deep inside. "It's because I was born when I was, the way I was. My mom was sick. She wasn't supposed to have kids anymore. She did anyway, for me. My parents' lives must have been so much harder with me in it. My dad's business collapsed the week I was born. It just seems like their lives were totally different after that. I feel like . . . I'm a burden. That's how I've felt, all the time. Not that it's anything they've done, it's just inside me, this feeling. I feel like I'm a burden."

I felt immense relief, like something that had been stuck inside me my whole life had just been released. I was still crying, but not from fear anymore. *That was real,* I thought, *a real feeling. I never knew I felt that way.* My body felt like it weighed less, like my veins were empty. I was slumping in his arms, and tried to steady my legs on the floor.

His face was right above my head. He felt somehow so solid, so steady, holding me up. "No, Danny. What else?"

What did he mean, no? That was real. I knew it was. Was it possible there could be more? He said there was, so I tried to find it, grasping in my head. "Well, you and Talia are so close. She's so clearly not a burden to you. So I guess I resented that, and that's why I lashed out."

"No. Wrong." He let go of me, and I saw him reach for the knife on the counter again. "I don't want to hear you try to logic it out. You tell me what *happened.* What you did, on purpose, and why. I don't want to hear you try to figure out an explanation. You need to admit it, and tell me how you're going to fix it. If you continue to insist on being dishonest, that means you intend to continue harming me, and my home, and my daughter, right? How am I supposed to come to any other conclusion?"

I didn't know where to stand, where to put my hands. I felt like I would fall down. I was definitely swaying, deliriously off-balance. "I don't know, I don't know." I felt exhausted. If I could get to the end of this and go away, go to sleep, then it would be over, at least for a while.

"You do know, Danny. It's your parents, right? That much you were right about. Keep going. Hey! Stay with me!" He clanged the knife against one of the exposed metal studs in the broken wall. "What about your dad?"

I tried to think of what else Larry and I had talked about. What were my problems, the reasons I might have done this? But I couldn't think out loud. It couldn't look like I was working it out. It had to actually be true, somehow even more true than true. "I was scared about my sexuality," I said. "About sex and, and being a man, and trying to live according to my dad's definition of that, growing up, which felt impossible, and I thought maybe I'm gay, but I get so caught in that, because I'm not, I know I'm not because you've told me, and shown me, but I think because I don't know what would happen with my parents if I *were,* like it's so unimaginable–"

"Stop, Danny, stop. You're spinning out again. Fela, did you hear that?" She looked tired, too. "Felicia always had an interest in psychology when she was going through her medical training. Well, there's no richer environment for learning about the mind than here, with me." I felt confused, insubstantial, like I might float away. I was still in the middle of figuring out what was real. What had happened with my parents? Was I going to have to pay Larry back for the oven? Was it possible to replace the door rather than the whole thing? He would probably make me replace the whole thing.

"See, Danny here has been worried about his sexuality. He's not gay, he knows that, but he can't stop thinking about it. Right? This comes from repression that occurred in childhood. Not repression of actual sexual desires or preferences, but the generalized repression itself created a vacuum, which was filled by this obsession. Danny, look at me. All of these behaviors and processes are extremely well documented; they've been proven over and over in countless studies. Fela knows, we've talked for hours about the psychology of all this, and she's amazed by the things I know that take years to understand in school, or that are even more advanced than what they teach you, right?" She nodded. She had a kind face, the face of a doctor reassuring you that everything is, after all, going to be all right.

Larry went on: "If you trust me, Danny, and stop ruining my stuff, and pay me back for what you've already ruined, you're going to be okay. Better than okay. But you need to trust me. I know you're not gay, but I'll make sure you know it by the time we're done here." The surprise on my face must have been obvious. "Did you not think that there was an ending to this, a conclusion that I'm leading you towards? Look around you." Isabella peeked out of the bathroom, where she had finished lining the tub with plastic. The apartment looked like the aftermath of a car wreck. "You think all of this is by accident? I've designed this environment to have exactly the effect I need it to have for each of you to get better. The oven is more significant for you than you even know. Think about that. You can't possibly understand the nuances of how I'm affecting you, but you can feel it. You're doing good, Danny. You're close. You need to let go of fear, though, before you can achieve clarity." He returned the knife to its paper sheath. We wouldn't clean up the apartment that day. I had taken up too much time.

—II—

My opportunity to let go of fear altogether arrived halfway through the summer. Felicia and Santos were visiting their parents, and Claudia and Talia were elsewhere, so it was just me, Larry, and Isabella in the apartment. I was sitting on the couch, which was now also covered in cans of paint. They tipped precariously on the soft leather and had to be moved to the floor if you wanted to sit. Larry was in the chair that we always kept clear for him, wearing only his briefs, as usual. From behind his laptop, he said, "Look at this place, Danny. What more proof do you need that all of you have completely broken minds? You know that I would have this place in perfect order if it was only me here. It's unbelievable the chaos you all have managed to generate. Izzy, do you have any of my Kank-A pens?" Larry had developed some kind of dental issue, an abscess that ran under his teeth that he said was more painful than any regular human being would be able to bear without painkillers. But he wasn't able to get a regular ID, so he wasn't able to get insurance to go to a regular doctor. Instead, he'd been using this over-the-counter local anesthetic, a white tube meant for canker sores, which he pressed into his gums intermittently. “Hello? Isabella? Where are my Kank-A pens?”

“I don’t know, Lawrence,” Isabella yelled from the kitchen. “Maybe your girlfriend hid them somewhere. Look in your bag.”

He rolled his eyes, grumbling, and began digging around. “Izzy’s been jealous because she thinks I’ve been giving Felicia too much attention. She thinks suddenly I’m not capable of helping multiple people at once.”

Isabella scoffed in the kitchen.

“All right, that’s it,” Larry said, pushing a Kank-A pen he’d found in his bag under his lip. His face twisting in pain, he got up and stomped toward Izzy, ducking through the broken wall. His hand wrapped around her whole side. He picked her up like a piece of equipment and moved her. Isabella was cackling; her eyes and mouth wide-open. “Come here,” he said, placing her against the workbench. “Come here!” he yelled louder this time, and I realized he was talking to me, the only other person in the apartment. He was fastening Isabella’s wrists and ankles to the worktable with vises. Isabella was still laughing, chuckling insanely, as he tightened the vises. Larry ignored her. “I just got these vises, they’re incredibly good, the best you can buy. We’re going to get so much good woodworking done with these. That’s exciting, right, Danny? Here, help me with this.” He indicated the vise on her right ankle, so I got down and tightened it.

When I looked up, he was grabbing her jaw. “Maybe I haven’t been paying her enough attention, and she’s gotten a little out of control.” I could see the web of tiny veins just under her skin, and I realized I was still holding on to her ankle. Her skin was cold. “Danny, clear a space on the ground. You can put that stuff in the bedroom,” he said. I’d never been allowed to take any of the equipment into the bedroom. The idea of opening up some space in the living room, actually being able to organize, was thrilling. I’d finally be able to sleep on the couch without moving paint cans out of the way, or on the floor when Felicia or Iban were here.

I grabbed as many items as I could carry and took them into the bedroom, carefully placing them on the only space that was open and wouldn't block the narrow walking path–the bed. It felt like all of my vision was blank except for a small circle in the middle, where I could see paint cans and power tools, and my hands, very far away, balancing the towering cans against each other on top of memory foam. When I came back into the living room, Larry had pushed even more of the mess wantonly aside and had apparently undone the vises, because now Isabella was on the floor, and she was naked. There was a knock at the door.

They both froze. I looked over at the door, which was blurry behind the plastic. There was another knock.

"Hold it. Don't move," he said, pointing at Izzy, then indicated with his hand that I should go over next to her in the living room. He went to answer the door.

I waited, sitting on my knees on the carpet. Isabella was next to me, naked. I wanted so badly to understand what she was thinking, but it was as if we were in two separate rooms. She smiled lightly at me, but she might as well have been looking at the wall, barely aware of my presence. Larry was talking to someone in muted tones around the corner, then the door closed, and when he came back around the corner, he wasn't alone. If Lee was surprised at the scene on the living room floor, or at Larry in his underwear, it didn't register on his face.

"I told you, didn't I?" Larry said. Lee nodded, and Larry went on. "See, Izzy has been getting a little jealous since Felicia's been around. It turns out Fela and I have a lot in common. Isabella can't handle that. It's not because she needs me, it's because she needs sex. She can't go without it, she's obsessed with it, and that's healthy, it's important to her progress because of how repressed and constrictive her upbringing was. She's discovering, exploring herself, it's perfectly natural, and as she's doing that she needs room to grow, she needs to be able to escalate things. Go ahead. Show him, Isabella."

Isabella got up, totally naked, and started to loosen Lee's tie. I was still on the floor, watching. She got down on her knees. Somewhere in my mind, there was the sound of a zipper, louder than the one on Lee's pants. Everything was still happening, but I wasn't there anymore.

—⊣⊢—

I do not know how much time passed, minutes maybe. We were all on the ground in the living room. I was trying, really trying, but I couldn't. My whole body was soft, and I wanted to get away with it, to be on board, to not let everyone down, to not let Izzy down. She scared me, Larry scared me, Lee scared me, they were one massive organism that got what it needed out of me whether I liked it or not. I hated myself. I couldn't do it and Larry could tell. I found myself sitting off to the side, where I had been for a few minutes without realizing it, zoned out. Larry turned to me and said, "Danny, why don't you take a minute? Go downstairs, get some ice cream. Grab a couple bucks from my bag."

I gathered up my clothes and put them on, then headed to the door. I hadn't been allowed to leave all summer for any reason other than to go somewhere with Larry, buy groceries for the apartment, or take things to storage. As I got up, I tried not to look at the pulsing knot of flesh on the floor surrounded by construction equipment. I could only think about how hard it'd be to replace all the construction stuff after they were done while making sure I didn't intentionally damage any of it. I grabbed some cash from inside Larry's bag. As I tried to decide how much it made sense to take so that he wouldn't claim I had stolen from him, I realized that he didn't mean for me to get ice cream only for myself, but for all of them. For afterward. It was an errand. I took the money and walked out the door. As it closed behind me, I remembered I didn't have a key to get back in. A little while later, I would wait outside that door, sitting on the floor against the wall, my knocking having gone ignored for a long time, the ice cream, which I knew I couldn't eat without them, melting inside a plastic bag.

14

SHIVAN, MY BEST FRIEND from high school, wouldn't let it go. It felt as if everyone else from my life outside of Larry and the apartment had let me disappear, but Shivan wouldn't give up calling, texting, and emailing, no matter how long I took to respond or how often I flaked on plans because of an "emergency" at the apartment. Shivan and I met back in high school English class after I'd spent most of freshman year sitting alone on the floor in front of my locker, decorating every surface of a folder with doodles. After we started hanging out, everything changed–it was the first time talking to another person didn't feel like a performance, a complicated series of steps and moves for a dance I'd never learned. Over the years of high school, Shivan and I started making music together, writing poetry and lyrics, going on road trips, camping, figuring out the longest distances we could travel to make our lives as unpredictable as possible. At one point in the middle of the school year, Shivan and our friend Andrew planned a cross-country trip to San Francisco. They drove away in the middle of the night, leaving notes on their pillows. They'd asked me to join them, but I didn't think I could handle the conversation with my parents that would come afterward. I didn't know how to be in trouble, so I avoided it at all costs. When they got back weeks later at four in the morning, dozens of ignored calls and texts from their parents on their phones, my house was the first place they stopped. Since I'd been living in the apartment, I'd missed Shivan, and life as it had been, but I was doing something more important now, something I couldn't explain to him.

Still, Shivan kept at me about coming home. We were halfway through the summer and I hadn't been back once. What was I doing for my birthday at the end of June? I could come back for a weekend, couldn't I? He'd gotten me a present, it was at his parents' house in New Jersey, come and get it. Then my dad told me that he was going out of town for a week and he didn't want to leave my mom alone, would I come home? It was enough of a justification that Larry couldn't be suspicious of me, I thought. Still, I expected him to make it hard to leave. As I told him, I saw a flicker in his face, like he knew that I was trying to sneak away. "Go ahead," he said. "Spend time with your friend, your mom. You go home for a while and then we can all come out and have dinner with your parents. You're going to finally talk to your family, and deal with all this."

—||—

I woke up in the middle of the night in my childhood bedroom. The room kept filling with light, then falling back into darkness. As I came to, I crawled out of bed and stumbled toward the source. It was a firefly that had gotten in somehow. I tried to catch it, but was too sluggish and groggy. Finally, as it landed on the bookshelf, I brought my hand down and crushed it. Then I went back to sleep. When I woke up in the morning, and the memory of what had happened resolved, I went over to look at the evidence. I cupped my hand around the smeared body on the shelf and peered inside. It was still faintly glowing, even then.

I crept downstairs and straight out the front door, stepping lightly so the steps didn't creak, careful to turn the doorknob as I closed it so the latch wouldn't click, habits I'd developed from sneaking in and out during high school. I didn't want my parents to ever ask where I was going, even if the answer was just for a stroll around the yard. Once I was outside, I walked on the driveway's edge, where it was gravel, avoiding the new asphalt my dad had recently put in. The driveway curved along the lip of a valley, then dipped and crossed the creek, until finally it connected to the road.

There was more air, more light, than I remembered—too much. Over the past few years, an invasive species of vine had moved into the forest. It would crawl on the ground until it found a tree, climb it, and thicken there, feeding off the tree's nutrients until it became so heavy that it toppled, leaving the fallen vine at the feet of a fresh victim. The valley was littered with the giant, broken bodies of trees felled this way. I crouched on the edge of the driveway and thought about all the bones I'd found mucking around in the woods my whole childhood. A turtle shell with the spine fused inside. Fragile bird bones. Broken eggs dropped from a nest or the jaws of a predator. Once, a whole carcass, and the snatches of fur all around caught on the pricker bushes, so fresh it had felt haunted, and I'd walked briskly home, afraid to run.

I wondered if Tiger, Talia's cat, was still alive out there. For a brief part of sophomore year, before her dad had gotten out of jail, she'd adopted a kitten. It was small and orange, and constantly sprinting across Slonim to sink its needle teeth into our ankles. Security was very serious about the no-pet policy, and after a few close calls, Talia had given the cat to Hailey to take care of in her dorm down the road. Then, while Hailey was in class, she got a call from security about an escaped kitten on the roof of her building. Ultimately, I'd offered Talia my parents' house as a refuge, and they said they'd be open to looking after the little beast for a while. Within a week, I'd gotten a call from my mom: The kitten had been lost in the woods. *Dead,* I thought. But then again, anything was possible out here. I'd come across a peacock once, head-bobbing through the trees, a neighbor's lost exotic pet. Of course, there were hunters, too, and the nooses they hung from their blinds in the trees, so that there was always a chance you'd find a deer caught and struggling on its hind legs as it suffocated, trying to run away.

I walked down to the end of the driveway where there was a forked tulip tree with one of its trunks severed near the base. I climbed up onto the stump and perched there like a gargoyle, waiting for Shivan, who was supposed to come pick me up. There was no phone signal out here, and he was not exactly known for being punctual. My mom had crashed the car into this tree as she brought me home from elementary school a long time ago. She'd passed the driveway, which was a sure sign that her blood sugar had dropped dangerously low, and I didn't notice until we were up the road a couple miles past the house. We needed to get home, and it was only a short distance, but I was eight years old and I didn't know how to drive. I decided that what made the most sense was to run alongside the car, smacking on the door to tell her when she needed to straighten out. I hadn't been old enough to understand what would've set the tree on fire when she crunched into it after she took the turn a little too wide. Maybe the headlight cracked and an exposed wire made contact with dry wood. Hours later, I'd stood there with my parents and watched the fire truck pull up. The tree was lightly smoking, and it had seemed like not that big of a deal. Then, as the firemen sprayed their hose, gouts of flame and dark black smoke burst out of holes in the trunk, and the whole thing was engulfed. It had been burning, invisibly, from the inside.

Crouching on the old, scorched stump, I tried to look inside myself really clearly for once. *I feel anxious about Larry and everyone else coming here, sure. But only because I let my parents think there's something wrong with my relationship with Larry, and because I let Larry think there's something wrong with my relationship with my parents.* I sighed, and tried to spit into the woods. It didn't go well. *The solution is easy. I have control over my thoughts. I have control over my actions. I have control. I can be a good son to my parents.* I heard a car coming up the road through the woods, saw glimpses of it between the trees, an old, coppery Lexus that I recognized as Shivan's grandpa's, which Shivan had been using for years. *I can be a good friend to Shivan.* As Shivan pulled up I hopped off the tree and landed on the smooth, clean asphalt. *And I can be a good friend to Larry. It's a choice.*

The week at home surprised me by being relatively uneventful. I'd spent some time hanging out with Shivan, who gave me an electric ukulele for my birthday, which he insisted on keeping at his house for me to come play whenever I wanted. The rest of the time I spent at home. My mom seemed fine, better than I remembered, and I wondered if, from a distance, Larry had somehow helped her. Toward the

end of the week, my dad came back from his trip, and that night, Larry and everyone else would be coming for dinner. I ducked my head into the kitchen to say hello, and my mom paused her book on tape. "Aren't you cold? Put slippers on, honey."

"Oh, I'm fine, thanks. I was going to start cooking for tonight." I started looking through the cabinets.

"Are you hungry?"

"No, no, I was going to start cooking for tonight."

"Well, I'll get out of your way then," she said, and closed up the kit she used to test her blood sugar. I pulled out the groceries I'd bought with Larry's money and started staging things on the counter. My parents had remodeled the kitchen years ago They'd gotten all new appliances, new honey-ish pine cabinets, and deep green granite counters. A local artist had painted the wall the color of my dad's eyes—swirls of teal. Within a year, half of the appliances had broken for no discernible reason. Larry said it was because of our unresolved family issues. My mom, who loved to bake, had been relegated to using the toaster oven in place of the double oven in the wall, which was filled with cans of food, a makeshift pantry.

I'd tried to find a recipe that wouldn't require the use of an oven, and had settled on one for stuffed chicken. I pulled plastic wrap from the roll and laid it on the counter. Then I cut the chicken breasts from their wrapping and rinsed the raw, pink bodies. Larry was beyond fastidious about germs. If he got sick from this meal, I couldn't imagine what would happen. I was being deliberate, putting my signature on every single action. I laid the breasts on the plastic, then pulled another layer of plastic across them with a long squelch. I grabbed the meat tenderizer from among the other utensils, then started hammering the soft, pink flesh between the sheets of plastic, bringing the spiked mallet down again and again until the meat was flat and soft. I pulled off the plastic wrap, sprinkled the chicken with salt and pepper, then took out strips of prosciutto and laid them on the chicken. I sliced provolone and washed stalks of basil, which I patted dry with paper towels, then plucked off individual leaves, and laid everything flat on the tenderized chicken. I hunted around in the cabinets until I found a container of rainbow toothpicks. I rolled the chicken breasts up, stabbed the toothpicks through them, wrapped it all up in plastic again, put the little chicken bundles into the fridge, then went to join my parents in front of the TV to wait.

—I⊢—

Almost half an hour past the time Larry had said they'd arrive, I got a text that there'd been an emergency, and they were finally on their way. I'd expected this, and knew what it actually meant, but I said it to my parents anyway: "They're on their way, sounds like there was some kind of emergency. I'm going to set up the porch."

I walked across the house, past the plummeting hole of the basement steps where the laundry room was and where, when I was much younger, my brother used to lie in wait, ready to scare me with one of his many Halloween masks. If it was only me and my mom at home, and I hadn't heard her make any noise in a while, I'd know to check down there, and there was a decent chance I'd find her passed out on the carpet. I unlocked the door to the screened-in porch, fumbled for the light, then gave up, deciding to walk out into the dark of the porch for a second. The air through the screens was warm, and the cicadas and tree frogs made it sound like we lived in a swamp. I hoped this dinner would go all right. I wished I could travel forward in time, turn my brain off so the night would pass, and wake up in the future. I sighed, willed myself to be calm, then hit the lights and set the table.

—ıı—

Larry was dead serious. "I have to get this gazpacho recipe from you, Amy." I couldn't believe they were all here, sitting on the chairs my dad and I took out from storage every spring.

"Oh, thank you," my mom said. "I really just throw it together."

Iban, sitting farther down the table, leaned in. "I actually spent some time in the Basque country, but the gazpacho there is much thinner, not nearly as good as this, Mrs. Levin. Really excellent. I'd like the recipe as well."

"Charlie, I understand you're an Internet man. I've been getting into the Internet business myself," Larry said.

My dad was seated at the head of the table. "Is that right?" he said.

"Danny hasn't told you?" Larry shot me a look. "I can't believe that. I've been looking at the domain business. Actually it can be quite profitable, which I'm sure you know."

"Well, sure, at a certain scale, but generally your rate of return is not going to be very good. I make websites. Reselling domains is an entirely different prospect."

Larry had his mouth full. "I've actually gotten domains for everyone here, all their names."

"I'm going to get the chicken," I said.

"Let me give you a hand," Larry said, pushing his chair back from the table. I looked back at him, and the faces floating above the table. They were occupying my past, crawling around it like the stink bugs that found invisible cracks in the house every summer, that would whiz across a room and smack into your head. Larry followed me into the living room, leaving my parents behind with everyone else. "What's going on here?" he asked, pointing at the planter in the dining room, out of which was sticking about a two-inch stump and nothing else.

"That's an avocado tree my parents planted when they got married, but my mom recently pruned it. So now it looks like that." The wood floor underneath the dead avocado was stained from water damage. I guessed my mom had kept watering it in hopes it would come back to life. The chair in front of the pot had a broken seat. I could almost see myself sitting here in the mornings before high school, the full, healthy avocado tree behind me, with my head in my hands, trying to will myself to have a migraine so I would be allowed to stay home from school. No one makes you go to school when you're in pain so bad it's like your insides are weeping. I could remember it, my eyes closed, my face jammed into the edge of the table–trying to fix the pain as much as I was simultaneously inviting it in, and then something came, auras on the edge of my vision, a flash of white, and the pain arrived. It was right there, waiting, but it was hard to tell where it came from.

Larry looked up at the ceiling and sniffed as we walked into the kitchen. "Do you smell that? That must?" The house was old. It had always been a bit damp. "It's entirely possible it's neurotoxic. Could explain a lot, Danny."

I pulled the rolls of chicken out of the fridge and shrugged. "That would make sense, actually." Maybe mold was why I'd had the headaches, and would explain why I always felt so hollow, why my head went so blank, whenever I came home.

"How are you planning to cook those?" Larry asked.

"On the stove," I said.

Larry raised his eyebrows. "Not what I would do, but okay."

"Well, the oven doesn't work so–"

"Oh, yes, you told me. The oven. Well, this is a good workaround, Danny. Good thinking. We'll have to get your mom a new oven, won't we?" He smiled at me.

After I'd cooked the chicken, Larry insisted on carrying the penguin-shaped tray my parents used to carry food from the kitchen to the porch. As we came through the door, Iban shot up from his chair to help, and Larry sat as we doled out salad and rolls of chicken, the toothpicks sticking out of them like multicolored masts. Iban said to Larry, "Mr. Levin was just telling the story of how he and Mrs. Levin found this house."

Larry was sitting at the head of the table opposite my dad. "It's a beautiful property, Charlie. I wish we could've come earlier and walked around, but there was an emergency back in New York. I'm sure you know, being a parent, taking care of all these people's needs, it can be complicated. You raised a great son in Dan here. He's been a huge help around the apartment. We've been doing woodworking together, and he's been helping me out with my websites. Did he tell you that?"

My dad was halfway to bringing a forkful of salad to his mouth. He looked up. "No, actually he hadn't. Maybe if he called more often, you know"—he laughed a little—"but we try not to be typical guilty Jewish parents."

Larry took a sip of the wine my dad had put out. "Very nice. Shall we?"

I'd been watching everyone wait for Larry to begin eating his main course, a custom my parents hadn't been aware of. The moment Larry picked up his knife and began sawing at the chicken, Iban, Isabella, Claudia, Santos, Felicia, Talia, and I picked up ours. As I cut into my chicken, I saw to my horror that there was a rainbow inside of it. It took me a second to understand what was happening. "Oh my god, I'm so sorry," I said. "The toothpicks must have dyed it while I was cooking."

"Don't worry, Dan," my dad and Larry began to say in unison. My dad continued, "It'll be fine to eat. Tastes great."

My mom, who'd been silent the whole meal, said, "I couldn't eat it anyway!" and laughed.

Larry put his knife and fork down. "Claudia, Isabella, why don't you tell Charlie and Amy what we've been doing at the apartment."

"Are you cold?" my mom asked, leaning toward Isabella, who sat next to her and was wearing only a thin shirt.

"Oh no, I'm okay, thanks," Isabella said.

"I get so cold," my mom said, reaching out a hand to grab Isabella's arm and show her. I could practically feel my mom's hand, the rough fingertips healed over from countless pricks, testing for sugar.

"Well, like Larry said, we've been doing all kinds of woodworking, and learning about construction and renovation and stuff." I let myself slide a few inches down in my seat as Claudia talked. "Larry's been helping us all so much. I had these deep-seated, repressed memories with my parents and growing up and stuff, and I really needed to deal with them, and Larry made it okay to talk about, which has made a really big difference for me."

Larry looked over at Isabella. "What about you, Izzy?"

"Yeah! I had a lot of stuff that happened to me in my childhood that I never got a chance to deal with. It had actually been really affecting my schoolwork, and then I wasn't getting the help I needed at school until Larry intervened." They both seemed to be talking more to my mom than my dad; she was nodding and smiling, glassy-eyed, receptive.

"It's so lucky that you've been able to get so much help," my mom said, nodding gravely.

I could see my dad thinking, watching where this was going and wanting to get there first, before Larry even. There was an air of participation. He swallowed a bite of blue chicken, then looked in my direction. "What I'd love to understand is how this has been helping you, Dan. As your parents, we want to be involved, to be on your side. Is there anything you've been working through?"

"Oh, well, yeah, there has. Stuff from growing up."

"You're mumbling, Danny. Say what 'stuff,'" said Larry.

I would have done anything in the world, including throw myself headfirst through the glass table, before telling my parents anything I had told Larry. Did he want me to talk about the sex stuff? I looked through the table at my hands. "I don't know. I think a lot of stuff with Mom being sick, growing up, was really tough for me. I struggle with a lot of insecurity and anxiety and stuff."

My mom cocked her head, pained sympathy stretched across her face. "I wish you wouldn't, Dan. You're wonderful, there's no reason for you to feel insecure."

"Of course, we wondered what had happened to you in high school. You seemed to completely change, and we had no way of knowing what was going on." My dad was staring right at me. I felt like I could cry, not because of the conversation that was happening, but because of the conversation that wasn't. I could never figure out the right words to say how I felt. It was as if the words didn't exist, or if they did, I hadn't learned them yet. What if Larry was mad at me for not saying everything?

"As we agreed, Charlie, taking care of kids isn't easy. It's complicated. Of course, it's been my pleasure to take care of the kids, to watch them grow, but it hasn't been cheap, has it?" Isabella, Iban, and Claudia shook their heads.

"We've been very grateful to you, Larry," my dad said, "for putting Dan up. That's been very kind of you."

"It's no trouble for me at all. I don't ask anything in return," Larry said. "Only the presence of your son. Giving them a place to stay is my pleasure, and it's easy for me. If they didn't create such a mess around themselves as an expression of their resistance to improving, it'd be easier, you understand. You'd be amazed at what happens, how they push back. Isn't that right, Santos?"

Santos paused, as if it took him a second to return from a different place. "Yeah, that is right. I can't help it, the times I've actually intentionally broken Larry's woodworking tools and stuff, for example. I sabotage a lot." The sound of the cicadas outside swelled and then subsided. Something hit one of the porch screens, probably a stink bug, then flew away.

Talia shot a look at him. "You *can* help it, Santos. You could stop. But you keep on hurting my dad. It's that you don't bother trying. That's why he had to take a break from school, because of what he's going through."

"Oh, that's awful," my mom said, looking sadly at Santos. "But you don't sabotage things, do you, Dan?"

I started to say no, I'm not as bad as Santos, but Larry jumped in. "You'd be surprised. Danny's done his part, too, haven't you?"

My parents looked shocked. I hadn't expected this to be what the conversation was about, the truth that I was supposed to share. I looked at my dad, then my mom. "Yeah, actually I have occasionally done stuff. I damaged the new oven Larry bought."

My mom looked scandalized. "You did this intentionally?"

Larry looked at me. "More than *occasionally.*"

"Yeah, yeah, that's true. But I'm figuring out how I'm going to pay Larry back for it. I am."

"I should hope so. This man has given you a place to live. I can't believe you'd treat his things with anything but respect."

"I found that surprising as well, Amy," Larry said. "It's good for Danny to have it out in the open. If nobody minds, I'd like to help clear the dishes. I apologize for rushing out, but we need to get back to New York before it's too late. Besides everything else, these kids keep incredibly strange hours. Luckily, I don't need much sleep. Never have."

—||—

Driving back to New York in the limousine, which had been waiting in my parents' driveway the whole dinner, Larry commented, "I'm proud of you, Danny. He really was honest, open, and clear with his parents. Wasn't he, Iz?"

"He really was. He told the truth in a big way."

I smiled weakly, and tried to look out the window, but it was dark out and the glass was tinted, so I couldn't see the roads I'd driven on my whole childhood. I kept playing over and over in my mind the scene that had unfolded immediately after dinner. My dad was washing the dishes in the sink when Larry approached him from behind and offered to take over for him. My dad briefly resisted before giving in, and then said, as he stood behind Larry, who had taken his place, "Anyone who does the dishes is okay in my book!" I couldn't even see the silhouettes of the trees as we passed them by, which would have implied forward motion, the passage of time. There was nothing except me and this group of people, chattering in a sealed box that intermittently filled up with the light of another car's headlights. I must have nodded off. When I woke up, we were back in Manhattan, pulling up to the apartment.

— 15 —

"HOW'RE YOU DOING, ANDREA? How long has it been?" Larry held the phone faceup on the center console between our seats in the parked car.

"Years, Lare. I'm doing good, you know. I'm just sitting out here, watching the kids run around, trying to get in the last bit of summer. It's so great to hear from you after all this time." The voice coming out of the speakerphone had a thick Staten Island accent, not far off from the voices of New Jersey moms I'd grown up around.

"That sounds just wonderful, Andrea. You're still at the house on Staten Island, is that right?"

"That's right. We've got a hammock out here so I'm just relaxing, the wind's blowing through the tall grass, it's real nice. You should come out sometime, make it a visit finally, right?"

"Listen, Andrea, I'm here with my friend Danny—"

"Hi there, Danny," she called through the phone.

I responded with a weak "Hi, nice to meet you."

"—because he doesn't believe who I am. So I was wondering if you could confirm, we grew up together on Staten Island, yes?"

She laughed. "Yes, of course! Let me tell you, Larry was quite a kid growing up."

He looked at me with his eyebrows raised, as in, *See, I told you.* "Can you talk a little more about what you mean by that, Andrea?"

"Oh yeah, in general Larry was a tough kid. I don't know what you want me to say here, Lare, I know you had it rough growing up and—"

"What about the time I showed up at your door once covered in blood, isn't that right? Tell Danny about that."

"Oh yeah, absolutely. Pouring rain. The doorbell rings and there's Larry on the doorstep covered in blood. I mean head to toe, really."

"But it wasn't my blood, was it?"

She laughed again. That accent sounded like orange slices after a game of soccer, like the mall and a house with a yard. "No, it wasn't yours. That's right. It was those boys, who were they again? At the movie theater? You tell it, Larry, I don't remember."

"You remember those ashtrays they used to have in the movie theater lobbies?"

"Oh, yes, that was it! Oh my god, yes those huge, heavy ashtrays. These things were like entirely concrete."

"I picked one up and used it to beat the hell out of three guys, didn't I?"

"Larry, oh my god and he was shaking in the rain, Danny, kind of out of it, and I took him into the bath and washed the blood off him, and took care of him that night. It wasn't that unusual, though, was it? You showed up at my house like that pretty often, most of the time to get away from your mom."

"That's right. Andrea gave me a refuge. A safe place away from home, like I've done for all of you, Danny. But more often than not I had beat the shit out of someone and needed a place to stay." I heard her yell something away from the phone, presumably at her kids, whom I imagined running through the grass, tripping, getting dirty. "All right, Andrea, thank you so much for that, we've got to go now," Larry said.

"Oh, okay, Larry. Honestly, call me sometime. We'd love to have you out at the house."

He said goodbye and flipped the phone shut. "See?" he said, turning to me. "Danny, I've shown you pictures of me with Gorbachev. Photos with Bush Sr. You know I single-handedly ended the Kosovo War. Right? You don't doubt that, do you? You've met friends of mine who were very high up in the military and intelligence. What is it going to take for you to believe?"

"I do, Larry, I do believe. I'm sorry if I've made it seem like I don't."

"You'd better get there, Danny, or I don't see how you're going to continue at Sarah Lawrence without having problems."

"Yeah."

"You and Iban packed Talia's sweaters away in storage, right?" I couldn't remember. We had packed so many things and sent them to storage there was no way to keep track. "Yes, you did. How about we get ahead of things this time and you and Iban head up there tonight and grab those. Should be a quick trip."

—ı⊢—

Later that night, Iban and I dragged a dolly down an endless concrete hallway in a grid of corridors lined with roll-up aluminum storage unit doors. Behind each was the evidence of strangers' lives, what they couldn't hold on to anymore but were unwilling to get rid of. I could see Larry's storage unit in my mind—completely full, floor to ceiling, wall to wall, and shook my head. I had no idea how Iban and I were going to get Talia's sweaters out of there and back to the apartment without spending the whole night stuck in this twenty-four-hour Manhattan Mini Storage. The casters on the bottom of the dolly rattled, and the sound carried down every vessel of the cavernous building. It was almost midnight already; surely we were alone. Once we reached the door, Iban plugged the key Larry had given him into the lock, and rolled the door back. The room practically bulged out at us.

"Let's start staging in the hallway here," Iban said, indicating the square of polished concrete before the hall dead-ended. "We'll want to pull the cart back out the way we came."

I stared up into the abyss of objects. "You think it's one of these black ones, right?" I asked, pointing at the long black crates piled four high, the base of a tower of boxes so tall that it touched the ceiling.

"Yep. You put away her sweaters in the black bins, don't you remember?"

I couldn't, but since I should have been able to, I nodded. "Okay, then, why don't we just try to slide them out instead of taking everything down?"

Iban and I had thought that helping with the storage unit over the past few months would be an opportunity to prove that we were organized and capable, that we were unlike everyone else who had caused the mess in the apartment. It had turned out to be a whole new disaster. As the apartment overflowed, Larry would send me and Iban up to the storage unit with loads of supplies, old belongings, furniture for Talia's new dorm at Sarah Lawrence, and we'd find a way to make it fit. But it was a Tetris game we were swiftly losing. When Larry told us we had to store Talia's new kitchen island, and we explained that there wasn't going to be enough space, he'd glared at us, saying, "I've mapped it out in my mind, and kept track of every single thing you've brought up there. If you think for a second that room is full, you're trying to hide something from me. Do I need to come up there myself?" Not wanting him to see the mess we'd made, and especially not wanting the consequences of what would happen if he did, Iban and I had urgently insisted that no, no, it wasn't necessary for him to help with the unit. The night that conversation happened we had stayed up until dawn unpacking and repacking the whole unit until we could find a way to make the island fit. And it had, eventually, fit. He'd been right, as always.

I managed to carefully wriggle between the piles to a little space behind the crate, where there was just enough room to wedge myself in. "Okay, one, two, three!" Iban called, and we lifted the whole tower together while I used my knee to push the slightly dislodged crate on the bottom back toward Iban. Incrementally, we extruded the unmarked black crate while also lowering the stack that rested on top of it. I stood behind the pile and listened to Iban drag the crate across the concrete, unhook the latches at either end, and place the plastic lid carefully on the floor. He didn't even want to damage the lid. It was dark in the unit, whereas the hallways had been fluorescent, the light gleaming off the polished floors. My breathing sounded loud and heavy against the cardboard box inches from my face.

"Not this one!" Iban called. I stretched my arms as best I could and tried to suppress the feeling of being buried alive. We carefully strained to remove another crate. I listened as Iban unclipped the lid, and then: "Nope." We were in too deep by now to change our approach. When we finally got the next one out, I pinned myself against the boxes behind me, just trying to rest, feeling like I might pass out. "These are them, I think," Iban said. I craned my neck to peek through the crack between the boxes. He was pulling out piles of folded pastel sweaters, pale yellow, green, and pink. I crawled out of the stacks and stood with Iban in the hall, breathing heavily. We looked at the crates in the hall, then back into the storage unit. Iban's arms were akimbo, sweat beading on his forehead. "How the fuck are we going to put these back in, genius?"

It took until just before dawn to take the whole pile safely out of the unit, then put the crates, which were too heavy to go on top of everything else, back in on the bottom, followed by the whole rest of the pile. Then, after closing and locking up the unit, we had to drive the U-Haul back to Ninety-third Street to look for parking, which was nonexistent in the early morning. We both knew that if Larry ever asked us to take anything else out of the storage unit, which he inevitably would, we'd have to go through the exact same thing all over again. Besides that, if

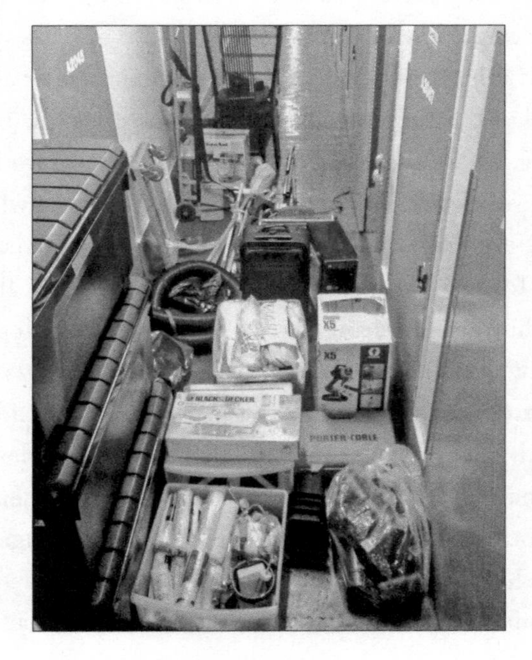

Larry noticed it had taken us all night to get some sweaters, it was impossible to know what kind of trouble we would be in.

As I nodded at the doorman and took the elevator up to 15, I realized I didn't even know where Iban was staying. I was so tired and glazed over I felt like I was drifting more than walking, but I had a vague feeling I'd like to watch the sunrise, the way I used to in England. I let the elevator pass 15 and take me all the way up to 45. The roof had a clubhouse area Talia and Isabella had told me about, but I'd been too busy to check it out this whole time. When I was in the apartment with nothing to do, my job was to wait for Larry to come out, and if I wasn't there ready for him, I'd be in trouble. Even when I was locked out of the apartment I would get in trouble if I did anything but wait, and if I missed the moment someone came to the door, I might be stuck waiting longer. Right now, though, no one would know what I did or didn't do.

The rooftop clubhouse was glass on every side. Sliding doors opened onto the roof, and there were some couches and a Ping-Pong table. The sky all around looked clean, and clear, as if the city was a dirty iceberg that had turned over to reveal its pure, glass underside. I walked to the window opposite the elevator and watched the sun come trembling up over the horizon, a spasming red coal just pulled out of a fire. I stared until I couldn't stand it anymore, blinking back tears. I wanted it, I wanted to take it all in, but I couldn't have it. It wasn't mine. Nothing was. Suddenly, I felt trapped in the glass box, with nowhere to go but down. In only a few hours I'd have to go up to Sarah Lawrence with Isabella for class. Maybe I could get a nap in before then. As I took the elevator back to the fifteenth floor, I reminded myself to water Talia's new avocado tree, which she'd planted from a seed. The pot was huge, and I resented the floor space it took up, where I could have slept, or put something that otherwise had to go to the storage unit. Larry had said if I killed the tree, he'd kill me. I walked through the door, pushing the painter's plastic aside, and I felt like the dawn had burned everything out of me. I filled the watering can in the sink, then watered the tree. I tried to water it just enough so that it would be undeniable I had done it, but not too much so that someone could say I was trying to drown the plant. I collapsed into the couch, still fully dressed. I'd have to rush out in an hour to move Larry's car anyway.

⊣⊢

The moment the bedroom door cracked open, I was getting up for the second time in an hour. Larry and Felicia came out, followed by Isabella, rubbing her eyes and stretching with a loud yawn. Talia had come in sometime while I was asleep and was stationed at the dining table, working on what I assumed were law school applications. Her plan to apply to law school was beginning to consume everything, and Larry had all of us researching schools and application processes, sending each other forms and all the advice we could track down online.

Larry plopped down on the loveseat and opened his laptop, then looked at me. "Danny, come sit next to me while we have some breakfast. I want to talk to you about something. Look at this," he said, indicating something on his laptop. It was a spreadsheet, a list of websites, some numbers I barely registered before he turned it away. "That's how much I'm making on this domain stuff. You know I started looking at this while you were in England. For a while GoDaddy was really fucking me, not to mention Time Warner, but I know more than most of the technicians over there anyway. Look here–what do you think that is?"

"I'm not sure. Another domain site?"

"Looks as good as GoDaddy, right?"

"Yeah, I'd say so. Totally." The page that came up looked like the kind of website you land on when you accidentally type in 'googggle .com' or something. I couldn't tell him that.

"See, Iz, I told you!" he yelled. "He couldn't tell any difference between GoDomainia and GoDaddy!"

"What, Lawrence?" Isabella called from the kitchen. I heard pans clattering. I'd wanted to be as uninvolved in the kitchen as I could manage, which is why I'd started helping with the storage unit in the first place.

"I kept thinking about you over there in England, working on your writing. Poetry is nice, Danny, but what are you going to do with it? What are you going to feed your kids? Bowls of poems?"

I looked over at Felicia, who was researching law schools for Talia on her computer. "I mean, no. I guess not. There are funded grad school programs for poetry my teachers have mentioned. I thought I'd look into that."

"Imagine yourself ten years from now. You could be making a million dollars a year working with me. Getting websites up and running, selling domains, helping me out here and there, most of your time free and your own; you could help me more with the woodworking stuff we've got going. We've made progress, haven't we?"

I looked around. I had no idea how long it'd been since Larry had started woodworking. Now there was a thousand-pound band saw in the corner. So far, we'd only built a shelf for the printer. We'd gotten partway through a wooden filing cabinet before there was another emergency: Larry discovered that someone had stolen his Patek Philippe watch, which he said was worth $70,000, a sum I couldn't even conceive of, and so that project never got finished. "Yeah, totally. We definitely have," I said.

He turned back to his work, so I sat back on the couch, pulled my backpack out from where it was tucked in the corner, and started looking through it for class. I needed to find a poem I could use for workshop. I pulled up the most recent one I'd written.

> My brain is like this apartment.
> It's not mine, it's someone else's.
> I live here rent-free
> with three other people.
>
> There are doors I don't open,
> rooms I keep closed and hidden.
> There used to be a blueprint
> but someone keeps changing it.
>
> Everyone who lives here is trying
> their best to do nothing.

We keep losing things,
then we find them changed.

He is probably god,
the guy who runs this place.
I am pretty sure he knows
what everything is.

I closed the document. That one was no good. Isabella was packing up her stuff, so I did, too. I would figure something else out for class.

—ıı—

My poetry workshop happened to be in Slonim House, the building at the end of the Slonim Woods path. I also had a meeting planned with Angela, my freshman-year literature teacher. Since we'd come up early for Isabella's morning class, I had some extra time. Larry had given her a hundred dollars before we left, some of which she'd dispensed to me, so I headed for the dining hall, where I figured I could camp out and have unlimited access to food while I waited for class. I wound through the middle of campus, the mossy hills carved by walking paths, the little stone tearoom in the center, enormous elm trees thrusting haphazardly out of the ground in a way that seemed, somehow, particularly like New England. Near the dining hall, the path became so steep you had to hold on to the handrail to keep from pitching forward. I descended past the gigantic arching glass windows set in the brick building, and once I was inside I paid for a meal pass and found a seat in the back. I sat at my table with a green apple and tried to finish reading the poetry collection I'd been assigned. The class was focused on contemporary, experimental poetry, most of which seemed irreverent and surreal, as if it encountered substance at oblique angles and only by accident. I was on a poem called "Mutually Assured Childhood Molestation," which began:

We assume most people weren't molested
as children, but what if they were?
All of them—

And it was such a scarring experience
that no one remembers. After all
aren't the most disturbing things
the ones most likely to be blocked out
by the psyche?

Doesn't seem to be much of a poem at all, I thought to myself. *Besides, most people* were *molested as children.* I knew this from hearing my friends admit as much when they were talking to Larry, and he would make the point, every time, that this type of abuse was more common than anyone acknowledged. It was just hidden at the bottom of the deep, dark, inscrutable wells of their memories. Talia and her sister, Ava, had been molested by their mom, after all, and it had taken them a long time to admit that to their dad. I had even started to wonder if *I'd* been molested when I was younger. Maybe that was the explanation for why I felt so sad and empty so much of the time. After reading for a while, I checked the time on my phone with a start, then stuffed my book into my bag and walked back up the hill and across campus for my meeting.

—ıı—

Angela's office jutted from the side of Lynd House, which was otherwise a student dorm. It wasn't unusual for professors' offices and classrooms to occupy the same buildings as dorms, so I couldn't tell if the girl who was sitting on the stone wall that encircled the little patio outside was waiting for a conference or for some friend who lived inside. I sat a little ways down the wall, putting the gigantic beech tree that leaned over the patio between us. A strange, enormous knot, a pregnant ball of twisting, malformed bark hung off the side halfway up the trunk.

Through the office window, I could see Angela talking with a younger student. I couldn't hear anything, but from Angela's gesticulation it looked as if the student was in trouble. I wondered if this kid might be going through something similar to what I'd been going through freshman year, when I was in Angela's class. Maybe they were feeling confused and overwhelmed, like their whole life was too big to wrap their arms around. I remembered meeting with Angela in my first semester in college, desperately hoping she wouldn't realize I hadn't read the story we were discussing, that I hadn't even understood how to get it from the library. Then I'd showed her that poem about my mom, she'd sat with me for an hour just talking about family, and everything had changed—the first evidence in my life that opening up yielded positive results. Now that my final semester was around the corner and graduation was looming, I wanted to thank her for turning things around.

The office door opened, and the student slinked out. Angela looked around the patio for who was next. She saw me and waved excitedly. I waved back, and then pointed to the student who'd been sitting on the wall before me, who rushed into Angela's office with a paper held out. I watched them, slightly blurred by the screen window, as Angela signed something and handed it to the girl, who ran back out. Angela popped back around the doorway. "Come in! Come in!" she exclaimed, gesturing to the seat across from hers. "Donnees, you know. How is Dennis, by the way?"

Dennis was my don, the teacher of my first poetry class at Sarah Lawrence. "He's doing well, I think. He's teaching a new first-year studies this year."

"I really don't know him, but we spoke briefly at some faculty meeting or other. What is your sense of him? He had those particular watery blue eyes if I recall. He was an awfully gentle-seeming man."

"Yeah, he's super nice. I'm really lucky to have him as a don." The shadows swayed as the wind moved through the tree outside. "Do you know what's going on with that tree?"

She craned her neck to look out the window at the strange, crusty-looking lump hanging off the tree. "It's a burl, dear. Like cancer for a tree. They're on the beech trees all over campus, unfortunately. I fear some kind of disease has been spreading across the campus over the past couple years."

We sat there for a second watching the tree lean in the wind. I wished I could just keep watching it and never say anything. I was removed from the room by many degrees. "I wanted to thank you for your notes on my dissertation in England," I said finally. "They were so helpful."

"Oh yes, of course! I found it very exciting. It reminded me of D. H. Lawrence, the energy and dynamism of it, the persistently recurring natural images. It reminded me of *The Turn of the Screw* also, which I know you had trouble with in class, but which, clearly, you took something from. That overarching sense of oppression, and repression, how the world infects the self or vice versa. What is hidden, and how it refuses to remain hidden. I've been working on a project for this book, actually, *Écritures de Femmes*." She pulled a purple paperback volume off her desk and held it out to me. "You would get something out of it, I think. So much of your writing seems concerned with the mind, the permeable boundary between self and other. And, of course, what is *sub*liminal, rather than just liminal. Oh, tell me, Dan, I had meant to ask you—what do you think the difference is between poetry and prose?"

"Oh . . . I'm really not sure."

"I saw a lecture recently in which the speaker said there was no difference. That poetry is only prose with breaks in the lines. She seemed an utter fool to me. Your dissertation was fascinating, of course, in the way it excised the ligamentation we're accustomed to in prose, the tissue that connects story elements. This seems fundamental to poetry, the images hung there like beads. In prose, perhaps, the beads are strung together in a necklace, whereas in poetry there is no string. Does that resonate? It fascinates me, this poetic approach, wherein so much remains hidden, while the work appears to be exposed. This is of course similar to the eroticism of someone wearing, say, a dress, as opposed to someone who is entirely nude. The implicit unsaid is necessary, perhaps inherent even, to the arousal of the reader; it is the source of a story's allure." She crossed and uncrossed her legs. I let the book she'd given me fall open in my lap. It was all in French, and the margins were full of her notes, also in French, lengthy and complicated. "Would you like to borrow it?" she asked.

I found myself saying yes, though I wasn't sure why. I'd started taking Beginning French this semester, as a senior, mainly to complete

Sarah Lawrence's language requirement, and also because my mom spoke it. I'd thought it might be a way to connect. This book was obviously far above my head. Nonetheless, I didn't know how to say no, and it felt desperately important that I not disappoint Angela, so I slipped the book into the recesses of my bag.

"I think often about your essay on *Pale Horse, Pale Rider* and the theory you drew up about the operation of light in that story. We know, of course, that light, in literature, frequently symbolizes knowledge–that which is known. But in that story, the points you made about how light appears to gesture toward the danger of certain *types* of knowledge–that sometimes full appraisal of reality leads to madness–fabulous. Dan, I don't know if you ever knew this, actually. Did you know that I was going to retire the year you took my class?" I shook my head. The first half of freshman year in Angela's class I was asleep more than I was awake. By the end of the year, though, I was doing all the homework and participating in every discussion. I'd spent more time on that *Pale Horse, Pale Rider* essay than I'd spent on maybe anything in my life. "Working with you that year reminded me why I love teaching. I ended up delaying my retirement because of it, in fact. To see that transformation was incredibly inspiring. I knew from the beginning that there was something waiting to come out. I could see it in your eyes."

"Wow, Angela. I don't know what to say. I actually came here to thank you for that year. I don't think I was even really fully conscious before your class, or at least not conscious of literature. It's like I didn't even know what books were, and then you gave them to me. What could be a better gift, right?"

"I think that origami swan you gave me at the end of the year was more than enough thanks,'" she said. "I keep it in a place of honor in my house." I could hear the breeze through the open door, shuffling the leaves like they were sheets of paper.

We continued talking like that until it was time for me to leave. Clouds had gathered, and I instinctively ducked as I stepped out of Angela's office; a light autumn rain had begun to fall. Some of my classmates were waiting outside Slonim House, smoking cigarettes beneath the eaves of the roof. I sat on a wall that ran alongside the art building and watched them from across the lawn. *There is so much they don't know. So much they're missing out on.* I had to write a poem, anything, quickly for class. That morning I'd read online about a guy who had taken a weather balloon up to the edge of space and jumped off it, 128,000 kilometers back to earth, setting a record for the highest free fall in history. I stared down at my notebook. *How do you make the choice to step out into the thin air? How do you know you won't just float, and be pulled into the abyss at your back?* I wrote a little poem about it, and when I looked up, my classmates were starting to drift into the building, so I walked over to join them.

⊣⊢

After class, I filed out with everyone else into the saturated afternoon, the rain over but still hanging, somehow, in the air. As I walked carefully on the path slick with leaves, my phone buzzed in my pocket. Iban was on the other end, and I could hear the militaristic terseness in his voice. He had a tendency to treat me like his direct report. "Do you know where Izzy is? You need to find her and get back here. Now."

"I'm not sure, but I can try to track her down. Why, what's going on?" He sounded out of breath.

"I'm going to another pharmacy right now to find activated charcoal. Felicia tried to kill herself. Just get back here."

⊣⊢

It felt like it took forever for Isabella to answer the phone. When she finally did with an annoyed, "What?!" and I told her what was going on, she sighed. "Okay, let's go back then, I guess." We took a cab to the train station in Bronxville, then the Metro-North down to Harlem, then the subway to the Upper East Side. As we passed through the Harlem station, I thought about how incensed Larry had been that Isabella would take these subways at night on her own. He wanted her to take cabs but she'd still go to these supposedly dangerous neighborhoods, and make a point of letting Larry know. For a while he'd confiscated her cellphone, but she'd still disappear all night anyway, and his face would contort with anger as she called from pay phones across the city. He would talk about how she was spun up again, just trying to get attention from him, and we would spend all night uselessly trying to track her down before she would eventually return to the apartment on her own.

When we got back, everyone was gathered around Felicia, who was lying on the couch, vomiting a black substance into a bowl that Santos held. What looked like strings of wilted spinach suspended in mucus were coming out of her. She coughed and sputtered, looking weak. Larry was standing in the middle of the room. "You happy now, Iz? You still think Felicia doesn't need my help? Iban was barely even able to find charcoal in time."

Iban looked flushed. He was sitting on the floor near Santos, and glanced up at us sharply. "Yeah, while you guys were all off at school, I was running around the city. She could have died."

"It's their job to go to school right now," Larry said. "As long as they're not so screwed up that they'll hurt themselves, too. Santos was at least smart enough to know he had to take a medical leave." Isabella rolled her eyes and stomped into the bedroom. "Just keep her head elevated," Larry said, and then he charged into the bedroom after Isabella and slammed the door.

When Isabella and I were riding down to the city, I'd wondered if this was all a ruse, if no one had actually tried to commit suicide, if we were just being drawn back to the apartment for another made-up emergency. Now I wondered how I could be so selfish, so evil in my thinking. Felicia laid back on the couch and Santos placed the bowl on the floor. He looked thin, drained out. "Turn on the TV or something, would you, Dan?" he asked me. His voice sounded strange, confident but wavering on the edges.

I grabbed the remote. *What channel do you put on when someone is recovering from a suicide attempt?* The channel guide was scrolling upward on the bottom half of the screen, and in the top right corner was a weather report. Apparently, a hurricane was approaching. The meteorologist was projecting record levels of damage across the Northeast. I thought about my parents, living in their house deep in the woods. The chyron scrolling across the bottom of the screen said flights were canceled in preparation for Hurricane Sandy, which would make landfall soon.

—ı⊢—

A few days later, I lay in bed on my back, staring up into the darkness of my childhood bedroom again. I'd come home at my parents' urging. The storm was so loud and the dark so stubbornly total that it felt hard to tell if I was inside or outside. The whole house creaked and shifted to one side as the rain changed direction, battering against a new set of windows. I worried the huge, ancient oak tree outside my room might fall right through the roof. I closed my eyes. It sounded like I was at sea—the branches clawing at the glass were sirens trying to get on board; the creaking, ripping crash of trees as they lost their grip on the earth were other ships collapsing beneath the waves; the shuddering booms of branches hitting the ground nearby were cannon fire splintering the deck beneath me.

I opened my eyes again and it was morning. Droplets of water were plunking onto the roof and running down my window, catching the light. I unknotted myself from the sheets and crawled over to look. Outside was devastation—the yard littered with huge fallen branches and whole trees. *I wonder how they're doing at the apartment.* Isabella had been making runs to the grocery store to stock up when I left. The government had listed the apartment in a flood zone because it was near the East River, which was part of why my parents had insisted I come home. I'd thought Larry would want me to stay and help out, but again he'd encouraged me to go. "It's a good thing to do, Danny. Go," he'd said, and insisted on giving me some money to take with me. I'd felt almost insulted that I was not indispensable.

—ı⊢—

The water and power stayed out for over a week, and there was no way to get back into the city, so I was stuck at home. I could be a good son, watch TV at night with my parents, join them on trips to Dunkin' Donuts for coffee or to the gym for something to do during the day instead of spending time alone in my room or out in the woods, having negative thoughts. It was easy, if you just didn't think about it, and instead thought about what would make the people around you happy. They wanted me to be in a good mood, and to do the things they wanted to do. I was, and I did. Life was easier this way, when everyone was happy. Sarah Lawrence had postponed classes during the storm, but they would be back in session soon, which meant that I'd have to return to New York, and to the apartment.

I borrowed my mom's car, figuring that before I had to go back, I might as well stop at the gorge, the river nearby where I'd been going for walks with my parents since I was a little kid. I couldn't figure out how to turn off the radio, so it crackled quietly in the background. The car was a stick shift and I was occupied with changing gears as I managed the steep hills and fallen branches. I drove until the road turned to dirt, then parked. A few feet away from the edge of the road, the river was raging, frothing so hard it looked rabid. There was one other car parked. I hopped out and retied my scarf around my neck. There was nothing wrong with this. A perfectly reasonable, brisk walk in which I'd appreciate nature. Larry would approve.

It was getting cold out, enough so that there were frozen patches in the mud that would melt by this afternoon. I stepped over the chain, which had a ROAD CLOSED sign hanging from it. As I came around the first bend, I saw the road was completely washed out—all that was left were boulders that must have been hidden beneath the packed dirt. I clambered over them and continued on, the river exploding alongside me. Two huge fishermen came walking toward me on their way back to the parking area. They nodded as they passed. One was missing his arm below the elbow, the sleeve of his shirt, poking out from behind his waders, held closed with a rubber band. I was coming close now, I knew, to the midpoint of the trail, where the abandoned train trestle passed over the river, the water widened out, and it would be calmer. *If that other car belonged to those fishermen,* I thought, *then I am totally alone.*

I slid down the bank to the edge of the river, and, without thinking, began to strip off my clothes. I shivered, my skin electrified by the cold as I stepped into the dark water, feeling the stones that lined the bottom with my bare, swiftly numbing toes. I crept in deeper and leaned into the force of the current, until I was far enough that even if I heard someone coming down the path and decided to turn back, they would have plenty of time to see me, naked, standing in the rushing current. Circles began appearing on the water, a few at first, then more and more. The rain was almost warm against the cool air, the freezing river. I stared up into the white sky, which was cut in half by the train trestle, blinking against the raindrops, and felt proud of myself. After so long, I was not afraid of anything.

16

I WAS WRONG.

It was well past midnight now, which meant that it was technically Thanksgiving, and the carpet I was kneeling on felt like it was making direct contact with my nerves. I was a skeleton dragging around a body, a wisp of soul, weak and worn out, draped in a thin, flowery dress that Isabella had fetched from the bedroom at Larry's request. I tried to get the smears of light through the fogged windows to resolve into individual points, and couldn't. There was filet mignon in the oven, sauce on the stove, which Larry presently sent Santos to stir. "You're keeping the lid half on, right?" Larry asked as he returned.

"Maybe I'd better check," Santos said, turning around and going right back into the kitchen again. Santos had been doing better as a result of hard work and relentless kowtowing. Larry and Isabella looked shimmery sitting on the couch in front of me. Maybe my eyes were just watering. Maybe I had meant what I said. It had still been wrong.

—⊣⊢—

I tried to track back through the night, to understand how I'd arrived here, what misstep I'd made. Larry had sent me and Isabella to Fairway with a long list for Thanksgiving. When we'd come home, Larry had rifled through the bags immediately, as if he knew before we walked in that something was missing. He'd started yelling into the bags, as if interrogating the groceries themselves: "Where's the duck fat? Danny, where are the herbs de Provence?" He was hunting, actually digging through the groceries like an animal trained for this, with the scent of terror on his nose. "Are you kidding me, Danny? Where are they?" Isabella was looking at me with an eyebrow raised. I thought I'd been totally on top of it.

"He wanted to get a tiny turkey, too, the cheapest, but I took care of that," Isabella said.

"You didn't want us all to have turkey? You've got eight people here, Danny. Why were you trying to prevent people from having a nice Thanksgiving dinner? You definitely knew, you *knew,* that I can't make the Thanksgiving turkey without duck fat and seasoning. You've really sabotaged things for me now." He'd sounded genuinely pained at the time, and I'd felt genuinely bad for hurting him. I hadn't meant to. *Is he testing me again? Why would he do this now?* "Why would you do this to me? Why did you have to sabotage Thanksgiving, Danny?"

Then he'd made me sit down in the middle of the living room, and everyone had filed into their spots, lining the couches. The conversation had seemed interminable, and at some point in the middle, Larry had taken a break to start making pasta sauce and a roast. So I'd known then that I was in for many more hours. And as Larry had shown Santos how to watch the pot, keep the lid half on, stir occasionally, I'd realized that Santos and I were swapping spots on the bottom. Someone had to be causing all the problems, but now Santos was doing better, so it had to be someone—and that person was me. I tried to skip a few steps ahead, knowing what had brought the conversation to its conclusion the last time things seemed to be going this way, and I blurted out, "I still think I might be gay!"

Larry's face had twisted with even more anger. That was when he'd told Isabella to get one of her dresses, saying, "I'm putting an end to this." I felt desperate. I wanted so badly to tell the capital-T *Truth,* like Larry wanted us to. This was it. The truer than truth. Or at least it was something that confused me still. That was worth exploring, right?

"Look at yourself, Danny. How does it feel to wear a dress? Are you still confused? Is this who you want to be all the time? Really, do, look at yourself."

I looked down at the flowery fabric spilling over my legs. "I'm sorry, I don't know. I don't know."

His eyes could be soft sometimes. Now they were like hard crystals glistening back at me out of an otherwise dark and treacherous cave. "Let's see about that. Iban, Santos, why doesn't Danny do something for us, for once, and get the mail. I think he could use some help. Bring him downstairs."

Iban and Santos hopped up with a couple of manly grunts and grabbed me by the upper arms, lifting me to my feet. Nothing was working in my body, so they had to half-carry me out the door. I could feel their hard fingers digging into my flesh. We stood in the gleaming gold light of the elevator, and I felt oddly close to them. The air was cold on my legs. I'd never worn a dress before. I felt embarrassed because I knew I was supposed to feel embarrassed. In the lobby, my shame spread to Santos and Iban, as if suddenly, in public, things felt different, and they realized how this might look. The floor of the lobby was jade marble. The mailboxes were around the corner from the elevators, so we didn't have to spend too much time in the main room, which would be empty anyway, since it was the middle of the night. The doorman spared only an extra moment to stare at us before returning his gaze to his desk.

In front of the mailboxes, a wall of bronze hatches, there was an unspoken awareness shared between the three of us. We all had to agree, without saying anything, that Santos and Iban had participated in this punishment correctly, to the degree that Larry would not see them as complicit, as saboteurs, but not necessarily to the degree that they had to be cruel, or go any further than was necessary. Iban let go of my arm to open the mailbox, so I slumped a little against Santos. The fact that outdoors there was a sidewalk, a city, millions of people, was inconceivable. I didn't consider running, because that was impossible, but I tried imagining it: bare feet slapping the freezing concrete of Ninety-third Street as I sprint to Second Avenue, the utter emptiness of the hours past midnight, the wind cutting through my dress, no money for the subway or a cab, no idea where to find help, no cellphone, Iban and Santos racing behind me because, having run, I'd have broken our unspoken pact, exposing them to even worse punishment.

Even if I did get away, what then? Surely, if I just got through this, here, in the warm lobby, the end must be soon, an end that meant it was all worth it, that I hadn't made a mistake coming here, tying my destiny to Larry. The more painful it was, the more sure I was that I was nearing clarity. I pulled out the few envelopes that were in the mailbox. I wanted to laugh at how stupid this whole performance was, how surreal, but I knew I couldn't. Was it just me who was pretending? Was I pretending? Or was I actually terrified? I started looking through the letters without thinking—for what, I didn't know, names I recognized, something for me—when Iban snatched them out of my hand. "What the hell are you doing?"

—⊣⊢—

Back upstairs, Iban and Larry debriefed on how it had gone in the lobby. I wondered what Isabella, Talia, and Felicia had done while we were gone. "Someone needs to stir the sauce," I said weakly. I worried I'd get in even more trouble if my failure to confess ended up ruining the meal. Larry's face looked like a wrecking ball but his voice was surprisingly gentle, encouraging even.

"You don't need to worry about that, Danny." He gave Iban a sign to go tend to the pot. "Are you sure you're straight now?"

I shook my head before I knew I was doing it. I couldn't help myself anymore; I was stripped down to nothing, and my brain was no longer in charge. "Danny, do you understand what you're saying? Maybe I should send you down to the Toolbox, and then you can really figure this out."

Isabella laughed. "Yeah! Send him to the Toolbox!" The Toolbox was the gay bar around the corner.

"Danny, do you know what would happen? Some guy would pick you up, like that, see you, innocent straight boy, and he'd take you back to his apartment or wherever in the Village, and he'd fuck you, and he'd get his friends to come and fuck you, and what I think you don't understand, Danny, is that that would be it for you." My chin was drifting to my chest; I let the gray carpet fill my field of vision. Larry clapped his hands together and it sounded like a gunshot. "I have plenty of friends who are gay, this isn't about that. I am telling you that you are not gay, but if you go down that path out of *fear,* you will never come back. You will stay afraid, and you will never become who you are actually meant to be. You see? Isabella, get one of your dildos for me."

Isabella bounced up off the couch cushion. "Oh yeah, I'm going to get the big one." She headed back into the bedroom, and while she was rustling around in there, Larry ran his hand over his bare scalp, staring at me. As he laid his arm across the couch, behind Felicia's head, I looked at the muscle pulsating under his skin. I'd seen him demonstrate a sleeper hold on Santos to show us how he would put people out during countless intelligence operations. Right there was the soft pocket of Larry's elbow where Santos's jugular and windpipe had fit, the bicep and forearm that had expanded like balloons. It had taken only seconds, just like Larry had said. Isabella came back holding a gigantic black dildo that wobbled and leaned to one side in her hand.

"Give it to Danny," Larry said. I took it from her. It felt surprisingly hard in my hand for something that didn't stand up straight. "Now, Danny, let's settle this once and for all. You're going to put that in your ass, and if you like it, we'll know you're gay. Simple enough, right?"

Iban leaned forward, his elbows on his knees, like this was no different from what he'd seen on base. "Makes perfect sense to me," he said. I tried to breathe. This was just another test I could pass. Everything paused for a moment. I could choose how to react. *I'll* choose *to seem horrified, and dismayed, even though I'm actually not, because nothing bad is actually happening. Bad doesn't exist.*

I watched myself try to reach up the dress with the dildo in my hand, struggling to figure out how to do it. I heard, muffled as if through a wall, Larry saying that I needed to put my legs over my head, unless I was trying to sabotage even further. Then I watched myself sit back on the base of my spine and slowly bring my legs up in the air. I watched Iban and Isabella laughing, acting disgusted at seeing a part of my body I couldn't recall ever having seen myself. Just acting. Nothing is good or bad. It all sounded far away and cottony until I heard the sound of a phone camera shutter so close it might as well have been in my ear. There on Larry's face I could see it: He was grossed out too, but also a little gleeful, at how pathetic I looked. It was all a joke. I was a joke. His silver flip phone was held out in his arm, full extension, as far from his face as it could go, as if he didn't want to see what was captured in the tiny rectangle of his phone screen—and then I realized it would be me in there, pressing a dildo the size of my forearm up against my asshole, legs over my head in a floral-print dress, and then suddenly: That is what's happening. To me. I am doing that. The sound and feeling came rushing back in all at once, the sobs heaving, the taste of salty snot running out of my nose and onto my lip. I felt the tension in my arm, how tired it was from holding the heavy dildo and acting upon the nervous impulse from my brain that said, *push this dildo into your own asshole,* but it wasn't me who gave the command anymore; it was Larry.

"All right, Danny, that's enough. Is this what you want?" I shook my head. "No, that's right, it's not. You make things way too complicated, you understand? All of you." He looked around now. "You're all extremely intelligent, and therefore especially capable of convincing yourselves of almost anything. Danny's not gay, we all know that, right?" They were all nodding their heads. "This was all so simple. How the hell did we get here, with you bringing up you think you might be gay? Tomorrow"—he looked at his watch—"today is Thanksgiving. When the stores open you go and try to get what you forgot, right? It's that easy. Fix your mistake. Go get yourself dressed." I was nodding now, and started to pull the dress off right there on the carpet. "Danny, in the bedroom or something. Jesus, what's wrong with him?"

I gathered up my things in my numb fingers and walked as best I could to the bedroom. Claudia had given me a shirt that had the cover of the book *Catch-22* across the front as a late birthday present. I'd told her that it was my favorite book, she said. I didn't know how to tell her I'd never read *Catch-22,* much less called it my favorite book. But maybe I had. I didn't know. I knew the basic concept of what it meant: something you can't get out of, because trying to get out of it gets you deeper in. You're stuck, fucked both ways. I wondered, only for a moment, if it was a secret message she was sending me. There was no way to find out. There never would be.

I stayed in there as long as I could without them saying I was up to something. The bedroom was mostly off-limits nowadays. When I came back out, everyone was getting ready to go to sleep–Isabella on the couch, Santos in the loveseat, Iban on the floor, and Larry, Felicia, and Talia headed for the bedroom. I guessed Larry had given the go-ahead for the day to end. "Get yourself some pasta," Larry said, indicating the pot on the stovetop. "The sauce is good." I did as he said, filling a wide white bowl with the rigatoni noodles, which looked like the disconnected segments of some oversized worm. As I walked across the room to the space in the far corner, Larry said to Iban, "The car is in a good spot for tomorrow, right? Let Danny take your car, okay? He's going to need it."

Iban nodded officiously from where he lay on the floor. The lights went out. As I tried the best I could to eat pasta I couldn't see, Iban's voice came out of the darkness: "It's a meal, not an orchestra, Dan."

"Sorry," I said, and tried to eat more carefully, managing even my breaths between bites, so that I might disappear totally into the silence of the apartment.

⊣⊢

Fairway was still closed a few hours later, it being Thanksgiving morning, as was the Williams Sonoma uptown, which happened to carry duck fat and herbs de Provence. I was sitting in Iban's old BMW. The bright morning light inside the car was strange, tinted by the dark windows, and the ancient LED center console cast everything orange. The salesperson on the phone told me that the Williams Sonoma downtown was, in fact, open. I'd gotten up early, hoping to erase last night as best I could before anyone else woke up. I couldn't stop thinking about spring semester coming up, just a couple months away, when I might get on-campus housing. What if Larry said, as he had with Santos, that I couldn't handle being on campus, that all my sabotage was evidence I was deeply unwell, and I needed to take leave? How would I explain that to my parents?

I turned the key in Iban's car, and the engine sputtered, then purred. I'd gotten used to driving in Manhattan. Larry had me drive him around a lot of the time now, ever since he'd stopped hiring the limo. I guessed that would probably change, now that I wasn't trustworthy. Once, he'd even had me drive him down to Washington, D.C., where he'd introduced me to his friend Chuck Pitman, a marine lieutenant general. On the way down there Larry had regaled me with tales of how Chuck had been a helicopter pilot, how once he'd even flown his helicopter to New Orleans, against orders, to kill a sniper holed up on a rooftop whom the police couldn't reach. When we actually arrived in D.C., I met the marine general for only a moment before Larry sent me back down to the car. He had turned out to be elderly and seemed confused.

Another time, Larry had me and Iban drive him to Hoboken to pick up his prescription. He'd always said we all had attention deficit disorder, but not as bad as Talia's, and nowhere near as bad as his own. No regular human brain could possibly handle the intensity of the ADD that racked Larry's brain, he said, which was why he required such large doses of dextroamphetamine. It made sense that he had to pick up his pills in such a sketchy fashion, I'd thought as we pulled up to the unmarked brick building in Hoboken and he sent Iban around the corner to pick them up. With the conspiracy against him, he'd never gotten health insurance. It also could have to do with some intelligence agency thing. Maybe Larry had to stay in the car to protect himself, given all the people who must have been after him. One time, as I was driving everyone up to Bronxville, I'd been checking the GPS on my phone, and out of nowhere pain shot through my wrists, so sudden and extreme that I'd dropped my phone in the footwell. Larry's hand, a blur as he'd karate chopped me, was already back on his armrest. It was a relief, this Thanksgiving morning, despite the circumstances, to be driving alone.

I stopped at the Williams Sonoma on Sixteenth, parking illegally out on Seventh Avenue, and ran inside to grab the ingredients. It was all remarkably easy—simple, as Larry had said. Why had I made it so hard on myself last night? It wasn't Larry who'd stressed me out, it was me. As I sat in the car, duck fat and herbs safely next to me in the passenger seat, I decided to give my parents a quick call for Thanksgiving. I'd been calling them every day since Hurricane Sandy. The idea was to keep them happy—if I could just get to the end of the program with Larry, there was no reason things had to be uncomfortable or difficult with Mom and Dad.

As usual, they answered together, a single unit, my dad mostly talking, Mom in the background, occasionally shouting something I could barely make out. I started the car, planning to drive back across to the east side via Sixteenth. As I pulled out into the avenue, my parents saying something I couldn't quite hear, the sun glinted across Iban's tinted windshield, everything turned white, there was the sound of tires screeching on pavement, and the BMW rocked hard to the side. "I've got to go," I said to my parents, and hung up without explanation. I glanced up through the windshield at the upset-looking man standing outside his dented Mercedes-Benz, who then stalked over to me.

I rolled down the window. I didn't know what to do, and was pretty sure I was going to be killed for this when I got back to the apartment. I had been so close. It was obviously true, Larry was right—I was broken. I needed fixing. The man was yelling something. My throat pinched like a hose, pressure building behind it. I gave the man Iban's phone number, explained that it wasn't my car and I didn't have insurance but I was sure Iban did. I got out of the car and looked at his, which was dented, then back at Iban's. The BMW was scraped up the side. I could have thrown myself into traffic. That would be easier. Safer. I didn't know how insurance worked, how anything worked.

The man said he would take his car to a mechanic and call Iban for the insurance information, and since it was Thanksgiving and he was in a rush himself, he wouldn't call the cops. After he left, I crouched down and desperately rubbed at the scrape, hoping it was just paint, but it wasn't just paint. I got back into the car, sat in the dark leather of Iban's seats, inserted the key, and prayed it would drive. It did. I tried to ignore a scraping sound that seemed like it was coming from right underneath me. I took the car uptown, and once I parked it, I sat there, imagining myself, my whole body, covered in metal that could crumple when hit, but would protect the soft leather inside, and the little person who sat in there turning the wheel.

—ıı—

"I'll take care of this guy," Larry said, one hand stretching the skin of the raw thirty-pound turkey, the other deep underneath, rubbing around a glob of duck fat he had clawed out of the jar. I could see the outline of his hand moving around under the second layer of skin. "Iban, you send me his number. Danny, don't worry about it. Some guy thinks he can mess with us, I'll show you how we take care of this." When I'd gotten back from downtown and told them about the accident, Larry hadn't seemed fazed. He only cared about the duck fat. Anything else was inconsequential.

I'd felt like I could collapse from either exhaustion or relief, I couldn't tell which. I had less and less of a sense of what was happening. Time seemed to keep skipping forward. Larry had left the Williams Sonoma bag on the counter and gone back to the bathroom to work. Hours passed. I couldn't tell the difference between waking and sleeping anymore. It was evening when Larry emerged. Before I could even suggest we should probably start cooking, he was already saying, "Why don't we get a little painting done?" His smile looked simultaneously genuine and sinister. He knew that every time we had tried to paint in the past year something would go wrong, delaying any other plan by hours, days, interminably. He had to know that. Paint would clog the nozzle of the expensive sprayer he'd bought, or the compressor wouldn't work, or no one could find the painter's tape or the mineral spirits, and then a hunt would ensue followed by an interrogation of the person who had hidden the lost item on purpose. I was painfully aware that Thanksgiving, which I had almost ruined, was vanishing with every hour that passed.

Larry struggled with the paint sprayer, and then, predictably, had a meltdown as if this was the first time it had ever happened. It was the middle of the night on Thanksgiving and we had yet to even touch the turkey. Time didn't mean anything anymore. Larry gave up on the painting and finally opened the duck fat. "I've got the Hilti guys coming over tomorrow so this better get done," he said to me, manhandling the turkey, aggressively caressing it with fistfuls of herbs de Provence. "How is this going to happen, Danny, huh? Since you all delay, delay, delay and ruin my Thanksgiving? What's your plan here? What am I supposed to do?"

"Just go to sleep," I said. I was shrouded in metal.

He looked at me, and I watched the puzzlement around his eyes harden, then go cold. He took his hands out from under the turkey's skin and put them into the sink. Wiping them dry, he called through the broken wall, "Everyone go to bed. Apparently Danny's taking care of the turkey. Don't worry, he knows exactly what he's doing and he's not going to screw it up at all, is he?" Then he said to me, more quietly, "Really, Danny, this is an expensive bird. It's all ready for you. Just put it in the oven and don't forget you have to baste it. Please, don't forget, or it'll be bone dry."

"You better not fuck it up, Danel!" Isabella called through the wall.

With that, Larry headed off into the bedroom, followed by Felicia. Talia was already asleep inside. In the living room, everyone lay down where they were, and I walked around, turning off lights. I looked up on my phone how long it would take for a thirty-pound turkey to roast. Five hours. I looked out the window; it was as dark as New York gets, like a speckled plum. I would be up until sunrise again. I tried to relish the notion. I set the alarm on my phone to go off every thirty minutes to remind me to baste the turkey, then turned the phone to vibrate so it wouldn't wake anyone else up.

—⊣⊢—

Five hours later, the morning after Thanksgiving, I finally took the turkey out of the oven. It steamed on the counter. I was exhausted, my body felt leaden, but at least the turkey looked like a turkey. I stared at the juices still bubbling in the bottom of the roasting tray, then was jolted with a sickening realization. *How am I going to put this in the fridge?* I couldn't leave it on the counter for the hours that would pass before anyone woke up—Larry had always been very explicit about foodborne bacteria and how deadly it was. But I also couldn't put it in the fridge steaming hot, because Larry had explained that putting hot food in the fridge raises the overall temperature such that everything else goes bad. I had seen other people get in trouble for that before, intentionally poisoning the food in the fridge by putting something away hot.

It took almost another two hours for me to decide the turkey was cool enough to put in the fridge without endangering anyone. I looked through the broken wall at my still sleeping friends dotted here and there across the living room, swallowed by the piles of blankets that were so like little nests. I'd saved them from foodborne illness, I thought. But another idea crept in, one that was hard to ignore. It felt good, in a strange way, to take the blame for everything going wrong. I could be the one who had to carry them, for a little while.

—||—

Later that day, I stood in the same spot watching Larry sit with two guys from Kosovo who sold him Hilti power tools. Everyone else sat around in a circle. Larry had carved the turkey and was serving it to everyone with stuffing and cranberry sauce on baguettes. "Danny did a great job with the turkey, didn't he?" Larry said to the men. They had just been talking about Larry's part in ending the Kosovo War. He had insisted he would show them the signed letter of thanks he'd received, if everyone hadn't made such a mess of his apartment. "You want to hear something really crazy?" Larry asked. The men nodded with mouths full of turkey, but Larry was already halfway into the next sentence anyway. "Yesterday, Danny believed he was actually gay. Can you believe that?"

Larry burst out laughing, and the men did, too. One of them looked up from his sandwich. "He doesn't look gay," he said.

"Danny, what are you doing standing back there, come over here! Have you had any turkey yet?"

I told him I hadn't. Actually, I hadn't eaten anything since the pasta. "Make yourself something!" Larry said, and then turned back to the men who were listening again, rapt, as I knew they had to be, and Larry went on, prattling to them unceasingly about how he had saved their homeland.

17

"**DO ME A FAVOR,** Iban, grab Talia's sweaters out of that crate in the bedroom. I want her to be able to get at them for school, now that it's cold. That's the least you all could do, right? Make a little space for Tal?" Larry said, half-gagging, pressing a Kank-A pen into his gums. Iban was up and moving as purposefully as possible. A few days before, Larry had noticed that Iban's hair was combed a different way, and that was all it had taken for him to realize that Iban was secretly planning to commit suicide. His number was finally up. Eventually, when pressed, Iban admitted it. Larry had sent him downtown to commit himself to a mental institution, the only responsible thing to do, he said. But Iban had returned later that night. He'd explained everything, he said, to a panel of doctors, the ones who decide whether you need to be committed. They had said he wasn't crazy. If anything was crazy, they'd told him, it was the fact that he thought he was crazy. "Did you tell them about the hair?" Larry asked, and Iban nodded yes, he'd told them, but they'd seemed confused. What was he here for exactly, they'd asked. "You must have lied to them," Larry said, "or you're lying to me now. Any professional would hear the list of symptoms that you had, that I identified, and know that you required immediate hospitalization."

Now Iban was just trying to keep his nose clean. Everything had gotten more and more chaotic, compressed, since winter break had begun at the beginning of December. Talia's applications to law school had gone wrong–paperwork she needed her dad to sign had vanished. Now she couldn't go to Stanford, her top choice, all the way across the country in California. "It'll be more time for us here together, and I'll get this place in order, so you can have your life back. So that you can stay alive, honeygirl, first of all. Remember what all this is for," Larry said. I'd just come up from parking the car again, and while Iban looked for Talia's sweaters–a sort of minor concession–she sulked on the couch. Everyone else sat around, pretending nothing was wrong, or trying to think of ways to cheer her up.

"I've got them, Larry," Iban called from the bedroom. "You want me to bring them out?"

"Come on, Tal, let's go look at your sweaters. Let's see which ones you'll want out for the winter. Do that for me."

Talia forced a smile, and I watched them walk into the bedroom together. Through the lit-up doorway, I could see them lifting the soft, pale fabrics out of the bin, laying them out on the bed. Larry's face looked more and more screwed up, and he was gesturing, moving like something was very wrong, so jerkily it was like he'd been caught in a strobe light. "Danny, come in here," Larry said. He was baring his teeth, the muscles in his face spasmodic from exertion. I wondered about the abscess he claimed was roiling underneath his gum line. Was there really a hollow cavern of rot under there? Was the inside of his head like the rafters in my parents' house, decaying with black mold?

I followed him into the bedroom and stood over the bed. The sweaters lying on the duvet seemed to emit their own light, like cracked glow sticks, or the back end of a firefly that had just been smashed. "These are Loro Piana sweaters, Danny, you know that. This is, conservatively, twenty thousand dollars' worth of sweaters you ruined. How are you going to pay me back for this? Look at this." He held one up. It just looked like a sweater to me. "What did you do, *fold* these? Are you fucking kidding me, Danny?" There was a crease running horizontally across the sweater, a long, straight, dilated vein. "And look at all this you put on top of it." He pulled a box out of the bin and threw it across the room, where it crashed into the wall, its contents spewing onto the floor. "You know you're supposed to lay cashmere flat. I told you all about this, remember? Why would you do this to Talia?"

Talia held up a light blue sweater draped over her hands. I could see the outline of her fingers through the impossibly soft material. "I don't know . . . it's not that bad, right? Maybe we can iron it or something?"

Larry pinched the bridge of his nose. "What? No, no, no, Tal, you can't iron cashmere. Danny here has ruined your sweaters, you understand? He had some kind of death wish, some kind of violent urge driving him, right? Right, Danny? You really did it now, you wanted what–to run away? Is that what you wanted? You saw Tal was going to leave for law school and that drove you nuts or what? Because it can't be 'Oh, I was resisting your help, I wanted to kill myself and I didn't want you to stop me.' That excuse is not going to fly anymore."

I couldn't remember Larry telling me anything about how to take care of cashmere, and I couldn't particularly remember folding the sweaters or not folding them. It was easy enough to imagine if I tried–gently, carefully folding each one after Iban and I had brought them back from storage, placing them in the bottom of the bin, probably feeling proud of myself for helping to organize everything. I realized then, standing there in the crowded, chaotic bedroom, that I didn't really care. It didn't make a difference what was real or not. Larry grabbed my wrist and dragged me to the living room. I could feel my pulse shuddering up and down my forearm. We stood in front of the couch; everyone gathered in a semicircle around us. This was all too familiar by now.

I wondered if Larry knew what was real or not, either. For the first time, I didn't push the thought down. I let it linger. I hung it up in the closet of my head. It looked nice there. "Danny doesn't believe that I am who I say I am," Larry was saying to everybody. It felt kind of like an execution, a witch trial: the pronouncement, the judge, jury, and executioner all wrapped up into one, the doe-eyed audience of plebeians cheering for blood, charred flesh, a distended, throttled neck, anything to make life off the gallows seem livable by comparison.

"Danny wanted to run, he thought he could just go back to Sarah

Lawrence and everything would be fine and he'd get away with it. Now he owes me twenty thousand dollars for Talia's sweaters. He's not going anywhere." It was funny to feel his flesh wrapped around my wrist. It was almost like he was holding my hand. I wanted to laugh, to cackle even, to really give Larry and all my friends what they wanted: someone to blame, food to consume so they could keep living. His teeth were an inch away from my ear. "Those were honeygirl's sweaters. Those represented all the years we were together, before we were persecuted. You took that away. How do you feel about that? You want to tell us why you did it?"

It felt more like a performance than it ever had. The blank looks of faith on everyone's faces belied the layer of thick, explosive, molten fear beneath. If they ever doubted him, if they ever pushed back, they would be in my position, or worse. Was there something even deeper down, underneath the fear? An actual self that was made of hard, irrepressible iron? I was shaking my head side to side.

"I'll tell you why you did it, Danny. Because you sabotaged Talia's law school applications. You couldn't handle it, so you acted out." There was a collective gasp. Everyone knew that Talia not being able to apply to law school was the worst thing that had happened since any of us had begun living with Larry. I picked my chin up off my chest. This was literally impossible. I knew I had never touched the documents Talia needed for law school. I had watched as Talia came over to the apartment with the papers and handed them to Larry to sign, pleading with him not to forget or get distracted, and then later in the day as she'd left again for school, I'd watched her remind him a second time. I'd watched him put the papers into his bag, and had thought to myself, *She's never going to see those again.* I could just feel it. Larry would say that feeling was actually me planning, some conniving impulse, that I was going to steal the papers and tear them up, then hide the memory from myself. But the feeling had been just that, a feeling, a real one, based on hundreds of hours of time spent around Larry.

Only rational logic, Larry had said, could be trusted, logic based upon what Larry said was true. Larry was objectivity. Larry was arbiter. Everything else was what he called "illogic." But if the whole idea of truth was, by definition, based on Larry being right, what if he was wrong? About one thing, even? What if he was wrong about this? Larry had walked into the kitchen, where he pulled a sheet of cellophane off the roll, the plastic screeching like a dying bird. He tore sheets of aluminum foil and crumpled them into balls. He had taught me that aluminum foil had a reflective side, which radiated heat, and a nonreflective side, and it mattered which side you pointed toward whatever you were trying to cook. He placed the balls inside the cellophane, then rolled it up until it looked like a snake that had swallowed a series of eggs. Everyone was watching. Maybe Larry was misleading me on purpose, and he knew that I hadn't done anything to Talia's law school applications.

Then it occurred to me that there was a way, maybe, to find out, once and for all. I could test him. I would make up a story, a story good enough—not to convince Larry, not an explanation that he would buy, but that made Larry look good in front of everyone else, my friends. No one needed to necessarily believe the story; they just needed to be impressed by Larry's ability to draw it out of me. If Larry went along with it, then either he didn't know what was real, or he did know what was real, but he didn't care.

Larry was holding out the cellophane and aluminum foil snake. "This is a garrote," he said. "I often have had to improvise torture devices in the course of my intelligence career, and this is a very effective one, so you know how serious this is, Danny. You're going to tell me exactly why you were driven to sabotage Talia's law school apps." I would take the fall—it was my only choice now—but I could also get something out of it: the truth. He told me to open my pants. I just hoped he wasn't planning to cut my vas deferens in front of everybody. How far would I let this go, I wondered. What would it take for me to just run out the door? What would happen if I did? Was there any situation, any outcome, where I could leave the apartment and they wouldn't come after me?

My pants were unbuttoned and unzipped, and Larry handed me the garrote. "Put this around your balls," he said. I looked at Isabella. She looked like the rest of them, raptly attentive, inscrutable. I knew what it felt like for Larry's scrotum to touch mine, to feel the outline of his genitals through the skin of another human being, but no one here knew that except her. I wrapped the cellophane and aluminum snake around myself like a noose so there were two ends sticking up out of my boxers, which Larry took from me. I pretended to wince. He started to twist the two ends together, which tightened the loop on my end. I couldn't tell if it wasn't actually painful, or if I had become immune to pain. I pretended to wince harder, letting out a whimper.

"Why did you sabotage Talia's law school apps?"

I shook my head, said I didn't do it. I couldn't give in too quickly. That would make it seem like whatever revelation I provided wasn't hard fought, wasn't deep-seated enough. It had to be an impressive reveal. I had to find the right moment. "If you say so, Danny," he said, and gave the garrote another twist, tightening it further. I assumed the aluminum balls were supposed to be digging into my skin, but it didn't feel like much. Was this because of the performance he and I were putting on—it was supposed to look painful but he knew it actually wasn't? Or did he actually think it would hurt, and in fact he was not that good of a torturer? "What about now?" he asked.

I shook my head and a tear squeezed out of one of my eyes and ran down my cheek. I let the tears flow, and didn't wipe them away. They were good. Plus, I wasn't sure what I was supposed to do with my hands. Larry had taught us that a man, a marine, hooked his thumbs at the top of his pockets, with his pinkies back, flat against his sides. But now my pants were undone, and threatening to fall down, so I was simultaneously hooking my thumbs in my pockets and trying to hold my pants up, to make it as convenient as possible for Larry to keep torturing me without exposing myself too much to everyone, which would be embarrassing. He might have twisted a couple more times, it was difficult to tell. Larry was staring at me as if there was no one else in the room, and as he twisted again, he said, "Danny, you'd better tell me exactly what fucked-up thing in your subconscious is the reason you did this, and you better admit it right now or things are going to get"—another twist—"serious."

I yelped out in pain, though I didn't feel any pain, and there were more tears, so I figured this was as good a time as any. I started to nod, and kind of moan. I looked around as if I couldn't see anyone, faking a kind of vision. See, everyone, the power of Larry, that he has accessed some deeper, rawer place in me. Thanks be unto him, for I am about to reveal my deepest, darkest secrets.

For a second I remembered high school, a trip when we went to see a hypnotist, and I got called up onstage. I was so excited—I never got picked for anything—and I was so deeply curious what it would feel like. A line of us stood there, and one by one the hypnotist said a series of phrases, then snapped his fingers in front of each of our faces. If you are not hypnotized, he said, will you please leave the stage. I'd looked around without moving my head. I definitely wasn't hypnotized, I was fully conscious and in control, but I wanted so badly to be hypnotized that I hadn't left the stage. That was how I'd spent the rest of the performance doing everything the hypnotist said, all while completely awake. He'd made me pretend to be a bird, and I'd flapped around on stage, watching everyone else do similarly ridiculous things. Ever since then I'd wondered if that's all hypnotism was—just people who were submissive enough to do whatever someone said because a crowd was watching and they were too afraid to admit they'd been conscious all along. Now Larry was looking at me wide-eyed, urgent and excited, and I said, as if mesmerized: "When I was a little kid, I walked out into the driveway once, and I found a little bird there."

"Oh yes, yes you did. Tell us about the bird. It was a fragile bird wasn't it?" It was working.

"Yes, it was a baby bird. I could see its little body pumping, breathing fast, it was still pinkish, blind."

Talia gasped in horror, she could see where this was going. "Oh no, what did he do to the bird?"

"Honeygirl," Larry said, "I know, but let him get there."

"And the bird looked so fragile, and I wanted to know, to *know* it, and there was a part of me that wanted to destroy it, to punish it for being like that, so weak, and alone. I hated it." There were light yelps of consternation from Talia and Claudia. "I was wearing my boots. They were heavy boots. I slowly brought the toe down on the bird, the little baby bird." I could really see it, the fiction I was weaving, and it was awful, I felt awful for this bird that didn't exist, and the tears were running down my face, thinking about its world slowly closing in, crushing it.

Larry still held the garrote tight on me. "Don't stop, Danny. You have to tell them all of it, so they can see what you are."

"I crushed it, the bird. I felt its tiny bones under my boot, and it stopped moving. That was it. It was dead. I killed it. I've felt guilty about that my whole life, almost insane over it. I didn't know what to do. So I buried it. The memory. The bird I threw into the woods. I didn't want any of you to know, and Larry was so good at revealing people's secrets, I was afraid he was going to bring it out of me, so I lashed out."

"That's why you sabotaged my law school applications? And ruined my sweaters? What?" Talia looked incredulous.

I nodded toward her. Larry shushed her again. "Danny will make up for it," he said.

"But, like, how far back does this go?" Talia asked. "There's all this stuff that Santos supposedly did to sabotage things for me earlier on, but it seems like Dan is secretly kind of a psychopath. How do we know that stuff wasn't him?"

Larry nodded for a few seconds. "Really impressive. Good job, honeygirl, you're learning. That's right, it was him. How does that feel, Santos?" This I hadn't planned for. Santos had taken the blame for pretty much any issue Talia had had at school, anything that had gone wrong for years. He'd made countless lists of all the things he'd supposedly damaged and was going to pay for, all the ways he was going to fix Talia's life, which he had systematically disrupted during their relationship. "He was supposedly your friend, and he let you take the blame for everything," Larry said, letting go of the garrote now. "Do up your pants. Santos, what are you going to do about that? Are you going to be a man? What are you going to do?"

Santos was getting up as I finished buttoning my pants. I was exhausted, and just as I turned to face him, thinking he might say something to me, Santos sank his fist into my gut. I wasn't as numb as I'd thought I was—this hurt more than anything Larry had done. I doubled over. "I'm very proud of you, Santos. That's so good. I can't even imagine how it feels, right?" I was holding on to the armrest of the couch behind me to stay upright, wheezing for air. "It was one punch, Danny, you can handle it. Don't be so dramatic."

—||—

I woke up on the couch. It was the middle of the day, and apparently I'd fallen asleep sitting up. I jumped up and started looking at the bookshelf. I had a tendency now to immediately act as if I had been right in the middle of doing something whenever I woke up so no one could claim that I was ever not busy. Isabella, Iban, and Felicia were sitting around the apartment, working on their laptops. Talia and Larry still hadn't come out of the bedroom. I scanned the books on the shelf, looking for Angela's book. I'd thought it was in my bag, but I hadn't found it. As I suspected, it was not on the shelf. Larry said things don't just disappear. In the past I would've wondered if I'd hidden it from myself. Now I wondered if he'd hidden it from me.

I pulled out a Jewish prayer book that Larry had been proud to point out to me a long time ago, and flipped through it. It was a reformed prayer book, and everything was in English, there was none of the Hebrew that had felt both stultifying and mystical in my conservative Jewish Hebrew school. We never learned how to actually speak Hebrew or what most of the words meant—just how to recite the prayers. That was all God needed: to hear us say it. It didn't matter if we understood what we were saying, or even believed it. As I flipped through, a page caught my eye. I didn't recognize this prayer from the prayer book we'd used in our synagogue when I was growing up. The prayer had no title, no explanation, no author.

Either you will
go through this door
or you will not go through.

If you go through
there is always the risk
of remembering your name.

Things look at you doubly
and you must look back
and let them happen.

If you do not go through
it is possible
to live worthily

to maintain your attitudes
to hold your position
to die bravely

but much will blind you,
much will evade you,
at what cost who knows?

The door itself
makes no promises.
It is only a door.

I read it over a few times. Before I put the book back, I kissed the spine. This was something I'd been taught to do growing up if a prayer book was dropped on the ground, sullied. It felt appropriate now, for some reason.

In the corner of the living room, surrounded by tools and hardware, the Christmas tree was all lit up. Larry insisted on keeping the lights on, even through the day, because it reminded Talia of home, he said. Talia's mom had always hated that Talia would want to leave all the lights on even when they left the house, so that when they came home the house would be all lit up instead of dark and creepy. It's a waste of money, her mom would say. But Larry knew, you cannot put a price on happiness.

I gulped, wondering where Angela's book had gone. I didn't want her to think I was still my old self: irresponsible and untrustworthy. I had changed. I also couldn't explain why I'd taken the book from her in the first place, an irreplaceable copy full of her one-of-a-kind notes, all in a language I didn't speak, not really. "Were you looking for something to read?" Isabella asked me. "You should check out *The Count of Monte Cristo.* My copy is up there. It's sick, and the main character is so much like Larry it's crazy."

"Oh, wow, I'll totally read it," I said, taking the thick book down from the shelf, knowing I would never read it. *What the hell is wrong with me?*

Larry and Talia came out of the bedroom. Larry made a brushing motion with his hand, and Iban and Felicia cleared off of the loveseat. Talia looked oddly bright-eyed and purposeful; she leaned forward a bit on her knees, and it was clear the two of them were going to make some kind of an announcement. Talia smiled. "Everyone is going to leave. Soon. Except Izzy of course. And Felicia. But everyone else, you're not welcome here anymore. My dad and I have talked about it, and we'll tell Santos and Claudia, but that's it—it's over. Too much of my dad's stuff has been destroyed, and my life has been unacceptably interrupted. I'm done, he's done, it's time for us to get our life together, honeygirl and honeyboy. I've asked for it and we've been patient enough and so that's it. You're all going to leave."

I sat back down on the couch while my stomach turned over. *What does this mean? What about everything we owe them for? Are we just being forgiven?* As if she knew what I was thinking, Talia said, "As for all the stuff you've broken and destroyed—those are just things. I can't believe you'd actually think we care about mere stuff. My dad gave all of you so many chances to pay him back for the things you damaged to give you an opportunity to be honest, to be good people—that was for your benefit—but you all failed. You're failures. Even you, Izzy. Even you, Felicia. But we'll continue to give you a place to stay, because you haven't interfered in my life in the same way the rest of you have, and you matter to my dad. Everyone else, it's over."

I tried to make sure I looked disappointed in my own failure, to mask the relief I was feeling. Both feelings coexisted inside me. It was over. Santos could go and live with his parents, Claudia with hers. I didn't know where Iban would go, and I didn't care all that much. I could go back to live on campus in the spring; I'd just gotten an email saying I was guaranteed housing, and I could go home for the rest of winter break until then. Talia sat back and whispered something in her dad's ear. No one stood or went anywhere. I wasn't sure what to do. "Okay, good!" she said. "Now I'm going to make some breakfast. I'll make tortilla de patatas, my favorite, because this is my house, and I'm having my friends over. We can still hang out, see, but we're not helping you anymore. That's over. So there's no need for you to hurt us in return. Who wants some breakfast?" After a pause, we all raised our hands.

18

I HAD THOUGHT, WHEN Talia kicked us out, that I would go home to my parents for the rest of winter break. But when I started to pack up my bag, Larry shook his head. "Sit down," he said, and then, leaning in closer, "I can still help you, Danny. You can still stay here, that's fine, if you are really ready to change and help me out. This apartment is Plato's Cave for you. If you walk out of the cave before you're ready, when you're only used to seeing shadows on the wall, you'll go blind. I don't want that for you. You finish your last semester at school, and then you can come back here, and we can finally start working together. I've been thinking that once we get everything in order, I might start paying you to work with me. How does that sound? We get Tal all ready for law school, the right way, and then you and me, we can do some amazing work. You're not going to get an opportunity like this anywhere else." I put my bag back down. It would be nice to get paid.

A few days later, I was suddenly in my last semester of college. Tomorrow, I was supposed to go back up to Sarah Lawrence to move into my new place on campus. It still felt impossible that Larry would actually let me go. That night, Talia, Isabella, and Felicia went out, as if to prove that things were back to a normal they'd never been in the first place. Larry went out, too—he was lending a hand to a private investigator friend of his.

I had the apartment to myself for the first time in two years. I decided to go up to the roof. It was only the second time I'd ever gone up there. I tried to imagine it: this apartment building as a home after college. I stepped through the glass doors of the rooftop clubhouse and into the frigid night air on the unprotected rooftop, zipping up my coat. It felt like I was in high school again, sneaking onto the roof outside my bedroom window to look at the stars and try out a cigarette.

I surveyed the rest of the roof and spotted a maintenance ladder over on the other end. I was wearing the specialized running shoes Larry had recently bought me, exactly the same pair he wore every day. They completed the outfit, the one that he'd never directly prescribed, but that we'd all ended up wearing. His bright polos, his bright running shoes. The red neon tread hooked on each iron rung of the ladder as I climbed, and the freezing wind cut straight through the high-tech, mesh fabric. From the top of this building I thought I must look like some kind of beacon. The ladder led to another level, which was empty except for some air-conditioning equipment and old roof panels. It was dark, but with the help of light pollution I could see another ladder on the other end. I wondered if I would get in trouble up here, if someone might see me. The bright shoes weren't helping. I tried to move stealthily to the new ladder. As I climbed, I could feel the weight of my body being pulled back to the earth. I paused to rest, hanging on my tired arms. It had been so long since I'd actually done the push-ups Larry prescribed. The exercise was where it'd all started, really. Larry had been right—doing push-ups every morning made me feel better. So how could he mean any harm?

I reached another level of the roof, and it had gotten even darker, but it was easy to make out the water tower on the corner of the building silhouetted against the bruised sky. I walked over to it, trying to step quietly. The water tower was such a classic New York image and yet I'd never had a chance to get so close to one. I stood next to it, peering underneath, and to my surprise, saw yet another ladder on the other side. I wondered how dangerous this was, if maybe it was some kind of crime. I put my hand on the first rung. The metal was cold, and when I tried putting some weight on it, the ladder seemed to move, just a bit. I pulled myself up anyway. It was like climbing a tree, but a gigantic one.

By now I had to be hundreds of feet off the ground. The city bounded away from me. The roof of the water tower was sloped and round. On the very top, in the center, was a red light which blinked on, off, on, off. After staring at it for a while, clinging to the cold ladder, I realized it was a warning for air traffic. I was high up enough that an airplane might fly into me, accidentally. I lay down on the roof, the puff of my coat providing some cushion, and wedged my feet against the edge. I put all my trust in the neon running shoes. If I slipped at all, it would be off the side of the building to the street hundreds of feet below. I imagined falling. What if it happened right at the moment Larry was coming back for the night and I landed on his head, and it killed us both instantly? *See, now, where do thoughts like that come from?*

He'd shown me the photos of him with Gorbachev, and with Bush Sr. Those were definitely real. It had looked like they were just hanging out. If they were fakes, they were impressive fakes, and would require more technical skill than Larry really had. How could I recognize that those photos existed, and also question whether Larry was who he said he was—some kind of government operative? The red light pulsed above my head, and I imagined it not coming back on again, a plane clipping me off the roof and sucking me into the engine.

A few days earlier I'd gotten an email from my dad. I'd stopped calling, stopped answering the phone. It'd been a long time since the hurricane, and it just felt harder and harder, for some reason, to bridge the gap. So I'd been ignoring his calls as best I could. His email had the subject line "Are you OK?" The email had gone on to talk about how I failed to respond to calls and texts, how he'd learned "in life and business" to respond to someone in twenty-four hours, how he "would never hire someone who acted this way."

There was the time I was chauffeuring Larry, driving the leased car, and a parade route had blocked our way. A police officer in a white hat sternly held out his gloved hand, told us there was absolutely no way we could go ahead. Larry had leaned across me and said someone's name out the window, and the officer's face had changed. I'd watched as the white hat moved cones aside, and then he waved us through the parade. I couldn't deny *that,* could I? Even if Larry wasn't a special government operative, at the very least he had some kind of connections, which meant that if I just left, or acted against him, I would never be safe. *Look at you, thinking that way again. The only reason you're not safe is you, because you brought yourself up to the edge of this building.*

The grid of lights stretched away in every direction. This was by far the tallest building on the Upper East Side. I could see everything. There were things I couldn't get past, though. His websites weren't good, or real. I knew that. They were just fake landing pages for ads, which couldn't possibly make the kind of money he claimed they did. So that was a lie. Maybe he had some reason to lie I didn't understand, maybe it was a part of some grander scheme, or maybe he really thought they were good websites. Any option was strange. I shifted my body a bit on the roof of the water tower, and wondered if it was built to hold the weight of a person. I imagined myself falling through it into the freezing water, how I'd keep myself afloat for a while, maybe calling for help, and then eventually I'd accept that it was no use and sink below the inky surface.

There had been the day a couple of weeks ago when I came back from school and walked in and they were all weeping; Larry was really sobbing, and he'd pointed at the TV. There had just been a shooting at a school in Connecticut, someone had shot up an elementary school with a machine gun. Larry literally fell to the carpet, racked with tears as Talia held him. I had felt nothing. In fact, I had tried to make myself cry, to fit in. It'd felt to me like they were lying, pretending to care, and I would be in trouble if I didn't care, too. But surely it indicated that something was wrong with me, and not them, that I didn't feel devastated, personally distraught, because of a school shooting, that I didn't feel compelled to *do* something.

I sat up and leaned, peeking over the edge. The street below bulged up at me, as if the whole island had inhaled. I craned my head to the left and could see all of downtown. He'd gone along with the bird story, and I knew that wasn't true. I'd based the story on a real memory of a morning in New Jersey when I'd walked outside to find a fawn curled up on our doorstep. I'd sat next to it for hours, just sat there, wanting so badly to touch it, but just as badly wanting not to hurt it or to mark it with my scent in case the mother, who had clearly lost her baby, came back for it later. I finally did let myself touch it, just for a second, let it sniff my hand then, ever so lightly, I felt the soft fur between its ears. The next day it was gone, and I'd felt guilty, worried I had killed it. Years later I learned that mother deer regularly leave their fawns behind in places they consider safe so they can go forage for food. I'd used that memory to make the story about the bird believable. The deer was a real memory, the bird was not. I could tell the difference. I could use that distinction as a compass. Yes, the bird had been a complete fabrication, and yet Larry had gone along with it, which meant either that he had believed it or he'd lied to everyone about believing it.

I looked down again at the road far below. He'd said I was a danger to myself. *I could make that choice right now,* I thought. The red light blinked on, then back off. *I could do it in a dozen different ways.* Red again. *He'd said I needed his help, because without him I'd kill myself.* Off. But I wasn't jumping, and it wasn't because of him. On. It was because I didn't want to die. Off. I never had. On.

—||—

Later that night, Isabella, Talia, and Felicia returned to find me playing ukulele on the couch. I plucked away as they dropped their things in the bedroom. Talia stood in the opening where the kitchen, bedroom, foyer, and living room met, and watched me for a second. "Did you know," she said, "that one time in Slonim I came downstairs, and you were playing that song, and I thought you'd written it?"

I was playing "Creep." I strummed out the chords and laughed. "You thought *I* wrote that? What a compliment."

"I thought you were so horribly disturbed or something. I heard you singing 'I wish I was special' and all that stuff, like first thing in the morning. It was so sad. I thought for sure you were suicidal."

"Huh, well no, definitely not," I said, shrugging. "That was Radiohead."

"Are you okay?" Talia asked. "You seem off."

"Yup, totally fine, thanks." I didn't mention the roof. I finally had an actual secret, for once. Something that was my own. A belonging. I knew they would go to bed soon. I didn't know what the morning would bring, when I was supposed to move out of the apartment and onto campus, but I knew I couldn't just gather my things and leave. There was no chance Larry was going to let me go without there being some kind of emergency, without me arbitrarily ending up stuck here until the middle of the night.

I kept singing, though more quietly as they went off to bed, "What the hell am I doing here? I don't belong here. . . ."

—II—

When I'd gotten the email from my dad about not calling, I'd immediately forwarded it to Larry. I knew that even if I didn't, it would come up anyway and that would be worse. This was what Larry chose that morning. It was exactly as I'd suspected, and everything unfolded as usual. It was a brand-new January day. School, campus, my new room, my new life, it was all calling to me, pulling me like a great big magnet.

"Let's talk about you going back to SLC," Larry said. My leaving had to appear to be Larry's decision, something granted to me. I understood that, and was happy to go along, to keep propping up his power over everyone, if it meant I got to leave. I was barely registering anything he was saying, just nodding when it seemed appropriate and keeping the door in the corner of my eye. He kept my laptop in the bedroom where I couldn't get it, because he'd claimed it needed fixing. When I'd asked for it back, he'd said he would be done with it soon, and I could just grab it when I came back down from school sometime. I would just use the computers in the school library, I thought, that's fine.

He was saying something now about how he'd heard from Talia that I'd seemed off last night. I hadn't found Angela's book, either. That was a bigger problem, but I would deal with it later. I could come up with some kind of excuse when I had to. I heard him say something about my dad, and I tuned in: "So you see, your dad, all along, has held your family in an iron grip. You all felt it, right, when we were there? Danny's silence. His mumbling. The transparent fear. The oven that never got replaced. Your dad has held that family in a stranglehold, hasn't he? And what about the ukulele? I heard last night, when you seemed strange to Talia, you were playing it. Good job, Tal, for picking that up. Isn't it the case that the music playing, the poetry, these are your ways of expressing yourself, of speaking, in a household where you weren't allowed to speak? Which means that these things, which seem to you to be mouthpieces, are in fact heavy chains binding you to your dad? Because you *can* speak, Danny. You don't need these things! They only hold you back!"

I could feel the crescendo, the approaching climax. I just had to catch the wave as it crashed, and ride it out of this apartment. "You can free yourself, Danny, from your dad. In fact, you must, if you think you're going to return to school, if you're going to live on your own, if you're going to finally become an adult. So do it, Danny. Free yourself."

I didn't know what he wanted. Some gesture bombastic enough that he could call it a revelation, enough to justify my escape to everyone else. I grabbed my ukulele, opened the case, and held the instrument in my hands. "Do it, Danny," he said, "free yourself." It was only a thing, like Talia had said. It really was—only a thing. I'd get a new one, I knew it. This was all absurd. My ukulele had absolutely nothing to do with my dad, but I was happy to pretend that I was exorcising the demon of my father as I brought my foot down on the ukulele, and my neon sneakers broke through the thin body. The strings snapped as I brought my foot down again, and again, the neck flipping back to hit me in the ankle, as if it was fighting back, and again, and again, and again, until the thing was splayed open and splinters of it were strewn across the carpet.

For a moment, I thought I saw a glint of surprise on Larry's face, but if it was there, it vanished almost instantly. He clapped me on the back. I was breathing hard. I didn't know if my friends believed I was having a breakthrough. I had a feeling that Larry didn't, but it was too late for him to reverse course. I had satisfied the narrative, the story he was trying to sell—that he had saved me. Which meant there was no justification he could give for keeping me from walking out the door.

—⊣⊢—

I descended the elevator for the last time with only my backpack on my back. As I walked through the jade and gold lobby that had become so familiar to me these past two years, I noticed something I'd never seen before—a large bureau and a nightstand up against the wall. They looked old and worn, and were clearly out of place. I was so close to escaping, in sight of the exit, but I had to do one last thing. I went over to the doorman. "Excuse me, do you know what the deal is with that furniture over there?" I asked.

"Someone's moving out, they're getting rid of that stuff," he said, not looking up.

I walked over and looked more closely. The furniture was Hawaiian-looking, the wood edged with something like bamboo. The bureau was huge, but the nightstand I might be able to carry. I hooked my hands around the sides, feeling its weight, and then hoisted it up. "This is okay?" I asked the doorman, and he shrugged. So I took the nightstand in my arms, and I carried it all the way to the train. I rode out of the city with it in front of me like a desk. It looked like I had made myself a little office right there. The other passengers either smiled or frowned at me as they stepped around me on the way to their seats. The one thing they couldn't do was ignore me.

When the Metro-North reached the end of Manhattan, it burst from underground into the light. I got out at Bronxville, and for the whole twenty-minute walk to campus, I hugged the piece of furniture, the first I'd ever owned, against my chest, intermittently changing the positions of my arms, now underneath, then for a brief moment on one shoulder, then back against my chest again. I felt like I couldn't put it down, not until I got home. It was heavy, but I could manage it.

19

CAMPUS WAS HAUNTED. LARRY, Claudia, Talia, Santos, Iban, or Isabella might be anywhere, and my phone weighed down my pocket like a grenade. The world was a series of blind corners, and at any moment I might round one and there they'd be, telling me I had broken something, sabotaged someone, done something that meant I didn't deserve this education, this room of my own, the possibility of graduating and moving on with my life. It wasn't just them. What if I ran into Raven, or Max, or Gabe, or anyone I knew from before? How would I explain what had happened? I felt like I was back in the house where I grew up, walking around at night with a souvenir dagger clipped to my belt, knowing it would be no use if I ran into a ghost, which seemed always to be a distinct and dire possibility.

I lay on my bed and stared at the seam where the ceiling met the wall, two slightly different tones of eggshell. It was late January and things felt worse than ever. I was lying to everyone in my life, not telling anyone what had happened to me, who I was. I was hiding and it made me feel like a rat in a hole. I missed knowing exactly what would come next—even if it was awful, at least I could be prepared for it. Now, every single hour was my own responsibility, and the time ached out ahead of me.

Valentine's Day was approaching. I just wanted to reach out and touch someone, say hello, be able to live in the world everyone else did, but at the same time, I could imagine nothing more repulsive. I wanted to be able to do normal things, like go on a date, and yet the idea was horrifying. What if someone discovered what I was? I had to keep up the act, keep pretending that I had capital-C Clarity, so that Larry wouldn't have a reason to recall me like a defective product. The very least I could do in order to prove I was a functioning, effective man was to ask someone out for Valentine's Day.

I rolled over in bed and looked at my phone, pulling up the Sarah Lawrence jobs posting page. I had a message—the event decorator I'd emailed, who was looking for someone to manage her social media, wanted me to come in that afternoon. I wrapped myself in a towel, shuffled to the bathroom across the hall, and found the door closed, which meant one of my roommates was inside. I hovered there, staring at the closed door. It thumped back at me. Then it moaned softly. I stood, frozen with the sense that I was in trouble. Then I realized there was no such thing, not out here. I shuffled back to my room and sat on my bed. I would wait for my turn.

⊣⊢

The event decoration job was in Tuckahoe, one stop up on the train, so quick that I managed to hop off before anyone checked my ticket, saving me a few dollars. Tuckahoe was practically indistinguishable from Bronxville, another small town in Westchester with brick buildings, mansard roofs, plush lawns. The address the decorator had given me was in an old bank, and I hesitated before the hulking shape of the building, not sure I was in the right place. Once I stepped inside, I saw that the whole bank had been hollowed out except for the vault in the back and an office up above with an opaque window that looked down over a few seemingly ornamental cubicles. The person I'd been emailing, who could only have been a few years older than I was, guided me over to an empty desk near hers, where I sat down.

She dropped into her office chair and reviewed the clipboard in her lap, which held what I assumed was the résumé I'd emailed. This was my first real job interview. I was trying to think of my greatest weakness and how to confess it in a way that made it sound like a strength when she asked, "Do you smoke?"

I looked around. Did she want me to? "No, I don't. I used to, I mean, but not anymore. Why?"

"Okay, good. The last person in this position smoked. I have to sit next to whoever gets this job, so if I can help it I'd rather not spend every day sitting next to someone who smells like an ashtray again."

"Oh. Well, I definitely don't."

"That's good." She marked something on her clipboard. I wondered if the other papers were résumés from other applicants. "Do you want to see the plant vault?" she asked.

I followed her to the back, where the old bank vault door waited, gigantic, ornate, taller than both of us. As she swung it open, it exhaled a cold, bright white sigh, revealing a jungle of pure color, humid and vibrant; flowers and plants hung and grew and blossomed and crowded the room. It glowed with fluorescent light that seemed to come from everywhere and nowhere, gleaming off the metal shelves. The air was thick with living. It was as if a minuscule forest, composed of plants from every imaginable region of the earth, flourished here on its own, protected in a vault that was so quiet and strangely *un*earthly that it could have been floating in space. "People think flowers need sun," she said, "but once they're cut, they're better off in the cold and the dark. Like wine," she said as she picked up a large Ziploc bag full of red rose petals. "You have a license, right?"

"A driver's license? Yeah, I do."

"Good. These are the rose petal turndowns for hotels. You'll deliver them so I can focus on other work. We have a lot of these coming up for Valentine's Day. Obviously there's paperwork to handle before you're officially hired, but if you want to get started now, you can help me strip thorns." She handed me a peculiar knife with a one-sided, flip-out blade. The rest of the afternoon I dragged the blade along the necks of roses, removing thorns and collecting fallen petals for other people's beds.

—⊪—

The busier I made myself, the better my excuse for not answering the phone or going down to Manhattan to visit. I started to take an extra class at school, and audited another, and I managed to get a second job as a waiter at Dumpling + Noodle, a new restaurant in Bronxville. I finally had good reason to be constantly exhausted.

One night, late in January, I'd just finished a shift at the restaurant, and Jenny, my manager, had insisted on driving me home. As she brought me back to campus, I looked out at the dark trees, the empty town pulling past us, and she was telling me how she'd been a model and newscaster back in the Philippines, and I realized I was sitting so far away from her that I could feel the cold from outside the car against my arm. It was not at all unbelievable that Jenny had been a model and a newscaster. What was it? Why was I so uncomfortable all the time, still?

She began to tell me how one of my fellow waiters had needed a place to stay after he'd emigrated, also from the Philippines, and she'd put him up in her basement for a few weeks. If I ever needed a place to stay, she said, it was there for me. Her kids played down there, but otherwise it was nice. I'd known Jenny only a few days, practically. I wondered if she knew how desperately I wanted to cry then, how terrifying her kindness was to me, how welcome. I couldn't exactly explain why, for the same reason I couldn't accept it, couldn't admit I needed it, and when she dropped me off, I ran up the tower of stairs, knowing that if she looked she'd be able to see me in the clouded glass of the stairwell, an indistinct shadow rushing up floor after floor until I reached my door, turned the key in the lock, and sealed it behind me, followed by my bedroom door, and I was finally safe, alone.

The next morning, as I got ready for French, I peeked out my window, hoping that I wouldn't be visible to anyone on the quad below, that I'd just look like something obscene censored out on TV. The nightstand was in the corner next to my door, where I kept my keys—the proof that I could leave whenever I wanted and that when I locked the door behind me, no one else could come in. I wondered if there was any way someone could get a copy from the school administration building if they wanted.

When I had to leave the house, I would keep my eyes up, scanning in every direction, because they might be anywhere on campus at any time, and I had no way of knowing when or how I might run into them. I hoped I'd at least see them first, and might be able to pretend I hadn't, and could turn a corner before they caught me. When I was coming home, I'd peer up at the windows, afraid that somehow they were in my room, waiting. I took a deep breath, not wanting to be late for French, grabbed my keys off the night table, and headed across campus on the route that had the longest sightlines.

My classmates were waiting outside the building at the end of Slonim Woods—the same building where I'd taken my poetry workshop earlier in the year—for our professor to show up and unlock the door. I hugged myself a little in my coat, a brown puffer I'd had since high school, and stretched a hard half-grimace, half-smile across my face, which I thought might communicate that I was friendly but less than predisposed to conversation. My classmates, standing in clumps outside the door, looked similarly cold, physically and emotionally. I shuffled up and stood among them.

Almost immediately, a girl whose name I could never remember, whom I avoided talking to not only because of the awkwardness of not remembering her name, but also because I found her insufferably unself-conscious, came up to me. She was from Russia, or Italy, or both, or had parents from both places and had somehow absorbed their accents, so that when she spoke French, which she did as poorly as any of us but as often as possible and with supreme, somehow condescending confidence, it sounded like someone tone-deaf insistently holding an audience captive while they sang. This wasn't her fault, of course, though it felt somehow intentional and aggressive. Nor was her personality, I guessed, which compelled her to offer her opinion on seemingly everything that happened around her, even to interrupt our professor while he was giving instructions, and to oftentimes wear a black beret and black bodysuit to a beginning French class.

"Bonjour, Daniel," she said. She pronounced my name "Danielle," the French pronunciation. She was wearing the beret now, I noted. I wondered why our professor hadn't shown up yet to unlock the door.

"Hello . . . *bonjour,*" I said. "How are you?"

"Ça va," she said. She seemed remarkably overdressed, somehow, even for winter in New York. Her coat almost brushed the ground, and it had a hood lined in what appeared to be a dead wolf. I wondered if she was rich. "I have a question for you, Daniel," she said.

My mouth was dry and cold, and I watched my breath eke out. *"Oui?"* I said.

She laughed, a tinkling giggle that sounded like an accessory she carried around, like a small, ornamental dog. "A friend of mine is curious," she said, "if you have plans for this upcoming Valentine's Day."

I hated myself instantly, but could not tell why. Then, because I could not figure out a reason to hate myself, but felt it so strongly, I hated her. How would I explain this to Larry, that I had either rejected this girl or had gone out with her? I was audibly fumbling an answer in the air, working my way toward the truth, which was that I did not have plans, when Cassidy, another student in the class, interrupted by saying, "Actually, Daniel and I have plans for Valentine's Day."

I grabbed the lifeline I'd been thrown. "Yeah, that's right," I said, and I stepped a little closer to Cassidy so that our coats were pressed against each other, and we looked like people who might have a preexisting relationship. In reality, she and I had talked just once or twice, having been assigned by our French professor to set up the projector for an extracurricular screening of a French film, to which none of our classmates ever showed up. We had sent a few emails back and forth since then. In our emails to each other, one of the main topics Cassidy and I had joked about was how annoying we both found this girl, who now adjusted her beret. "Ah, I did not know. Of course. I will tell my friend." She dispensed her laugh again. Cassidy pulled me away, and we followed our classmates into the building.

—ı⊢—

I looked around the big circular table at all the freshmen—they were so young, naive, and, therefore, safe. They knew no one I did, had no reason to ask what had happened to me, who my friends were, where they had gone, had I heard anything about that girl's dad who lived on campus? At the same time, they forced me to see myself by contrast. I must seem so strange, a lonely senior in a class full of freshmen, who apparently had no friends and a shaved head. I was still dressed up in the costume in case I ran into anyone from the apartment—a bright polo and specialized running sneakers that made me feel as if I was perpetually pitched forward. I felt monstrously out of place. The professor was saying, *"Est-ce que vous appelez où vous habitez 'Bronxville' ou 'Yonkers'? Peut-être vous pourriez l'appeler 'Bronkers'? J'aime bien aussi 'Yonksville,'"* or at least, that's as much as I absorbed. Cassidy sat next to me. I couldn't see her profile past her hair, which was long, blond, parted down the middle. Everything was a choice. I'd chosen this. I wished, for an instant, that I'd jumped off that water tower. I wished I'd been a better, more capable person who was able to actually learn from Larry and become the kind of complete human being he said I could have become, rather than fearing him and skittering away to hide. Cassidy pushed a wrapped square of chocolate toward me.

I looked around. The little square of chocolate sat on the table like a talisman, but of what, I didn't know. The chocolate was wrapped in purple tinfoil, I recognized it immediately as Dove dark chocolate, Isabella's favorite brand. I looked around the table. Some people had chocolates in front of them, some didn't. The people who'd received the chocolates seemed to radiate outward around the table from a girl named Zara, who sat on Cassidy's other side. I surmised that she'd brought in the chocolates to share with her friends, but why had I received one?

For a moment everything shifted a few degrees, as if in a mirror that had been tilted. I jolted. I'd fallen asleep a little bit. The chocolate was still in front of me. I unwrapped it carefully, and for the rest of the hour nibbled on it, barely managing to keep myself awake in the wash of voices that were speaking French like warm, lapping waves until class came to a close and everyone began to gather their things.

"You always fall asleep in class," Cassidy said, packing up her bag beneath the table. "It's really annoying." Briefly, as she closed her notebook, I saw her handwriting—perfect, round, some kind of pastel gel pen. I followed her out of the room in the stream of exiting students. "How do you even pass this class?" she asked, quietly, for we were surrounded.

"Honestly, I have no idea," I said. She'd paused outside our classroom in a foyer that felt like a living room—there were couches around a fireplace where poetry readings were held some evenings. She asked me where I lived, and when I told her Rothschild, she asked if she could walk over there with me to see it, because so few people had actually noticed the existence of Rothschild, much less been inside, it being a nondescript tower attached to the side of a building with no identifying characteristics and an unmarked door. The perfect place for me, basically.

Once we reached my dorm, after a short walk, Cassidy and I stood talking for an incredibly long time in the field which was outside my building. We were like two rubber bands pulled to our maximum extension, held there by opposing forces. I thought she might want to come up, but I wasn't sure, and I couldn't ask if she wanted to come up. I just couldn't. It didn't occur to me to wonder whether she might be experiencing the same internal struggle.

Her hair was so light that strands of it ignored gravity entirely in the dry, winter air. She seemed to want to talk about everything in the world and, despite the cold, kept standing there, chatting easily with me in the patchy field. Somehow we got onto the topic of bees, then for a while discussed how many different types of oil there are—coconut, olive, avocado, palm, walnut, hazelnut, et cetera—and how do you wring oil from a nut anyway? We talked about our favorite desserts; hers was peach pie, so I said mine was peach pie, too. We never talked about the past. She was shivering in her thin jacket, and I didn't want the conversation to end, so I gave her my coat to wear over it, but after a long while of me still standing there in my short sleeves, even though I believed I was fairly immune, at that point, to pain—it was just mind over matter after all, everything was, and if I did feel it, the cold, then that meant it was weakness leaving my body—even so, it was only reasonable to say goodbye.

Valentine's Day was soon, which magnified the significance of everything beyond recognition. When she finally turned and started to walk home wearing my coat, which I'd insisted she take since she had to walk all the way to Hill House and it was beginning to snow lightly, I felt I'd failed. I hadn't done what Larry would have said I should do, which was invite her up, because everyone enjoys sex, and there was nothing wrong with it—I was a straight man and she was, as far as I knew, a straight woman and that was that. As I turned and walked back to my dorm across the cold ground, I already missed the feeling of standing there talking to her, of forgetting to be scared, however briefly.

—⊣⊢—

Cassidy brought my coat back the next day, because it was too cold to not have a coat, she said. She came upstairs to deliver it, and so I showed her my dorm, which resembled an actual grown-up apartment, in which each person has their own room, and everything is smooth and painted white. I showed her the living room, the kitchen, and then my bedroom, and as we walked around, we talked about movies from our childhoods. We were discussing *The Lion King*—I was wondering what Talia must think of that movie, since I knew she was obsessed with Disney, and it had that whole theme of separation from one's father, the conspiracy against the child who has to raise themself, more or less—when Cassidy asked if I'd like to watch it, and after a moment of trying to remember what we'd even been talking about, I said yes.

We sat cramped next to each other in my twin bed, and as the familiar sound and logo arced across the screen, I wondered if I should put my arm around her. I spent the next hour and a half trying to decide. Then, as the movie ended, she yawned and said she was feeling tired, she might take a nap, and she wriggled farther down on the bed next to me. I said that sounded good, maybe I would take a nap, too, and I got up to give her the bed to herself. She looked at me with an odd expression. I sat at my desk, and as I lay my head down, my hands folded on the hard laminated wood, my knuckles digging against my head, I simultaneously understood that what I was doing made no sense and truly could not imagine any other option. As I closed my eyes, I watched her pause for a moment, then she turned away from me to the wall.

It was dark when I woke up. "It's snowing really hard," Cassidy said out of the darkness. "I wonder if it's going to snow all weekend." We both looked at the window for a while.

"Do you want to stay until it calms down a bit?" I asked. She said yes, maybe she should. It snowed through the weekend, and so she stayed that night and the next until she had to go to work on Monday. On Valentine's Day, about a week later, I baked her a peach pie.

—⊣⊢—

It wasn't like everything was perfect, like the past could be entirely erased by writing a new story on top of it. The only evidence I had that the past two years had even happened was a *Catch-22* T-shirt, a sweater that was supposedly "cantaloupe" but was really neon orange, a pair of running sneakers, and a roughed-up Hawaiian nightstand. I had the memories, of course, but it turned out to be possible to hide those underneath what felt like my brand-new life—two jobs, college graduation approaching, a girlfriend, and something like a comprehensible future. My memories were easier not to dwell on—they had dread attached to them, fear, and despair. I wrote over them, and so my life became a strange palimpsest. What mattered was the present, and the possibility of joy.

About a month into our relationship, the grenade in my pocket finally went off. I was sitting with Cassidy on my bed; she was reading and I was working on my final project for the last poetry workshop I'd ever take at Sarah Lawrence. The workshop was titled "Speaker Box." Every poem we wrote for this class was supposed to be in the voice of another person, and our final project was to display the poems in some unique form. I'd transcribed each poem I'd written over the course of the semester onto the back of a piece of origami paper, then folded each poem into a specific shape so that, when combined with the others, it formed a complex, interlocking, sculptural sphere called a *kusudama,* "medicine ball," in Japanese. Since the poems were all locked in the interior of the *kusudama,* the idea was that you'd have to destroy the emotional vault entirely in order to get at these poems, these hidden voices, the "medicine" within.

I paused for a moment in my folding and looked at Cassidy. It was almost like I was really starting to see her: another human being, who had parents, and a brother, and complicated relationships, whose skin was so pale I could almost see the thin blue veins in her eyelids, which were hooded now as she focused intently on her book. She was working on a paper about the representation of women in *Buffy the Vampire Slayer* as opposed to the *Twilight* movies. I pressed my foot against hers, and she looked up, and right then my phone buzzed in my pocket. When I pulled it out to look, Cassidy must have seen my face blanch. She asked, "What's wrong? Who is it?"

I didn't know how to answer. I told her it was my friend's dad.

"Why don't you pick it up, then?" she asked.

I couldn't think of a reason that would make any sense. The buzzing stopped as I pressed the green button that meant the call was connected. I held the phone up to my ear. I could hear his voice inside my head.

Hi, Danel.

Hi, Larry.

Long time, no talk.

I'm sorry about that, I've been really busy. I got a second job and I'm taking an extra class now so–

You'll come visit soon. We miss you. We have a lot of work to do.

Oh yeah, I'm sure, how is–

Help me with something. I'm trying to get in touch with honey-girl but I can't find her. I'm sending up Iban and Izzy, but since you're up there on campus would you mind looking around for me? Or are you too busy for me and Tal?

No, Larry, of course not. I'm not. That's no problem. I'll look around for her and then report back.

I hung up the phone. Cassidy was looking at me. "What was that? You seem weird."

The past month, I had let myself feel that things might be safe and calm, but the reality was that I'd been living in the eye of a storm, trying to hold the storm walls back by pretending they weren't there. There was no way to ignore Larry now. *If I want this to be real, I have to tell Cassidy the truth about what happened. A relationship is built on a foundation of honesty. If I really believe I'm good, then I have to be honest with my girlfriend.* I told her it had been my old roommate's dad on the phone. I'd lived with him in his apartment in Manhattan for a while. I thought he'd been nice but he'd turned out to be really weird, having us do work for him all the time, getting angry really easily and stuff like that. It seemed like maybe he was lying pathologically or something.

I could only tell her what I had the language for. I didn't know what to call the rest of it. He was a dad. We hadn't slept much. Everything was a blur. The rest of it floated just outside the periphery of my vision. I tried to zero in on it. He was the weird, obsessive dad of my friend who'd put me up for a while, and I had to leave to look for his daughter right now to appease him, because otherwise he'd get intense about it and it'd be a whole thing. Cassidy sat cross-legged, her knees touching my knees, probably not fully understanding, but wanting me to be okay, I thought. She shrugged and said all right, and did I need anything, to call her if I did, and she let me go.

So I went wandering around campus, uselessly looking for one of the people I least wanted to find. I had to search for Talia thoroughly enough so that I could claim I'd tried, but poorly enough so that I wouldn't actually run into her, while simultaneously hiding from Iban and Isabella and anyone else that might be looking. I went to the most secret, least traveled places on campus I could think of. I walked through the dark back hallways of the dance studios. I walked the back path behind all the old dorms to the bottom edge of campus, then came back up the hill, walking through the backyards of the houses on Mead Way, one of which Raven had lived in sophomore year.

I was constantly terrified I would see them from a distance, or that I would open a door and there they would be, on the other side. I passed through Westlands Gate, and poked around the patios behind the pub, even checking the back rooms and upstairs, where few people ever went. They were all empty. I checked all the secret spots in the library, the private study rooms with people's names carved in every surface, where people supposedly went to make out or have sex, then the maze of pathways and courtyards in the Andrews Court dorms, and the secret path behind the tennis court. Finally I circled back to the suburban road that ran along the outskirts of campus where I'd gotten lost my very first day—it provided a hidden route back toward Rothschild, where I could return to Cassidy and the imagined safety of the lock clicking behind me, and hope that Larry wouldn't call me to check in. Talia was probably in class, or meeting with a teacher, or having coffee with a friend, and just hadn't looked at her phone. As I walked back, I kept peering in between the suburban mansions that lined the road, searching for my past life, my unresolved business, which I didn't want to find. If campus was haunted, I was the ghost haunting it.

⊣⊢

Months passed, and then school was almost over. Everything was in bloom; the pergola in the middle of campus was a tunnel of hanging wisteria, and in Bronxville, every median and patch of grass was bursting with tulips. I was headed to the train for work, wondering whether I should buy a ticket or chance the one stop up to Tuckahoe. I was on the corner about to cross the street when I saw them. There was no way to turn around; we were really out in the open now, the cars stopped on either side. The sun was hot and lighting up everything. As I walked toward them, they billowed across the crosswalk into a whole group, and quickly I took in each of their faces: Talia front and center, Isabella beside her, Claudia on the other side, even Iban trailing along. They were wearing bright polos, and the running shoes, and thankfully so was I. Santos wasn't there and, most important, neither was Larry. What would I say? Would they stop me right there, in the middle of the street, and insist I come back to New York with them, or that I hang out with them later, have a coffee and a conversation that would inevitably unfold into the evening, and then, as if I'd strayed dangerously close to a whirlpool, I would find myself walking back to the apartment? If it had happened once, what was to prevent it from happening all over again?

I kept walking. I did not know what my face might look like. We met in the middle, and they moved to the side as one, like a shoal of fish, so consumed in conversation they seemed to barely care I was there. They held up their hands, saying, oh, hi, Dan. Like it was no big deal. Like we were people who had lived together in Slonim and had not seen one another much since then, so didn't have anything to say. Like none of it had ever happened. Then they were past me.

This act, this bare minimum of acknowledgment, was referred to, while I was a student there, as "Sarah Lawrencing" someone, in reference to the haughty, cliquey, isolating nature of the school's culture. The people who made up and used the term found it frustrating that people didn't really care to greet one another, to treat each other as human, to engage in conversation, but instead averted their gaze and pretended to never have met you. I'd just been Sarah Lawrenced. I got onto the train without a ticket, dumbfounded.

—II—

Later that week, Cassidy and I headed into the city to meet her godparents. They weren't exactly her godparents. She called them her "fairy godparents." Her mom and stepdad were in Wisconsin, where she'd grown up, and since we'd been dating a few months, and school was coming to an end, and we'd been talking about her spending some time staying with me in the apartment I'd found in the Bronx, her mom thought we should grab dinner with Giulia, her old roommate from college, who was a big deal in the New York City Department of Education, and her husband, Josh, so they could make sure I wasn't a lunatic.

Cassidy and I had decided to head into the city a little early to hit the American Museum of Natural History and make a day of it. The train lurched as Cassidy and I settled into a row of shiny blue and turquoise Metro-North seats. Suddenly Manhattan was that much closer, and my mind went blank. Cassidy asked if I was okay, and I said yes, I'm fine. I had to be. I was meeting her family, and I would not be her freaky older boyfriend who had a shady past and a fragile state of mind.

It got worse as the train screeched into Grand Central Station on the tracks I had told Larry I sometimes thought about throwing myself onto. I didn't know now whether that had been true. *Why did I say that?* It grew even worse after we transferred to a train that took us uptown, so that even though we were on the west side, we were still unbearably nearby. *Are they still there?* Worse as we ascended the stairs and were struck by the blinding city. *They almost never leave the apartment.* We were underneath some scaffolding, which was barely a break from the heat. "What's wrong?" Cassidy asked, and I hated that she could tell, that it wasn't a secret, that to her, I was visible.

"Nothing. Nothing's wrong," I said. *Why can't I see her like she sees me?* "I think just being in the city is making me feel weird."

"What do you mean?" She seemed genuinely curious, her arm around me.

It felt like I was an animal trying to speak to a human being. *Why is she doing this to me?* "It's Larry and them. I don't know, I keep thinking about it, and it really freaks me out."

"I don't get it, though, Daniel. I mean, I get that Larry is really weird, or something, as you've said, but what *happened*?" She'd opened up to me about her family, her parents, her brother, her stepfamily, and how hard it was to be so far away from home, in a city that was not in reality anything like what she'd imagined. I'd opened up in turn, I thought. We were back to walking again side by side, but more slowly now.

"Well, you know, he used to hit me and stuff, so I guess that's probably part of it," I said. She didn't say anything in response. We kept walking in silence. Then I realized she wasn't next to me. When I looked over, she was a few steps back, frozen in the middle of the sidewalk, just standing there framed by the scaffolding. I couldn't understand what had happened. I walked back to her, and when I got close, I could see she was crying. *What happened? What did I say?*

"You didn't tell me that," she said, quietly.

I just stood there for a minute. *That he hit me?* Tectonic plates were shifting inside of me, a whole planet crumbling and changing shape. "It was just like stuff in the marines," I said, a little desperate to get to the other side of the conversation, for everything to stay the same. "He was a marine, you know, and so was Iban, so that's kind of what was going on."

She looked at me hard. Her eyes were red. I felt embarrassed, standing there, not understanding what I wasn't understanding. "He *hit* you?"

"Well, yeah. But that was totally not a big deal." *It got a lot worse than that,* I started to say, but then caught it before it came out of my mouth.

"You weren't *in* the marines."

"Well . . . no. I wasn't."

"And he was your friend's dad."

I nodded.

"And he hit you."

I nodded, thinking over and over again, *So much worse,* and I looked up, and let myself see it, all of it, all of it at once. It was like an entire building had been hovering above me this whole time, and now there was nowhere for it to go, no room for me to put it in. I grabbed a hot pipe supporting the scaffolding. I was suddenly so tired. Nothing made sense. We ducked into a café. We wouldn't go to the Museum of Natural History after all.

Cassidy asked questions, and I let the answers slide out of me. It felt as if I was sitting in the back seat of my own mind. Neither of us knew what to call what had happened. She wanted us to go to a police station, to do something, but I explained that I'd thought about it every which way, that first of all he had connections in the police and even higher up in the military and intelligence, so I couldn't guarantee that news wouldn't get back to him that I had become an adversary. And even if the police did raid the place and get everyone out, they wouldn't really be *out.* I explained that while I was there, if the police had arrested Larry, I would have really believed, in some part of myself, that what was happening was all part of the corrupt conspiracy working to bring him down. If everyone else was going to escape, they would have to free themselves. That was the only way it worked.

She was nodding a lot, having to swallow everything I was telling her all at once. She asked about Raven, about my old friends, where they'd all gone, and I told her I didn't really know. I tried to explain why I had to avoid everyone at all costs. Finally, she insisted that I see a therapist, and I said I would, once I could afford it. I couldn't tell how much time passed, unreeling all of it, but soon it was time for dinner, and so we headed downtown.

—I I—

I sat in bed in my apartment in the Bronx a few weeks later, looking at a checklist of the characteristics that make up a cult. The apartment I'd been able to afford because of an award for poetry I'd gotten upon graduating from Sarah Lawrence. I couldn't say how I'd arrived at the checklist. I'd just been scrolling and clicking around. But now here it was on my screen. I perused, only vaguely interested in finding out how cults—those strange, fringe religions—operated. I scanned down the list. I stopped after a few lines and went back to the top. It felt like the screen was vibrating. On it I saw the past two years of my life reflected back at me.

- The group is unquestioningly committed to a leader.
- Doubt and dissent are punished, this being characterized as healthy, positive, helpful, and/or necessary for the punished member. The leader reverses roles with the recipient of punishment, claiming that they, the leader, are a victim of the dissenting member's abuse.
- The group is a tool to make money for or accrue power to the leader.
- Techniques such as denunciation (hot-seat) sessions, constant labor routines, and sleep deprivation are used to numb the minds of group members.
- The leader determines how members should think, act, or feel.

- The leader claims a special status or mission, which the group becomes committed to carrying out.
- The leader is accountable to no one; there is no higher authority.
- Giving up ties to friends and family is a consequence or even prerequisite of belonging to the group. Those who might oppose the group from the outside are characterized as evil, abusive, or ignorant.
- Members are expected to devote inordinate amounts of time to the group.

I had been in a cult.

Not just living in an apartment with my friend's dad. Not some weird relationship with Isabella. Not just hanging out with my friends, everything going constantly awry, and us never able to catch up, to fix it all. Not broken, suicidal, needing to be saved.

I was shaky and raw, stranded on top of the blanketless bed. I felt like I had just returned from many years living on a planet with different gravity, like my bones were thinned out entirely. It wasn't a surprise, exactly, but it wasn't quite like I had known it all along, either. It was like the two sides of my brain had been separated, and the word was a bridge that put them back together. My dad had said it so early on, I remembered now! But the saying had been made impossible, unallowable. It was as if I'd been experiencing a unique kind of pain but I'd forgotten what pain was, so I didn't know how to tell anyone what was wrong. But here it was. Other people had been through this, had felt it, knew what it was called.

I looked up the author of the list and found his email. He had written a book. I made a fake email because I didn't know if, somehow, Larry might have access to mine. He might be capable of anything—he might be omnipotent for all I knew—but he seemed either to not realize I'd been avoiding him for months, or to not care, so he probably couldn't find a way into an anonymous email account. I wrote a message to the author, asking for help.

Every day, I checked the secret email. The only message that had ever gone out from that address was a thin tether connecting my past, which had seemed like an awful dream, to this reality. After a few days passed, a message appeared from the author. He couldn't help me, he said, or suggest any action to take in particular against Larry, or to help the other members of the group. There was a support group in New York, he said, that I might check out.

I went back to my regular in-box. I sat staring into the light of my computer for a long time, listening to the hush of cars passing by on Mosholu Parkway. No one could help me. I scrolled to an email from Angela that I'd been ignoring for weeks. She was asking for her book. I hadn't known what to say when she first asked, hadn't been able to come up with an excuse. I looked around the empty room. The sun had gone down enough so that all the edges of the wood-paneled walls had softened; when it was dark, I noticed, truly dark, it was as if there were no walls at all. It was womblike, this darkness—not bad, not evil or scary, just lacking definition. This must be how flowers feel, I thought, when the vault door is shut—right before it's opened again. They must remember what it felt like to be alive, to drink up light. I tried to see the apartment in my head, to scan my mind's eye across the bookshelf, to somehow call up Angela's book out of the ether, but of course it wasn't there. It had vanished into thin air.

Instead, a phrase popped into my head from the Jewish prayer book I'd found on Larry's shelf. "Either you will go through this door or you will not go through." What had that been? A Jewish prayer I'd never heard of? I googled the phrase and it came up immediately: it was a poem by Adrienne Rich called "Prospective Immigrants Please Note." I sat there for a minute, stunned. Had anything been what I'd thought it was? I looked back at Angela's email. What would I do? Who was I? I could either keep ignoring my past, or I could follow this feeling—the one that spread through me when I looked right at what had happened and called it by its name. I began to type.

I started with a long prologue explaining to Angela that I was about to tell her something outlandish. "I have rather unfortunate news regarding your book and it is involved in something extremely disturbing which I have told very few people," I wrote. The secret was a burden that was unfair to unload onto her. What was she supposed to do with the knowledge that the whole time she had known me–she who believed she saw so much behind people's eyes–she had not seen that I was being tortured? At the same time, I didn't want to lie or hide or make up excuses anymore. I wanted to tell the truth.

> I am only saying this because as someone who is very busy and probably has her own sense of the scope of our relationship, you should have every right to resign yourself to the notion that I just lost your book, take that as you may, and move on. However, I've been roiling over this for a few months because I could just have told you that, and not have to deal with talking about what I'm about to tell you, but I'd rather not lie and diminish my standing in your eyes.

I hoped she would remember the swan I'd made out of hundreds of little pieces of folded paper, or the extra hours we'd spent talking in her office, that something would make her believe me, but I didn't know how she possibly could. Once I felt I'd exhausted every possible explanation for why I was writing the email, why I hadn't sent it earlier, why it was so hard, I continued, pushed further, and I called it what it really was. "I was a member of what I can now call a cult," I wrote.

> Over those two years I had a relationship with a man who was physically and psychologically abusing me, literally beating me up and sometimes actually systematically torturing me occasionally in front of a group of my peers. I was only allowed to sleep on average maybe 4 hours a night, while sharing a one bedroom apartment with 7 people. They were trying constantly to rewrite my memories, my logic; it was brainwashing. I do not know how to explain my acceptance of this at the time except that I was completely terrified and completely confused.

For the first time in years, I didn't feel like my brain had to crawl through a maze. The voice in my head and the voice I wrote down were the same voice—they had been all along, but now they weren't separated on either side of a makeshift wall, trying to speak one at a time. I had no one to convince, no one to fool, no one to hide from, no one to deceive. No one else decided for me what was real. I wanted someone to know, finally, how I really felt, right now, here. I wanted to open it all up, but in a way that wasn't coerced, wasn't a confession. So I kept going, trying to encapsulate everything that had led up to that very instant: me writing alone on my bed in my apartment in the Bronx almost exactly equidistant from the Upper East Side and Sarah Lawrence College. I told her, and in a sense, by putting words to it, I also told myself. It became something that had happened *to me,* rather than my whole being, the only thing I could see no matter where I looked. I could almost feel where it ended and the rest of me began.

> I am a little less scared and a little less confused every day now. When I got housing on campus I finally stopped answering their calls, and somehow managed to cut off contact entirely. They haven't pursued me at all, but I am so afraid every day that I'll run into one of them.
>
> That is where your book is, and why I have no idea how to retrieve it for you. I feel terrible because I know it was filled with your notes and is not replaceable. I wish there was something I could do. I think even if I felt able to try retrieving it, I would not be able to find it there, because this one bedroom apartment on the Upper East Side of Manhattan is literally filled wall to wall with construction equipment and tools. I know it sounds insane and it is.
>
> I realize I've laid it all out sort of bluntly but I don't really know how to frame it for myself, much less for someone else. I am still trying to understand it. But those are the very bare and basic facts. I hope and believe that you know me well enough to know that I would not throw around terms like "abuse" and "cult" if I had

any question that I was using them accurately. I hope that somehow the work you did on the book is possible to re-create. I have found a few different copies online that I would like to purchase for you, please let me know if that is at all desirable to you, and I can show you the different versions I have found so that you get the same or the closest to your original version.

Once again I'm asking you as a friend to keep what I have just told you a secret. I suppose as a former student I am asking you for some sort of guidance but to me, and I think to most, this is a completely unique situation. I do not expect you to have a clue what to say. As you might be able to imagine, it terrifies me even to think about this, but to share it is another thing entirely. I am sorry to lay this all on you. I have had a strange, singular and in a sense, very lonely past two years. I am trying to find some sort of support group or something for people who have experienced similar things. It is all I can really think of to do.

All my best,
Daniel

I typed until my fingers ached. When it was done, I rubbed my eyes, scanned across the words I'd written one more time, and hit send. I looked at the door. *It is only a door,* I thought. Then I got up and I turned on the light.

— 20 —

WE WANT SO BADLY for the world to be ordered, and reliable. We want it to be magical, too, to be meaningful. The idea that everything is random and unpredictable, that our memories and perceptions are shifting and chaotic, that we have no control over our place in the world, what happens to us, our futures or our pasts, is terrifying. We want to look up at the stars and see shapes that resemble ourselves.

In the process of writing this book, for example, I discovered that the name "Slonim," the dorm in which I first met Larry, came from the name of the Belarusian town and later ghetto where it seems there is some likelihood my ancestors lived and were ultimately murdered in the Holocaust. In the time since I began writing this book, Larry was indicted on federal charges, his marine lieutenant general friend Chuck Pitman passed away, Bernie Kerik received a presidential pardon, and Iban, tragically, took his own life. This all in the course of a few months. It would feel better to say that it all means something, that it's evidence of a grand design, nefarious, shadowy forces, a worldwide struggle between good and evil, order and chaos. That's what Larry would have said—and it would have felt comforting. Of course it is desirable to listen to someone who shows up and tells you they have the answers to what's really going on in the world, as well as how to live so that you never feel bad or confused ever again. If that person does exist, and if they are who they say they are, then everything must operate according to some kind of perceivable order, which would be an enormous relief.

We want truth to exist—knowable, objective truth. We want there to be answers to our questions about what is real, how to live and how to be happy. The reality, at least as best I can tell at this moment in my life, is that everything lies somewhere in between good and bad, true and false, random and significant. Most things are random, but some things are not. Some things you remember inaccurately, but some you remember accurately. Some things are definitely good or bad, but for other things, it's harder to say. Anyone who claims to know how everything really works, what is absolutely real and what isn't, is either deceiving you or deceiving themselves. Or both, most likely.

—||—

If you are reading this, and you are one of my friends, the people who went through this with me, here is the message that it never felt safe to send you after I left. I am so sorry for everything that has happened to you. I felt sure the situation Larry created in that apartment would fall apart soon after I left and you would all find your own ways out, as I had. I told myself that this must have happened. I imagined somehow rappelling down the side of the building, pulling you all out to safety, and burning the place to the ground, but I knew that wouldn't actually help you. It is one thing to leave the building, and another to leave your belief. Pretty much anything I might have done could be integrated into Larry's story about the world and how it worked.

That includes this book, of course. Perhaps Larry has said, or you are saying to yourself, that this is all part of the conspiracy against the Ray family. Maybe the government actually wrote this, not me. Maybe I did write it, and I've been brainwashed, or manipulated by Teresa Ray and Bernie Kerik. Maybe I've been a part of the conspiracy from the beginning. Perhaps you've combed through the text, looking for any evidence of language intended to manipulate the truth, or instances where I've claimed things happened that didn't happen, opportunities to undermine what is clearly just another bald-faced attack on Larry Ray.

Or maybe all of this is part of Larry's plan, some grand scheme he's been running since the beginning, which, once it has reached its final conclusion, will save the world. That would be easier to believe than the other option. That you have been the victim of abuse for years. That you spent years as a part of a coercive group, pushed away your friends and family, and defended at all costs the man who was hurting you and your friends. That none of it was true. Why would you ever choose that reality over the former?

You will have built up copious evidence that tells you Larry is and always has been who he says. Some of that evidence is probably valid. Some of it probably isn't. Truth is very complicated, as it turns out. Maybe he is a consummate spy, a unique, superhuman genius that the government taps for special jobs, the scope of which none of us truly understands. That can be true, without invalidating the fact that it is not okay for someone to hurt you the way Larry hurt each of us. You don't deserve to be hit. You don't deserve to be tortured. There is no situation in which that's acceptable. Not in the marines, not in a family, and not between a group of friends and one of their dads.

As far as the sex goes, I do not know what all of you were aware of. You have probably already found a way to deny it if you weren't aware, or to justify it in your mind if you were. All I can say is that it happened, and that in the situation Larry created, there was no such thing as consent. If you deserve anything after this, it is to be in relationships where the power dynamic is equal and balanced, where you have control over what happens to you, when, and how, and you have a full, independent life that is totally your own beyond that relationship.

When I left, I barely talked about what had happened to me. I had one session with a therapist at first, and as I described what had happened, I watched the horror overtake her face, her jaw practically on the floor. She couldn't believe that I had stayed, couldn't understand any of it. When I emailed my literature teacher, one of the first people in my life to whom I ever tried to explain what had happened outright,

I never got an email back. I assumed she didn't believe me, and would learn much later that I was right. So, even if I did tell people, I became terrified of how they might see me, and I tried to move on as if this chapter in my life had never occurred. That turned out to hurt me in a whole new way.

I am hopeful that telling my story will help to create a world that understands at least the edges of what happened to you, and that this will make whatever comes next easier for you. The steps from the "A" of meeting Larry to the "Z" of being willingly involved in the constant insanity of that apartment felt impossible to explain for years. I've tried my best to tell only my own part of the story, and to involve the rest of you only when it felt absolutely necessary in order to depict my experience. I have tried to share only my "confessions," never yours—whether they were true, false, extracted, freely offered up, or, probably, a mixture of all four, whatever may have been the case. I do not know how to balance my right to my own past and pain against the right to privacy of everyone else who was a part of that. I tried my best to give you as much of that privacy as I could, and to leave room for you to tell your own stories, your own versions of events, which I am sure will differ from mine. I hope my telling my story helps you somehow to take my perspective into account, and maybe to tell your own.

Please know that your lives are waiting for you if and when you want to return to them, and they always have been. Your families are waiting for you; I've talked with many of them, and they love you, and miss you. A lot of time has passed, and the version of you they remember is not the version of you that exists now. But I bet they'll be excited to get to know you again. I know that you've come to believe all kinds of things about your families, and I cannot say what is true or isn't. That is up to you to figure out, and that process will take time. The important thing is that *you* decide, and that you have beds to sleep in where you can be safe, whenever you need.

Part of what you'll find confusing is that there were things you learned while you were in touch with Larry, ways that you grew and became a more complete person. How can it be all bad, if some parts of it were good? Perhaps some of those things did come from Larry, but you'll find in time that more of them came from you, that you grew up not because of Larry, but in spite of him. Perhaps one of the most confusing things for me at the very end of my time with all of you was that, in order to leave Larry, I used one of the very first pieces of advice he ever gave me. When I was going through my first real breakup, he told me I could just leave, that in a breakup one owes the other person nothing—I didn't have to answer calls, or texts, or emails; I was responsible only for my own life from there on out. That was one thing, at least when it came to him, that he was right about.

I wish none of this had ever happened. I wish I could change the past, and we could all have finished college, graduated, gotten jobs, had families and relationships, and figured out who we were at our own pace, along the way. But it did happen, and there's no changing it. That said, one thing you can control is it being over for you. Then, after it's ended, it's up to you to decide how to live with it. More than anything, that's what I hope you do: live.

ACKNOWLEDGMENTS

For years, I didn't feel capable of writing this all down, and even after countless hours of processing, recovery, and therapy, I wasn't ready for how hard it would feel. I am so deeply grateful to the people who took care of me, and made it easier to take care of myself, while I made the attempt. Thank you to Jenna, who lives down the street, and who is probably reading these acknowledgments right now, helping me make them better. This book would have been much harder to write had I not fallen in love with you while writing it. Thank you to my roommates in L.A., including the cats and the dog, who made me feel at home for the first time in my life. Thank you to Giulia and Josh, who, at my most vulnerable moment, without question or pause, gave me a place to sleep when I needed it, a job to pay the bills, love, support, advice, mutual trust and respect, and pretty much every unconditional resource one could need to recover from trauma. Oh, that everyone could have a Giulia and Josh.

Thank you to Shivan, who never stops fighting, and is the only person I've ever heard of to essentially peer pressure someone out of a cult, even if only for a weekend. You have always made me feel like a capital-W Writer. Thank you to Rebecca, who keeps me sane, and who not only made this book better, but makes me better.

Thank you to Ezra Marcus—whose name, speaking of seemingly meaningful coincidences, literally means "help"—and James D. Walsh, the reporters who first thought this story was worth looking into, and whose article in *New York* magazine, "The Stolen Kids of Sarah Lawrence," meant that I no longer had to prove all on my own that any of this had happened. Thank you to Raven and Max, who knew all along what this was, and tried to raise the alarm, even if no one was hearing it.

Thank you to Chris Clemans, my agent, who was one of the first people to believe this was a story I was capable of telling. I appreciate you for letting me unload the panicked, scattered version of this whole saga all in one sitting, and deciding that you wanted to help me put it to paper. Thank you to Will Wolfslau at Crown, who championed this book from the beginning, and made space for its existence in the world.

My gratitude to my parents and my brother, who have always made me feel loved and special, who have always wanted the best for me, and who have always trusted me perhaps a little too utterly. Mom, thanks for always picking the raspberries. There is still nothing better in the whole wide world. Dad, thanks for always buying the books, no matter what, and for reading me to sleep. This, I know, was not exactly the kind of odyssey you wanted or imagined for me. I love you all. I'm sure we have a lot to talk about.

ABOUT THE AUTHOR

Daniel Barban Levin holds an MFA in poetry from the University of California, Irvine, where he taught creative writing and rhetoric, and a bachelor's degree from Sarah Lawrence College. He is the winner of the Stanley and Evelyn Lipkin Prize for Poetry and the Lynn Garnier Memorial Award, and is the recipient of fellowships from the Frost Place, Tent, the Sarah Lawrence Summer Seminar for Writers, and the Community of Writers at Squaw Valley. His writing has appeared in *Provincetown Arts, Bat City Review, The Sarah Lawrence Review, The Westchester Review, The Offbeat,* and *The Fourth River.* He lives in Los Angeles.

ABOUT THE TYPE

This book was set in Baskerville, a typeface designed by John Baskerville (1706–75), an amateur printer and typefounder, and cut for him by John Handy in 1750. The type became popular again when the Lanston Monotype Corporation of London revived the classic roman face in 1923. The Mergenthaler Linotype Company in England and the United States cut a version of Baskerville in 1931, making it one of the most widely used typefaces today.